Just Immigration in the Americas

Just Immigration in the Americas

A Feminist Account

Allison B. Wolf

ROWMAN & LITTLEFIELD
Lanham • Boulder • New York • London

Published by Rowman & Littlefield
An imprint of The Rowman & Littlefield Publishing Group, Inc.
4501 Forbes Boulevard, Suite 200, Lanham, Maryland 20706
www.rowman.com

6 Tinworth Street, London SE11 5AL, United Kingdom

ISBN: HB 978-1-78661-333-2

British Library Cataloguing in Publication Information Available

Library of Congress Cataloging-in-Publication Data

Names: Wolf, Allison, 1975– author.
Title: Just immigration in the Americas : a feminist account / Allison
  Wolf.
Description: Lanham, Maryland : Rowman & Littlefield, [2020] | Includes
  bibliographical references and index. | Summary: "Using testimonies from
  immigrants and examples of immigrant policies, this book proposes an
  interdisciplinary, feminist approach to immigration justice"— Provided
  by publisher.
Identifiers: LCCN 2020024787 (print) | LCCN 2020024788 (ebook) | ISBN
  9781786613332 (cloth) | ISBN 9781786613349 (epub)
  ISBN 9781538149843 (pbk)
Subjects: LCSH: United States—Emigration and immigration—Government
  policy. | America—Emigration and immigration—Social aspects. | Women
  immigrants—America—Social conditions. | Feminism.
Classification: LCC JV6483 .W65 2020 (print) | LCC JV6483 (ebook) | DDC
  325/.7—dc23
LC record available at https://lccn.loc.gov/2020024787
LC ebook record available at https://lccn.loc.gov/2020024788

To Ari and Naomi, my favorite immigrants of all

Contents

Acknowledgments

This project came to fruition because of the support, kindness, and generosity of so many.

I want to begin by thanking Simpson College, in particular Heather Priess Groben, Meave Callan, and Katie Smith, for always having my back and for our great lunches over the years. I also want to say *muchas gracias* to the University of Costa Rica's Philosophy Department and Institute for Philosophical Investigation for buttressing the early stages of this research. I am especially grateful to Gabriela Arguedas, Carlos Sandoval Garcia, Mario Solís, and Abileny Soto for all of their collaboration, intellectual exchanges, and friendship. Además, quiero expresar mi gran agradecimiento a Olga Retana. Gracias, no sólo por haberme enseñado cómo hablar español, sino también cómo amar el español, amar a Costa Rica y amar a la gente de Latinoamérica. Espero que sepás el lugar especial que tenés en mi corazón.

While this project began in the United States and Costa Rica, it concluded in Colombia. Thank you to my new colleagues in the Philosophy Department, the College of Social Sciences, and the Law School at Universidad de los Andes in Bogotá for welcoming me and for supporting my work. I am particularly grateful to Gracy Pelacani and Carolina Moreno for letting me tag along to observe free legal clinics and helping me learn Colombia's immigration system and policies toward Venezuelans. Ana María Forero Angel, thank you for helping me discover new directions to take my research and for welcoming my family and I to Bogotá with such warmth and wit. And a very special thank you to Catalina González Quintero; you have been a brilliant and generous colleague—listening to ideas and reading drafts of chapters with a careful, insightful, and encouraging eye—and you have become a dear and treasured friend who makes me so happy that I moved to Bogotá. Muchas muchas gracias por todo.

I am so lucky to have a wonderful group of philosopher colleagues and friends in the United States who, for the past twenty years, have attended conference presentations, helped brainstorm projects, read drafts of essays, and consistently encouraged me to persist. Gaile Pohlhaus Jr. and Alison Bailey, thank you for our always reinvigorating writing weekends and for your continual wise mentorship. Sonya Charles, I owe you a huge debt of gratitude for reading almost every chapter of this book, often on a short timeline, and for offering excellent feedback that undoubtedly made it better. And Sonya, Jennifer Benson, and Barry DeCoster, thank you for being the best friends anyone could ask for—whether it is moving, traveling, having children, debating philosophical theories, coming up with innovative pedagogies, or just sitting around having a glass of wine, you have always been there for me, loving both "Buddhist Allison," and "Stressed-Out Allison" as the occasion demanded. I am so fortunate to have you all in my life.

Finally, I want to thank my family. Thanks to my beloved Grammy, Lenore Moss, for building up my confidence with your constant bragging and for teaching me that women to need to have their own lives. I miss you so much. Thank you to my parents, Laurel Wolf and Kenneth Wolf, for always telling me that I could accomplish anything, even when doing so took me to states and countries far from you. Thank you to my sister, Wendy Wolf, for always being there for me, for giving me my incredible niece, Emma Madison, and my spectacular nephew, Jaxon Luca, and for reminding me that, sometimes, I do need to care about fashion. I love you sista! I owe a very special thanks to my children, Ari Seth and Naomi Devon, for letting me have my special writing spot on the couch (even when they wanted to sit there) and for loving me even when I could not hang out because I was working. You are the loves of my life and I am so proud both of who you are and that you are my kids. I could not ask for better. Last, but certainly not least, thank you to Daniel Klass. Thank you for telling me that I would really enjoy majoring in philosophy, thank you for always pushing me to continue to grow personally and professionally, and thank you for always playing guitar so beautifully. I love you.

Introduction

Starting to See Global Oppression in Immigration Policies and Practices— Why It's Time for a New Approach

May 21, 2002. I landed at Costa Rica's Juan Santamaría International Airport for the first time. I had never been south of Mexico and, frankly, I was not overly enthusiastic about the undertaking; I only went because I thought I would regret passing up the opportunity for an all-expenses-paid assistantship in what I was told was one of the most beautiful places on earth. So I went . . . and I was quickly won over. Ticos were so welcoming and the nature was, indeed, breathtaking. I walked the streets of San José every day with a sense of ease and belonging I had rarely felt before. I became obsessed with learning Spanish. But best of all, I had the privilege of staying with a wonderful host family, which is how I got to know Mateo.[1]

Mateo was a Nicaraguan immigrant who came to Costa Rica in the 1980s. He was dating my host mom for a while and, once the romantic part of the relationship ended, they stayed very close friends. Mateo helped her maintain the house and she gave him food and a family life. Mateo was able to find relatively stable work in construction and he lived with multiple other Nicaraguan men in San José. He had a daughter in Nicaragua who, by then, was in her early twenties (though he had not been able to see her since he migrated, their principal contact being phone calls). One day, I noticed that Mateo had lost part of his thumb and had scars on his hand and arm. I asked him what had happened, and he told me that he was injured when he fought with the Sandinistas. I asked him if that was why he came to Costa Rica, and he simply said, "Sí." It was hard, he said—being called "Nica," making enough money, finding a decent living situation, and, most of all, missing his daughter and the rest of his family (all in Nicaragua)—but he knew that he had done the right thing. We never discussed it again, but my curiosity about his story, that of other Nicaraguan immigrants, and the stories of Latin American immigrants throughout all the region never ceased. And it led me to write this book.

1

IMMIGRATION IN THE AMERICAS

I think it is fair to say that we are living in a contested time with respect to immigration. While the United States continues to refer to itself as "a nation of
immigrants," since the 1980s, in particular, it has transformed into an increasingly hostile place for those who want to seek a new life, especially for those
from Latin America. In 1986, the Immigration Reform and Control Act required employers to verify the immigration status of their employees, prohibited them from hiring undocumented immigrants, expanded border security
and enforcement,[2] and introduced a criminal alien program designed to deport
convicted felons.[3] In 1988, the Anti-Drug Abuse Act created provisions for
deporting noncitizens who have committed aggravated felonies.[4] In 1994,
California passed Proposition 187, or the Save Our State Initiative, which
aimed at creating a state-run citizenship screening system and prohibited undocumented immigrants from receiving nonemergency health care, accessing
public education, or receiving other state services.[5] In 1996, President Bill
Clinton signed the Personal Responsibility and Work Opportunity Reconcili-
ation Act, which included provisions to deeply cut federal aid to immigrants
during their first five years in the country, and the Illegal Immigration Reform
and Immigrant Responsibility Act, which expanded the list of aggravated
felonies for which one could be deported to include petty theft, minor drug
offenses, and DUIs, and required mandatory detention of noncitizens who
had completed their prison sentences.[6] Spending on border enforcement has
skyrocketed, increasing from almost $7.5 billion in fiscal year 2002 to over
$17 billion in fiscal year 2010.[7] In fact, since "the creation of the Department
of Homeland Security in 2003, the federal government has spent an estimated
$324 billion on the agencies that carry out immigration enforcement."[8] Ef-
forts at comprehensive immigration reform have gone nowhere. Walls have
been built on different parts of the U.S. southern border with Mexico and $1.6
billion was allocated in fiscal year 2019 to build even more in the Rio Grande
Valley Sector.[9] Whereas Pat Buchanan was rejected in his 1996 presidential
bid for being a fringe racist running on an anti-immigrant platform, Donald
Trump was elected by demonizing immigrants. And on his watch the United
States has responded to influxes of Central American migrants by detaining
pregnant women, separating families, building detention centers, and asking
other nations to prevent them from even getting here in the first place.

Immigration crises and anti-immigrant backlash are not limited to the
United States, however. These issues are also taking center stage in Latin
America. Mexico manages a population of undocumented Guatemalan immigrants and has been caught for many years between Central American migrants (and others) who want to travel throughout their territory to reach the

United States and U.S. demands to prevent them from doing so. Costa Rica is receiving Nicaraguan immigrants fleeing from violence in their home nation, often, at least in part, fomented by U.S. interventions. And South America, most prominently Colombia, is in the midst of trying to accommodate millions of Venezuelans. Indeed, large swaths of the Americas are in the midst of figuring out how to proceed.

CURRENT APPROACHES TO IMMIGRATION AND WHY WE NEED A CHANGE

There are many fascinating practical and political issues around immigration throughout the United States and Latin America. But what I am interested in here are the philosophical issues raised by these empirical realities, particularly the question: What constitutes a just (or unjust) immigration policy, process, or practice? And that is the central question of this book.

Like a good academic, I began searching for the answer in the philosophical literature. Unfortunately, as much of the nation's (and the world's) focus on immigration has increased, philosophers have tended to ignore or drastically undertheorize the topic. Those who do write on immigration ethics or immigration justice tend to offer analyses that are too often irrelevant or too abstract to provide guidance on concrete realities. While Mexican immigrants face systemic violence as they travel to the United States, philosophers primarily debate whether states should have open or closed borders or whether there is a right to emigrate from one's home country.[10] While increasing numbers of undocumented immigrants are deported after decades of living peaceful and productive lives in the United States, philosophers are debating the abstract existence of a right to stay.[11] As the Trump administration forces thousands of Central American asylum seekers to await their hearings in treacherous conditions in Mexico, philosophers interrogate the conceptual status of refugees.[12] While immigrants face exploitation, police harassment, and daily humiliations, philosophers investigate whether they are entitled to basic human rights protections.[13] And while Costa Rica and Colombia struggle to settle record numbers of Nicaraguans and Venezuelans, philosophers say absolutely nothing. We can do better.

I do not want to give the false impression that no philosophers are engaging these issues; that is simply untrue. Amy Reed-Sandoval distinguishes two schools of thought about immigration within this philosophical literature: the "Classic Open Borders Debate" and the "New Open Borders Debate."[14] According to Reed-Sandoval, the Classic Open Borders Debate has the following characteristics. First, the philosophical inquiry is strictly focused on two questions: (1) Can states justly exclude perspective migrants? and (2) Is there a universal right to migration? Second, these investigations rarely, if ever, reference particular borders or migrants of specific identities, instead exploring what they take to be universal concepts and searching for general principles about immigration. Third, methodologically, the Classic Open Border Debate tends to occur in the realms of ideal and/or institutional theory and employ core ideas of liberal, democratic, political thought.[15] Fourth, these discussions often offer "utopian" proposals that have little chance of becoming enacted. Finally, the Classic Open Borders literature tends to avoid specific debates about nonideal immigration. Reed-Sandoval places authors like Michael Walzer, Joseph Carens, David Miller, Michael Blake, Peter Higgins, Kieran Oberman, and Phillip Cole into this camp. While these are valuable areas of inquiry, they are largely too abstract or disconnected from the realities of immigration policy to effect change in this area.

In contrast to the Classic Open Borders Debate, the New Open Borders Debate is evolving out of feminist theory, critical race theory, Latin American philosophy, and other nonideal thought. Specifically, Reed-Sandoval suggests that this immigration literature makes normative claims about the questions of the Classic discussion on open borders while also expanding those questions using the methodology of nonideal, feminist, and/or critical race theory; drawing on particular migrant experiences; referring to specific nation-state borders; presenting new ways of thinking about borders and migration; and discussing aspects of migration unrelated to open borders,[16] like detention, derogatory language, brain drain, domestic and sexual labor flows, etc.[17] Among other theorists, Reed-Sandoval places Natalie Cisneros, Serena Parekh, Grant Silva, José Jorge Mendoza, Carlos Alberto Sánchez, and Shelley Wilcox into this camp.

MY PROPOSAL: FEMINIST IMMIGRATION JUSTICE

I situate my work within this burgeoning New Open Border literature. I aim to present a new way of thinking about specific immigration practices, policies, and norms throughout the United States, Mexico, Central America, and Colombia that draws on insights from feminist, decolonial, and critical race theory and that centers oppression as the central concept of immigration justice. That is to say, I do not take traditional Western theories of justice, such as those proffered by Rawls, Nozick, and Walzer, to be useful bases for immigration justice discussions—they are too abstract, conceptualize immigration justice as being about achieving an ideal policy rather than trying to identify and rectify current injustice, and operate on problematic metaphysical premises. Instead I take my cue from feminist political thinkers, such as Iris Marion Young, Shatema Threadcraft, Naomi Zack, and José Medina, who start from actual injustices, identify the oppression in them, and seek to correct the issues as best as possible. Specifically, the point of departure of my approach is that the core tenet of feminism is true—oppression, in all of its forms, is wrong. And, given this, any policy, practice, or norm that creates, reflects, or perpetuates oppression is wrong and unjust.

Applying these ideas to the context of immigration, I take it as fundamentally true that oppression against immigrants exists, that it is wrong, and that any immigration practice, policy, norm, law, or enforcement mechanism that creates, reflects, or perpetuates oppression domestically or globally is unjust. Given this position, an essential function of immigration justice is to recognize where oppression exists in relation to immigration and try to correct it. Now as these thinkers have taught us, oppression includes both distributive and non-distributive elements; it expresses itself in the social, political, and epistemic realms; and it affects people's public and intimate lives. Given all of this, evaluating immigration issues via the lens of oppression requires assessing all of these aspects of immigration policies, practices, and their effects.

In this book, my focus is applying this understanding of immigration justice to specific immigration policies, practices, and norms throughout the United States and Latin America. Specifically, I will interrogate immigration issues involving the United States, Mexico, Guatemala, Honduras, El Salvador, Costa Rica, and Colombia and the degree to which they create, reflect, or perpetuate domestic and global oppression. My hope is that, in doing so, we will better understand what is happening in the region with respect to immigration and thus be better positioned to act and improve Latin American immigrants' lives.

OUTLINE OF THE BOOK

The book is set up to answer the following questions. First, why should we adopt a new approach to philosophical assessments of immigration policy? Second, what new lens should we use when exploring immigration policy? And finally, how do we apply that new lens to evaluate specific immigration policies and practices? The first question, I hope, has been addressed in the previous section—we need a new approach because our current discussions are incomplete, too abstract, and not especially useful in addressing current issues in the United States and Latin America. The second question was also just answered partially—the new lens is a feminist one that centers oppression in both domestic and global contexts. But it will be addressed in more detail in the two chapters that comprise part I. The chapters of part II are dedicated to answering the third question. With this in mind, here is a brief summary of what you will find in these pages.

Part I of the book presents the theoretical pillars of the feminist approach to immigration justice I am advocating, namely that a feminist approach to immigration justice would affirm that immigration systems, policies, practices, norms, laws, and enforcement mechanisms are just if they help alleviate oppression within nations and globally and they are unjust if they create, perpetuate, or reflect oppression in any form in the public or intimate realms. The problem, though, is that that while we understand oppression in the domestic context, we do not have an account of *global* oppression. But immigration is inherently global, and a great deal of the oppression perpetrated in this context is global oppression, not domestic oppression. So in order to incorporate analyses of global oppression into our probes, we need to remedy that. And the first chapter does this by offering such an account of oppression.

While the account of global oppression detailed in chapter 1 fills in many key conceptual gaps, the problem is that oppression goes beyond the political and social realms to include the epistemic. If we are to account for all oppression in our analyses of immigration, though, we need an account of epistemic oppression. So in chapter 2 I offer a schema of how to understand epistemic oppression and explore various instances of it in the context of immigration to detail its nature.

In part II of the book, I turn to utilizing and applying this new understanding of immigration justice in relation to current immigration issues and policies in the United States, Mexico, Central America, and Colombia. Chapter 3 is the first of three chapters with a central focus on U.S. immigration policy. There I explore Trump administration efforts to increase deportations, through a push to end the Deferred Action for Childhood Arrivals program and increased raids, by analyzing the underlying reasoning to justify these efforts, namely that they should be pursued because undocumented immigrants came to the United States "illegally." I maintain that such rationale is both philosophically flawed and morally misguided because of its connections to oppression globally and within the United States.

In chapter 4 I turn to the Trump administration family separation policies and explore what, exactly, makes them so wrong. While many scholars condemn the policy as cruel, I argue that when we explore the reasoning behind the policy, the way it has been enacted, and the nature of cruelty, we see that cruelty is not the operative injustice. Instead the most apt description of the injustice in the family separation policy is the fact that it reflects, perpetuates, and creates global oppression.

Chapter 5 interrogates the longstanding practice of the United States exporting its immigration policy to Mexico and Central America. Specifically, I explore Plan Frontera Sur (the Southern Border Plan), Migrant Protection Protocols (more commonly known as the Remain in Mexico Policy), Third-Country Agreements, and tariff threats to reveal their fundamental injustice. In particular, I argue that requiring Mexico and other nations to enforce or help enforce U.S. immigration policy treats Mexico and the nations of Central America as mere derivatives, while simultaneously rendering thousands of Central American citizens powerless and vulnerable to systemic violence.

In chapters 6 and 7 we move further south. While most of the United States is focusing its attention on the South-North immigration involving Guatemalans, Salvadorans, and Hondurans, there are also South-South migration crises affecting nations in Southern Central America and South America. And the final two chapters focus our attention there. In chapter 6, I explore the treatment of Nicaraguans in Costa Rica and how it stands in stark contrast to the treatment received by immigrants from Europe and the United States. By assessing what could explain this differential treatment, I propose that this divergent treatment is a manifestation of global oppression in the form of coloniality and cultural imperialism.

In the final chapter, chapter 7, I explore femicide against Venezuelan immigrants in Colombia and what it illuminates about immigration injustice in the South American nation. Doing so reveals that femicide itself is a form of immigration injustice that must be included in our analyses. Beyond this, though, exploring Colombia's efforts to address the problem illustrates that Colombia is both a perpetrator and a victim of immigration injustice in this context.

A FINAL NOTE REGARDING OPEN BORDERS

Before concluding, I want to highlight two benefits of the oppression-centered approach I am proffering here. First, it complicates the open/closed borders discussion in a way that, I think, is desperately needed. Though debates about open and closed borders dominate traditional philosophical literature on immigration, we all know that, in reality, no border can be (or is) completely open or closed. So many see these discussions as unhelpful for providing practical guidance on admissions policies and philosophers remain ignored or excluded in the public discourse.

If we follow the path I am suggesting, though, then the abstract discussion of open or closed borders loses its pull; whether a specific state should or should not have open borders becomes a question whose answer can only be determined after considering the particular histories of the affected parties and the effects of different policies as they relate to oppression.[18] If we want to know how many Mexicans the United States should permit in the country and vice versa, we do not explore abstract arguments about open or closed borders but rather we explore what levels would create or reduce oppression and choose the best option. Admissions policies, in other words, should be based on how various decisions worsen, maintain, or reduce oppression globally and domestically, not principles of open or closed borders.

A second benefit of my approach, I suggest, is that the oppression-centered model better reflects the needs and concerns of Global South nations. Most of these nations, for example, are not struggling with open or closed border policies. For them, immigrants come from the Global North and Global South regardless of whatever open or closed border policy they have in place. But my approach may help better manage this. For example, European, Canadian, and U.S. citizens have increasingly moved to Costa Rica, buying up real estate in both the mountains and the beaches. Consequently, prices have skyrocketed, and many Costa Rican citizens cannot afford housing or food. If, in response to this, Costa Rica decided to limit immigration from these groups (while still allowing it for refugees and other Central American neighbors that have traditionally migrated throughout the isthmus) or limit the privileges those groups can enjoy in Costa Rica, like access to buying land, the global oppression standard provides a more useful way to determine the justice of such a policy than abstract open border discussions. Even better, it does so by capturing the underlying issues, such as global poverty, wealth distribution, and national economic concerns. So my proposed account better encapsulates issues facing Latin American nations while moving beyond abstract discussions of open or closed borders.

In the end, I hope this book expands our conversations about immigration injustice philosophically and geographically. I hope that its readers see the value of emphasizing the relationship between oppression and immigration. I hope it encourages more feminists to engage in the topic and more traditional scholars to see the virtues of exploring it via a feminist lens. I hope that it motivates more scholars to investigate immigration as a *global* matter and undertake projects exploring immigration throughout Latin America and not solely on the U.S.-Mexico border. Finally, I hope these words will inspire us to do our part to improve immigrants' lives throughout the region so that people, like Mateo, receive the respect and dignity they deserve.

NOTES

1. Name changed to protect his anonymity.
2. Immigration Reform and Control Act, 1986.
3. Patrisia Macías-Rojas, *From Deportation to Prison: The Politics of Immigration Enforcement in Post-Civil Rights America*, (New York: New York University Press, 2016), 59.
4. Ibid.
5. Gustavo Arellano, "1994 California Proposition 187: Timeline of Anti-Immigrant Law," *Los Angeles Times*, October 29, 2019, https://www.latimes.com/california/story/2019-10-06/proposition-187-timeline.
6. Macías-Rojas, *From Deportation to Prison*, 61.
7. Mahwish Khan, "CHARTS: Border/Enforcement Spending and Deportation Levels Continue to Skyrocket Under Obama," *America's Voice*, May 25, 2019, https://americasvoice.org/research/charts_enforcement_spending_and_deportation_levels_continue_to_skyrock/.
8. "Fact Sheet: The Cost of Immigration Enforcement and Border Security," *American Immigration Council*, October 14, 2019, https://www.americanimmigrationcouncil.org/research/the-cost-of-immigration-enforcement-and-border-security.
9. Department of Homeland Security, *FY19 Budget Brief* https://www.dhs.gov/sites/default/files/publications/DHS%20BIB%202019.pdf.
10. See, for example, Brian Berry and Robert Goodin, eds., *Free Movement: Ethical Issues in Transnational Migration of People and Money* (State College, PA: Pennsylvania State University Press, 1992); Joseph Carens, "Aliens and Citizens: The Case for Open Borders," *The Review of Politics* 49, no. 2 (1987): 251–73; Carens, *Ethics of Immigration* (Oxford and New York: Oxford University Press, 2014); Michael Walzer, *Spheres of Justice* (New York: Basic Books, 1982); Shelley Wilcox, "The Open Borders Debate on Immigration," *Philosophy Compass* 4, no. 5 (2009): 813–21; Wilcox, "Immigrant Admissions and Global Relations of Harms," *Journal of Social Philosophy* 38, no. 2 (2007): 274–91; Lea Ypi, "Justice in Migration: A Closed Borders Utopia?" *The Journal of Political Philosophy* 16, no. 4 (2008): 391–418; Sarah Fine, "The Ethics of Immigration: Self-Determination and the Right to Exclude," *Philosophy Compass* 8, no. 3 (2013): 254–68; Phillip Cole and Christopher Heath Wellman, *Debating the Ethics of Immigration: Is There a Right To Exclude* (Oxford and New York: Oxford University Press, 2011); Veit Bader, "The Ethics of Immigration," *Constellations* 12, no. 3 (2005): 331–61; Kieran Oberman, "Immigration, Global Poverty, and the Right to Stay," *Political Studies* 59 (2011): 253–68; Arash Abizadeh, "The Special-Obligations Challenge to More Open Borders," in *Migration in Political Theory: The Ethics of Movement and Membership*, eds. Sarah Fine and Lea Ypi (New York and Oxford: Oxford University Press, 2016); David Miller, *Strangers in Our Midst: The Political Philosophy of Immigration* (Cambridge, MA, and London, England: Harvard University Press, 2016); Paulina Ochoa Espejo, "Taking Place Seriously: Territorial Presence and the Rights of Immigrants," *The Journal of Political Philosophy* 24, no. 1 (2016): 67–87; David Miller, "Is There a Human Right to Migrate?" in *Migration in Political Theory*, eds. Sarah Fine and Lea

Ypi; Anna Stilz, "Is There an Unqualified Right to Leave?" in *Migration in Political Theory*, eds. Sarah Fine and Lea Ypi.

11. See, for example, Oberman, "Immigration, Global Poverty, and the Right to Stay"; Fine, "The Ethics of Immigration."

12. Carens, "Aliens and Citizens"; Carens, *Ethics of Immigration*; Chandran Kukathas, "Are Refugees Special?" in *Migration in Political Theory*, eds. Sarah Fine and Lea Ypi; David Owen, "In Loco Civitatis: On the Normative Basis of the Institution of Refugeehood and Responsibilities for Refugees" in *Migration in Political Theory*, eds. Sarah Fine and Lea Ypi.

13. Miller, *Strangers In Our Midst*; Carens, *Ethics of Immigration*; Sarah Song, "The Significance of Territorial Presence and the Rights of Immigrants" in *Migration in Political Theory*, eds. Sarah Fine and Lea Ypi.

14. Amy Reed-Sandoval, "The New Open Borders Debate," in *The Ethics and Politics of Immigration: Core Issues and Emerging Trends*, ed. Alex Sager (New York and London: Rowman & Littlefield, 2016), 13–28.

15. Ibid., 14.

16. Ibid.

17. An excellent example of where this is beginning to take place is the essays in the 2016 recent anthology titled *The Ethics and Politics of Immigration: Core Issues and Emerging Trends*, edited by Alex Sager.

18. I want to thank Santiago Amaya for helping me with this point.

PART I

Chapter One

A Feminist Account
of Global Oppression

In 1983, Marilyn Frye conducted a philosophical investigation into the nature of oppression.[1] Then (as now) the word "oppression" was a contested term; various, even contradictory, claims were made about what oppression was and how it worked. For example, countless women maintained that they were victims of oppression, while just as many men either denied that such a thing existed or claimed that men, too, were oppressed. How could this be? What was it that so many women were sure they experienced and so many men thought either did not exist or was so pervasive that they too were victims? Frye set out to investigate and, in her essay "Oppression" clarified its nature.

In the context of immigration,[2] I believe it is more appropriate to speak of *global* oppression (as opposed to oppression more generally) given the international character of the policies, practices, and norms governing it. But based on the public discourse, it is clear that we do not have a clear sense of what "global oppression" is. For example, while immigrants experience global oppression because of U.S. immigration policies and how they are enforced, critics respond either that there is no such thing (because immigrants are getting the treatment they deserve) or that the true victims are native U.S. citizens (that is, white) whose lives, livelihoods, and culture are under threat from immigrants. How can this be? What is it that so many immigrants clearly experience and so many U.S. citizens think does not exist or think is so pervasive that they are its true victims? This is what I set out to investigate in these pages. Specifically, this chapter aims to clarify the nature of "global oppression" through an exploration of Mexican and Central American immigrant experiences in the United States. I will start to do so by returning to Frye's landmark account.

FRYE'S THEORY

As Frye explained, the root of the word "oppression" (in English) is "to press." She says, "Something pressed is something caught between or among forces and barriers which are so related to each other that jointly they restrain, restrict, or prevent the thing's motion or mobility."[3] This "pressing," however, is neither random, accidental, occasional, or avoidable, nor is it the result of bad luck or the actions of a few bad apples. To the contrary, this pressing results from a systematic network of forces and barriers "that work *together* to reduce, immobilize, and mold the oppressed."[4] As such, oppression is structural.

Of course, says Frye, the mere existence of barriers that restrict and press does not yet constitute oppression. After all, everybody faces barriers, but clearly not everyone is oppressed. To distinguish between cases where restricting choices constitutes oppression and cases where it does not, Frye introduces the concept of the double-bind.

Under oppression, structures work together to catch, restrict, and impede the oppressed by placing them in a double-bind. A double-bind exists when the oppressed's "options are reduced to a very few and all of them expose one to penalty, censure, or deprivation."[5] Put differently, no matter what they do, they could face negative consequences. A common example of a double-bind is young women's sexual expression. If young women have sex, then they are called "whores," but if they abstain, they are called "prudes," "teases," and "frigid." If they masturbate (if that can even be conceived), they are called "crazy," "gross," or "hypersexed." Regardless of their choice, young women are vulnerable to censure. So the distinguishing factor between oppressive and nonoppressive barriers is whether they trap the oppressed in these double-binds.

To be clear, to say that these networks of systems and barriers are set up to restrict and immobilize the oppressed does not mean that oppression is conscious, calculating, or necessarily done with malice (though this clearly could occur). Rather, because of its structural nature, oppression can (and often does) result from well-meaning parties doing what they were taught was appropriate. The problem lies in the structures and norms being upheld in the policy, not the individual character flaws or intentions of the perpetrator. And this means that oppression is located in structures, values, and practices, not in individuals.

A consequence of this is that detecting oppression requires utilizing a macroscopic analysis—one must see how everything is connected (history, politics, laws, social norms, etc.) to determine whether a particular instance is a random, unfortunate event or part of a larger system of oppression. Frye describes this via the metaphor of the birdcage. If one examines how a birdcage traps the bird using a microscopic, individual approach, the answer will be elusive because one will only see a single wire or one wire at a time rather than how the wires come together to prevent the bird from flying away. But, the cage only works because of how all of the wires are connected. Similarly, the only way to identify oppression is to take a macroscopic view of the various relationships among barriers and how they are connected.

Frye's birdcage metaphor raises a key question—who or what does the bird represent? In the domestic context, the answer is almost always social groups. Put differently, when someone finds themselves in a "cage" and asks "why am I in this cage?" (that is, why am I caught in this double-bind?), the answer will not be that individual's actions but instead will be: "You are in the cage because you are a member of a certain social group." For example, the U.S. practice of racially profiling Black and Latino men. Under these circumstances, there is nothing an individual Black or Latino man can do to avoid the police pulling them over—driving too fast will be cause since one is speeding, while driving too slow or driving the speed limit will be cause because both are viewed as suspicious. In these cases, the man is not stopped because of his actions (all of which many white people, including myself, do on a regular basis), he is stopped because he is Black or Latino. In this way, one is oppressed because of one's membership in a social group.

Of course, we have multiple social group memberships and allegiances. And consequently this means that individuals or social groups may sometimes be the perpetuators of oppression and, at other times, be its victims. Upper-class, cisgendered, heterosexual white women, for example, are often victims of gender oppression. However, this same group of women may also be perpetuators of oppression against men and women of color. Similarly, men of color may be victims of racist police violence as well as perpetuators of gender oppression. This is because oppression is perpetuated and experienced in various ways. To capture this, I will build on Frye's foundation by turning to Iris Marion Young's account of the five faces of oppression.

YOUNG AND FACES OF OPPRESSION

Iris Marion Young builds on Frye's account and expands it to capture the fact that oppression is experienced in multiple ways. Young explains that this is because oppression has multiple expressions or faces—exploitation, marginalization, powerlessness, cultural imperialism, and violence. I will briefly define and illustrate each one in turn by referencing Young's work in conjunction with specific immigrant experiences.

Exploitation refers to the systemic transfer of the labor from one social group to benefit another,[6] while marginalization refers to systemic forces that marginalize entire groups of people. In essence, marginalization occurs when society and its institutions cannot or will not use certain groups such that a "whole category of people is expelled from useful participation in social life."[7] By contrast, exploitation occurs when entire groups are used almost exclusively for the benefit of others.

Often exploitation and marginalization lead to the third face of oppression, powerlessness. Generally, those who are powerless systemically, institutionally, and culturally lack power over various aspects of their lives.[8] As Young puts it, they must take orders but rarely, if ever, can give them. The powerless have little work autonomy, often face disrespect, and are not taken seriously in public spaces. Young argues that we can best explain powerlessness negatively: "the powerless lack the authority, status, and sense of self in at least three ways."[9] First, they lack the ability to develop their capacities to improve their position. Second, they lack autonomy over their work life. Third, they do not command respect in larger society and are denied authority. Osiel López Pérez's experience captures all three faces. Here are the details:

A Guatemalan immigrant, Osiel was just weeks past his seventeenth birthday, too young by law to work in a factory, but he got the job at Case Farms with a driver's license that said his name was Francisco Sepulveda, age twenty-eight. On April 7, 2015, Osiel sanitized the liver-giblet chiller, a tublike contraption that cools chicken innards by cycling them through a near-freezing bath, then looked for a ladder, so that he could turn off the water valve above the machine. As usual, he said, there weren't enough ladders to go around, so he did as a supervisor had shown him: he climbed up the machine, onto the edge of the tank, and reached for the valve. His foot slipped; the machine automatically kicked on. Its paddles grabbed his left leg, pulling and twisting until it snapped at the knee and rotating it a hundred and eighty degrees, so that his toes rested on his pelvis. The machine "literally ripped off his left leg," medical reports said, leaving it hanging by a frayed ligament and a five-inch flap of skin. Osiel was rushed to Mercy Medical Center, where surgeons amputated his lower leg.[10]

López Pérez's experience illustrates these first three faces of oppression—exploitation, marginalization, and powerlessness. He faced exploitation as an undocumented Guatemalan migrant in that the benefits of his labor as an undocumented immigrant were transferred to the owners and management of Case Farms. Because of laws prohibiting the legal hiring of undocumented workers, though, this group is also marginalized and excluded from the formal labor market. Worse, because of this marginalization, immigrants like López Pérez are unable to complain about their exploitation out of fear of losing their jobs or being deported. As a result, U.S. employment law joins immigration enforcement structures to render them powerless. And because of these structures and the marginalization and exploitation they provoke, he (and other undocumented immigrants) lacked the ability to improve his position because he had no documents, lacked authority over his work life, and did not command respect from the larger society. To most, especially his employers, he is "just a pair of hands."[11]

Young explains that "exploitation, marginalization, and powerlessness all refer to relations of power and oppression that occur by virtue of the social division of labor—who works for whom, who does not work, and how the content of the work defines one institutional position relative to others."[12] All three of these faces directly affect people's material lives. The fourth and fifth faces, cultural imperialism and violence respectively, while indirectly affecting people's material existence, cause different types of harm.

According to Young, "cultural imperialism involves the universalization of a dominant group's experience and culture, and its establishment as the norm."[13] In situations of cultural imperialism, in other words, one culture's experience is dominant by being equated with what is considered "normal"; all others are weird, odd deviations. In framing the dominant culture as normal, nondominant groups are made invisible or demoralized merely by differing from "the norm."

Cultural imperialism is expressed via increasing occurrences of white U.S. citizens demanding that people stop speaking Spanish in public[14] and pushes to create "English-only" laws.[15] In these cases, citizens are trying to enforce English as the "official" language of the United States in an effort to promote (impose) the view that English and English-speaking people are the norm and all others are deviant, wrong, or abnormal, and thus not "true Americans." As a result, non-English speakers are portrayed as threats to U.S. culture and must be confronted. Sometimes protecting cultural imperialist norms leads to violence, which is the fifth face of oppression.

The final face of oppression that Young identifies is systematic violence. This face occurs when "members of some groups live with the knowledge that they must fear random, unprovoked attacks on their persons or property, which have no motive but to damage, humiliate, or destroy the person."[16] And this violence again occurs because one is a member of a social group. Young explains that "what makes violence a face of oppression is less the particular acts themselves, though these are often utterly horrible, than the social context surrounding them, which makes them possible and even acceptable."[17] This systemic violence is not simply about the violence itself but also the knowledge that members of targeted groups share that they are targeted. Christina Madraso's experience provides one such example.

Christina Madraso, a trans woman, sought asylum in the U.S. after being badly beaten for her gender identity in Mexico. However, her nightmare began when she was detained in the Krome Service Processing Center, where she was placed in the men's ward, and faced harassment by guards and other detainees. She was then transferred into an isolation unit, where she was then sexually assaulted twice by the same guard. After the second rape, INS officials told her that she could either transfer to a mental institution, county prison, or give up her asylum claim.[18]

There are clearly numerous injustices in Christina Madraso's case, and systemic violence is one of them. The specific actions—sexual harassment, rape, and being placed in a classic double-bind with nonviable choices of having to choose between going to in a mental institution (implying that her identity made her mentally ill), going to prison (for what crime?), or dropping her asylum claim (and being forced to endure more systemic violence)—all assured that she would be vulnerable to violence because of her identity as a trans woman and as an immigrant. And because ICE and the border patrol rarely face oversight and complaints against this sort of behavior are rarely heard, let alone addressed, this violence occurs in a social context that makes it possible and acceptable. Beyond this, this violence on Christina's person had the sole motive to destroy and humiliate.

THE SIXTH FACE: DERIVATIZATION

Exploring immigrant experiences demonstrates that oppression includes another face that Young does not discuss—derivatization.[19] Ann Cahill explains that to derivatize someone is to fail to recognize them as a distinct being, instead apprehending them as a mere extension of another. She states, "To derivatize something is to portray, render, understand, or approach a being solely or primarily as the reflection, projection, or expression of another being's identity, desires, fears, etc. The derivatized subject becomes reducible in all relevant ways to the derivatizing subject's existence."[20] The derivatized subject is one who is seen or treated as a being who is reducible to another. She is not a subject who matters in her own right, she is simply a projection of another's will, desires, identity, and fears. So the problem with derivatization, in other words, is failing to recognize the subjectivity of the other apart from oneself; it is failing to recognize someone as a distinct ontological subject rather than as an ontological extension of another. They are not recognized as having their own interests, traditions, identities, or goals—they are merely projections of the derivatizer's will, desires, and fears.

The case of Jorge Garcia is an example of derivatization in U.S. immigration policy. Here are the basics of his experience:

Jorge Garcia was brought to the U.S. by an undocumented family member when he was 10 years old. Today he has a wife and two children, all of whom are U.S. citizens. He's been trying for years to find a path to live legally in the U.S., with he and his wife spending $125,000 in legal costs and fees since 2005. Garcia had been facing an order of removal from immigration courts since 2009, but under the previous administration, he had been given stays of removal. But because of the Trump administration's immigration crackdown, Garcia was ordered in November to return to Mexico. His supporters say he has no criminal record—not even a traffic ticket—and pays taxes every year. Nevertheless, Garcia had to be removed, said Immigration and Customs Enforcement (ICE). On Monday morning, accompanied by ICE agents at Detroit Metro Airport, Garcia went through security as supporters around him held up signs that read, "Stop Separating Families."[21]

Garcia was derivatized in at least two ways. First, he was reduced to "an undocumented immigrant" and not understood as a complex human being with many social identities (that is, husband, father, employee, community member, immigrant, etc.); he was been stripped of his own unique subjectivity. As such, nothing about his circumstances were deemed relevant—it did not matter that he is married to a U.S. citizen, has two children (who are also citizens), is employed, had paid his taxes every year, or had not had so much as a parking ticket. All that mattered was he "broke the law"[22]—he was simply an "undocumented/illegal immigrant," a mere extension of his migration status. As such, his identity as a subject was denied/erased by the deportation policy.

Garcia was also derivatized in that he was apprehended as a mere extension of the will, fears, and desires of a certain U.S. citizen—one who fears immigrants and sees them as "threatening others."[23] In other words, Garcia must be deported because some white U.S. citizens fear that he and others like him are taking jobs away from U.S. citizens, committing crimes, and poisoning our children with deadly drugs. As such, he was not a father, a husband, a law-abiding citizen, a good neighbor, and a hard worker, he was a thief, a criminal, and a murderer. It did not matter whether this is actually true, because to consider that would be to recognize Garcia as a subject, as a human being who exists beyond the imaginary of the frightened (or simply racist, nationalistic, nativist) U.S. citizen. Garcia was portrayed and reduced to a projection of someone else's will and consciousness.

GLOBAL OPPRESSION: A FIRST PASS

The previous discussion provides a foundation for beginning to understand the nature of *global* oppression, in particular how it is similar to oppression as feminists have come to understand it. Like all oppression, global oppression is structural and systematic; it does not result from one or two policies or practices but rather occurs when policies and/or practices are interrelated to work together to reduce, immobilize, and mold the oppressed. Moreover, these networks of forces and barriers are not "accidental or occasional and hence avoidable" by affected parties but rather (unintended or not) they come together to create double-binds. And finally, like all oppression, global oppression can be experienced and perpetuated in multiple ways. For example, sometimes it will appear in the form of exploitation and at other times it will appear as violence. Sometimes, the faces will overlap. The point, though, is that, like all oppression, global oppression is multifaceted.

Despite these common foundational features, though, we must not ignore the *global* in "global oppression"; global oppression is neither identical to oppression more broadly nor reducible to it. Global oppression always relates to policies, practices, and norms involving multiple nations, societies, or transnational communities and their members and is primarily concerned with global, international, multisocietal structures, even if those global structures, norms, and policies play out within the borders of a specific territory. The targets and agents of global oppression are not those Frye and Young describe. And the nature of the faces also differs. So in our quest to offer an account of *global* oppression, I will now turn to discussing these unique features.

DIFFERENT "WIRES": GLOBAL STRUCTURES AND PROCESSES

Like all oppression, global oppression is structural and systemic. However, what differs in the case of global oppression is the specific structures and systems it encompasses. In global oppression, the specific policies, practices, and norms involved in forming the metaphorical cage are global in nature—global norms of business and economic interaction; policies and practices that involve multiple nations, societies, or transnational communities; structures and systems of international governance; and norms and structures governing various nations' foreign policies (including those with respect to immigration). In other words, a key aspect of global oppression is its specifically *global* character.

If global oppression involves global structures, then identifying it requires macroscopic analysis of global policies, institutions, practices, and norms, then this entails at least two things. First, all global norms, institutions, and policies, including well-entrenched ones such as national sovereignty, are within the scope of evaluation. One way that global oppression is furthered is presuming that the global order is fixed or beyond question. This is especially true in relation to immigration, where some critics question or support policies on the grounds of respecting the rights of sovereign nations to self-determination. But this global norm or principle is not universally accepted (nor is it accepted that nations can do *anything* they feel is necessary or right to exclude immigration).[24] More broadly, all norms, practices, policies, and structures that govern the global order and relations between nations and transnational communities are in the scope of global oppression. So investigating global oppression in immigration would include, for example, an analysis of the role of national sovereignty doctrine in the issue under consideration, along with global institutions, structures, and policies that influence immigration policies and practices in specific instances.

Second, because global norms, structures, policies, and practices do not arise out of nowhere, we must look at the history of those policies, institutions, and structures in identifying and confronting global oppression. To be clear, this is also true in a domestic context. However, in the case of global oppression, the specific histories that must be investigated are those involving multiple nations, societies, and international organizations and the global order in which they exist, their relationship to each other within that global order, how that global order is upheld (justly or unjustly) because of that relationality, and those entities' policies with respect to each other. At a basic (and probably obvious) level, for instance, we cannot truly understand the nature and effects of global policies, institutions, and practices outside of their historical contexts; we cannot understand how they came to be, the interests involved, the ways that global power structures are reflected in the policies, etc. without the historical context. That means that we will not be able to identify the existence of global oppression without exploring the history, history and processes that led to, generated, and support global policies, practices, and norms under evaluation.

The central role of globally focused, macroscopic, historical analysis is revealed when we explore Mexican and Central American immigration to the United States. U.S. policy surrounding immigration is largely a twentieth-century phenomenon. Before the Mexican American War in the mid-1800s (1846–1848), what we now consider the Southwestern United States (California, Utah, Nevada, Arizona, New Mexico, and part of Colorado) was Mexican territory. Once the war concluded, Mexicans living in those territories were suddenly living in the United States and there was free movement across the border. In fact, from this time until the end of the nineteenth century, the border with Mexico was not patrolled at all and, when the first immigration control laws were passed (for example, in 1924), Mexican immigrants were exempted.[25]

To be accurate, a border patrol was established in Texas and later in Arizona and California after the Mexican American War. However, it was woefully underfunded, lacked clear authority, and its mandate to enforce the Immigration Act of 1917 did not make it a force to be reckoned with.[26] Members of the Border Patrol did not even have uniforms to distinguish them from ordinary citizens until 1924.[27] And its purpose was not about keeping undocumented migrant workers out of the country so much as to police the behavior of Mexicans in the United States.[28] This is because the border patrol worked closely with agriculture to ensure that migrant workers from Mexico *were allowed* into the country to work for them.[29]

One example of this occurred during World War I when agribusiness and industrialists complained that restrictions imposed in the Immigration Act of 1917 hindered their access to Mexican workers. As a result, these workers were exempted from those regulations.[30] Some of this changed post–World War II, when the border patrol came to be seen as more important. As historian Kelly Lytle Hernández characterized it, "in many ways, World War II was a re-birth for the national police force that had long ago yielded to local control."[31] In this process, a new program, the Bracero Program, was created to help meet labor demands of this sector.[32] The postwar economic boom, combined with the relatively unregulated nature of the border, according to scholars of the U.S.-Mexican border Paul Ganster and David Lorey, led to unforeseen consequences, namely that many jobs for migrants were being created in cities rather than being seasonal labor. And as a result, the migrations became more permanent and included many more families instead of just men.[33]

With this combination of new programs and new professionalism from the border patrol came new enforcement techniques along the southern border. This along with the changes to migration just mentioned caused a great deal of annoyance throughout the borderlands. The local population did not want permanent migration, but local ranchers also did not like the border patrol "taking their workers" and "interfering in their way of life."[34] But it was not until "Operation Wetback" in 1954 (which was an operation to find, capture, and deport large numbers of unsanctioned Mexican workers in the United States) when we began to see tactics of apprehension and other forms of en-forcement, like detention.[35] Given all of this, we can say that, for all intents and purposes, regulating the border in the ways that we think of it today is a very recent phenomenon.

This is even more apparent when we trace the rise and types of legal reforms and increased border security on the southern border that suddenly declared it a crime to enter the United States without papers and made it more difficult to cross into the country. In 1965, the Immigration and Naturalization Act made it a crime for Mexicans to cross the border without permission. In other words, the act "had the effect of converting, almost overnight, the status of a large portion of the long-established Mexican migrant-flow from legal to illegal."[36] Mae Ngai highlights an additional connection between the 1965 Immigration and Naturalization Act and the creation of a substantial number of "illegal" immigrants, namely the imposition of a 20,000 annual cap on Mexican immigrants, which "recast Mexican migration as 'illegal.' When one considers that in the early 1960s annual 'legal' Mexican migration comprised some 200,000 braceros and 35,000 regular admissions for permanent residency,"[37] it is clear that a consequence of the 1965 act was to render what had, up to that point been considered normal migration from Mexico illegal. But we must note that all of these new "illegal immigrants" who entered the United States "without documents" did so legally at the time because documents were not required—they became "illegal" almost overnight with the change in legislation, not change in behavior. Almost immediately after the 1965 Immigration and Naturalization Act, Mexicans were increasingly profiled and presumed to be in the country unlawfully until their legal status could be confirmed.[38]

For various reasons, it became clear that the 1965 law needed reform and in 1986 the Immigration Reform and Control Act was passed. While this law did give legal status to undocumented immigrants who entered the United States before 1982, it also included a requirement that employers verify the immigration status of their employees, prohibited them from hiring undocumented immigrants, expanded guest worker programs for agricultural workers, and expanded border security and enforcement.[39] This law, however, began a cycle of reforms and legal measures that focused on making it harder to cross the border. Ironically, though, it was this increased focus that actually led to increased numbers of undocumented migrants in the United States.[40] As José Jorge Mendoza explains, the reason for this is simple:

> In the past, most immigrants who came to the United States came for work and followed a pattern of circular migration, where they would work in the United States for a limited time and then return home. Few migrant workers came with the idea of remaining permanently in the United States. The increased focus on border enforcement disrupted this pattern of circular migration. As it became more dangerous and expensive to enter the United States through clandestine channels, undocumented immigrants simply began to stay in the United States permanently and eventually sent for their spouses and children to join them. In other words, the increased focus on border enforcement trapped undocumented immigrants in the United States.[41]

In other words, previous to these laws focusing on border security and enforcement, many migrants from Mexico operated on a cycle in which they came to work in the United States when needed and then went back to

Mexico. It was only because of border security that they decided to remain in the United States to avoid the hassle, dangers, and expense of crossing the border. So what was intended as a fix to undocumented immigrant issues actually created a higher population of such things; legal reforms to curb immigration only increased it.

I suggest that this brief and no doubt overly simplified review of some of the history of U.S. immigration policy toward Mexicans demonstrates why it is crucial that we assess U.S. immigration policy and its effects within a historical, global framework. It is through recounting the history, for example, that we get a more complete picture about how individual wires (that is, specific immigration policies) actually fit together. This history also reveals other elements of the policies, such as the ways in which, despite neutral rhetoric, they were directed at Mexican nationals as such. And this is not random or accidental but rather a systemic, structural aspect of U.S. immigration policy that targets nations and transnational communities and their members in ways that place them in harmful double-binds only because they are members of those nations or communities. In other words, what appear to be isolated incidents are actually incidents of global oppression that play out in specific contexts. The crucial point, though, is that the role of history must be explicit in analyses of global oppression. Beyond this, including history in our analyses better helps to reveal why we have issues with immigration justice and undocumented workers (in part because of laws that created crises) and more potential questions, such as why the southern border with Mexico is so much more policed than the northern border with Canada.

THE "BIRD" IN THE "CAGE" OF GLOBAL OPPRESSION

Like all oppression, global oppression is neither perpetuated by nor aimed at individuals as such. Whereas the agents and targets of oppression are social groups and their members, the targets and agents of *global* oppression are nations, national governments, territories, international organizations (such as the World Bank, International Monetary Fund [IMF], and the United Nations), and transnational communities. This is true for at least two reasons. First, individuals as such (meaning as random, private citizens) cannot promote policies or practices at the global level. Instead, to the extent that an individual can affect the global order, it is in the capacity of some institutional role, office, or position they occupy in a nation, international organization, or transnational community. For example, Donald J. Trump cannot negotiate trade agreements as an individual or a mere citizen but rather as the president of the United States.

Second, Hye-Ryoung Kang argues in another context that neither nationalism (which identifies the main agents of global justice claims as nations and national collectives) nor cosmopolitanism (which identifies the agents of global justice as individual citizens of a cosmopolitan world) capture many of the core injustices of the global order. The nationalist model fails to capture many significant features of the current global economic structure and often excludes marginalized voices in ways that obscure the concerns of marginalized groups. At the same time, the cosmopolitan model wrongly relies on a liberal social ontology that is inadequate for capturing injustice; focusing on individuals obscures, rather than illuminates, structural issues at play. But the problems of immigration need a collective, systemic response. So agents of global oppression cannot be individuals.

Still, Kang is cautious that we should not only see the targets and agents of global justice (and I argue global oppression) as nations, nation-states, and national governments because doing so will ignore the fact that the category relies on certain concepts, like national sovereignty, that many will reject. Beyond this, doing so would miss many key aspects of the global order and how it functions to produce global oppression. I agree. But this does not mean that we should deny that identities known as nations exist, negotiate treaties, enact policies, etc. that form the global order. Similarly, international entities like the World Bank or the IMF create and enforce global policies that can cause or alleviate global oppression. So despite understandable concerns, we must include nations and national governments as targets and agents of global oppression. Still, there are international entities like international organizations and transnational communities and societies, such as Indigenous groups, that should also be understood as targets and agents of oppression. In light of this, the agents and targets of global oppression should be seen as being nations, national governments, transnational communities and collectivities, and international organizations.

Now, just as was the case with oppression, we must explain a real issue—individuals, including immigrants, do appear to be facing global oppression as individuals. And, president or attorney general or not, there are often identifiable individuals creating policies and practices that enforce global oppression. How can that be if I am right about who the targets and agents of global oppression are? To answer this, we can return to a question: Why is this happening to me? Why I am in this cage? The answer will be the person in question's nationality or collective membership (not individual actions as such). For example, Central American immigrants face global oppression via the family separation policy of the U.S. government because of their nationality (as evidenced through numerous statements of government officials stating that the policy targets Central Americans), not their act of coming to the United States. It is not *what* they did, but *who* did it that leads to their oppression. People are victims of global oppression because of their national, territorial, societal, or communal membership.

The previous point leads to another, which is that a nation and transnational collectivity or community *itself* can also be the target or agent of global oppression. In this case, when one inquires as to why a policy, practice, or norm is being applied to them in a certain way, the answer is their geographical, global, economic, and/or historic position in the global order. For example, the United States has invaded and interfered in Central American affairs for well over a century. In part, this is because of the proximity of Central America to the United States. In part, this is also because, following the Monroe Doctrine, the colonial world order permitted the United States to maintain hegemony in Central America (and Latin America more broadly). In part, this is because the geography of Nicaragua and Panama coincided with U.S. business interests of building a canal and Guatemala's climate and proximity to the United States coincided with the needs and interests of U.S. fruit producers. Finally, the fact that Honduras and Costa Rica simply bordered Nicaragua to the north and south made both nations targets of U.S. interference and foreign policy. In all cases, the reason the nations of Central America were targeted were not random or the result of their specific actions, but rather was due to their geographic, economic, and historical position in the world. As such, the nations themselves were targets and agents of global oppression.

Before leaving this section, allow me to highlight that, as is true for oppression more broadly, it is possible to be both a target of global oppression in one context and a perpetuator of it in another. Mexico and its citizens may be victims of global oppression via U.S. immigration policy (for example, when the United States targets Mexicans for deportation and then sends massive numbers of deportees to Mexico when they are ill equipped to handle it), while also being perpetuators of it (in the case of the Southern Border Plan, for example).[42] Similarly, Costa Rica may face economic exploitation and cultural imperialism from the United States as a result of U.S. economic and foreign policy but also may be perpetuating exploitation and systemic violence against Nicaraguan immigrants. So a nation, government, transnational community, or international organization is not simply a victim or an agent of global oppression but could be both depending on context.

In summary, then, the targets and agents of global oppression are nations, national governments, transnational communities, and international organizations. They are targeted or are targets of global oppression specifically because of their national or collective identities in the cases of individuals or because of their geographical and geopolitical positions and histories in the cases of nations, collectivities, and international organizations themselves.

Because these positions and histories are complicated, it is possible to be both a victim and a perpetrator of global oppression.

SIX FACES OF *GLOBAL* OPPRESSION

All of the factors just discussed change the nature of the various faces of *global* oppression. In most cases, this will be about *who* or *what* is experiencing the face in question, though sometimes it will also relate to other things. So let me briefly detail how the six faces of *global* oppression differ from their counterparts.

In the case of global oppression, we should understand the face of exploitation as being about the transferring of labor from one nation, national government, or transnational community to benefit another. In essence, when exploitation is expressed as a face of global oppression, one nation's, national government's, or transnational community's labor and activities are used for the benefit of other nations, national governments, or transnational communities. This is fundamentally what I take to be the core concern being expressed about "brain drain"—one nation educates and provides for the well-being of its citizens and then another nation reaps the benefits.[43]

Similarly, marginalization as a face of global oppression refers to global systems, practices, policies, and norms that exclude an entire nation or transnational collective of people from useful participation (because of their national membership) within the global sphere or within a nation. One example of such marginalization is immigration policies that refuse refugee status to members of entire nations because the receiving nation does not approve of the actions of the refugee applicant's home government. Another example of marginalization can be seen in the way the global order excludes stateless people from being able to participate in most activities within nations and globally.[44] In all cases, global policies, practices, institutions, and norms exclude an entire nation and its members from participating in the global order or domestic life.

The definition of powerlessness is relatively unchanged in global oppression; global oppression still sees powerlessness as systemic lack of control over various aspects of one's life. However, in the context of global oppression, this powerlessness stems from one's national or communal membership. Again, we can see this in the treatment of refugees. The United Nations respects sovereignty and thus nations' decisions on how to control who enters their borders. In this way, though, one suffers powerlessness in two ways—they are powerless to improve their lives in their home nation and they are powerless to choose where to reside instead. As such, global norms and global rights of exit and entry expressly render refugees unable to develop their capacities to improve their positions, and deny them both autonomy over their professional and personal lives, as well as respect on the global stage, all because of their membership.

Cultural imperialism in the context of global oppression refers to various ways in which the cultural norms of a nation(s) are presented as normal, civilized, and superior and others are rendered deviant, primitive, barbaric, or odd. This occurs throughout Latin America in relation to the United States and Europe; the United States and Europe are disputed as civilized, educated, and places of opportunity, whereas Latin America is portrayed as violent, poor, and stagnant. As a result, the desire to migrate to the United States or Europe is seen as normal in Latin America, whereas migrating to Latin America from the United States or Europe is crazy or dangerous (unless one is a retiree, in which case it is smart to receive your U.S. or European pension but live on the cheap).

Systemic violence occurs in global oppression when one is vulnerable to violence only because of one's nationality or geopolitical/graphical location. For example, the nations of Central America and their citizens are vulnerable to systemic violence because of global structures that place the United States in a position of such power that it faces no real consequences for perpetuating violence against these nations. The United States, for example, has been condemned by the International Criminal Court for its actions against Nicaragua and ordered to pay billions of dollars to the Nicaraguan state but never did and never will because it chooses not to recognize the jurisdiction of that court. And because of its power position along with the rules of the International Criminal Court that allows nations to opt in to its jurisdiction, nobody will really challenge the United States in this. Similarly, immigrants from Latin America are more vulnerable to systemic violence from U.S. immigration officials because of how they enter the country. Europeans, who primarily enter via airports, do not face this violence. So the United States can act with impunity, thus placing the nations of Central America in a position of being vulnerable to systemic violence from the United States.

Finally, we can see how derivatization functions as a face of global oppression. When a nation, social group, community, or international organization fails to recognize the ontological or political existence of another apart from itself, then derivatization is present. The oppression lies in the failure to recognize a nation, community, or social group as having its own existence, desires, fears, objectives, and culture apart from those who maintain power in the global order. In addition to the political violence, cultural imperialism, powerlessness, marginalization, and exploitation that coloniality and colonialism yield, derivatization captures the ontological erasure of nations, social groups, and communities. As such, if it exists, then there is global oppression that must be rectified.

One example can be found in the U.S. actions toward Costa Rica in the 1980s. In 1949, Costa Rica abolished its army to divert funds to social programs, such as health care, pensions, and education. At that time, it became illegal to have a military presence in the country or involve Costa Rica in military endeavors.[45] But during the 1980s, the United States was waging a covert war in Nicaragua and wanted to open a southern front in Costa Rica in an effort to force Costa Rica into the war. Because Costa Rica was resisting out of a long cultural history, it was not moved. In fact, eventually Costa Rica prohibited these acts, and the United States interpreted the moves as an affront to its power, not the result of Costa Rica's own cultural norms and laws. In retaliation, the United States engaged in various acts of terrorism and set up illegal military operations from Costa Rica. When Costa Rica shut down such operations, the United States threatened (and followed through) with various reprisals. For them, Costa Rican law did not exist; only the U.S. agenda was recognized. The United States could only interpret Costa Rica's actions in relation to its own policies and could not conceptualize Costa Rica as a nation in its own right; Costa Rica was reduced to a derivative of the United States.

SEEING THE BIG PICTURE: APPLYING THIS ACCOUNT OF GLOBAL OPPRESSION

Before concluding, I want to return to the experiences of Osiel López Pérez. Doing so will help us do at least two things. First, it will help clarify the similarities, differences, and overlaps between oppression and global oppression. Second, it will demonstrate the necessity of distinguishing oppression as Frye, Young, and other feminists employ the term and *global* oppression. Specifically, it will illustrate that without this distinction, our analyses of immigration will be incomplete, thus leading us to misidentify global oppression, miss its presence, and/or yield ineffective suggestions for confronting immigration injustices. With that said, let's return to Osiel López Pérez.

Analyzing López Pérez's case through the lens of oppression broadly (rather than global oppression specifically) reveals the presence of exploitation, marginalization, and powerless as I discussed earlier. And this is not random or coincidental. Case Farms has a long pattern of searching for a cheap, malleable workforce and targeting undocumented Latinx immigrants and using their undocumented status to foment these things. Many immigrants, fearing lack of rights and retaliation, were manipulated at Case Farms to buy false documents or face constant threats of deportation if they complained about working conditions, tried to organize, or had workplace injuries. And according to *The New Yorker*, this is part and parcel of Case Farms' playbook, noting that they have a "decades-long strategy to beat back worker unrest with creative uses of immigration law."[46] In 1993, for example, around a hundred Case Farms employees refused to work in protest against low pay, lack of bathroom breaks, and payroll deductions for aprons and gloves. In response, Case Farms had fifty-two of them arrested for trespassing. Then, in 1995, more than two hundred workers walked out of the plant and, after striking for four days, voted to unionize. Three weeks after the protest, Case Farms requested documents from more than a hundred employees whose work permits had expired or were about to expire. And in a final example, in July 2008, more than a hundred and fifty workers went on strike. For nine months, through the depths of the recession, they picketed in a cornfield across the street from the plant. In the winter, they bundled up in snowsuits and protested from a shed made of plywood and bales of hay. According to the N.L.R.B., when the workers walked out again in 2010, a manager told an employee that he would take out the strike leaders "one at a time." All were fired.[47]

Even before Osiel López Pérez came along, then, there was a long history of exploiting Latino migrants and using their labor to benefit the business and not the workers. Clearly, oppression exists here. But the analysis is not complete; there is more to the story, which is revealed when we explore the *global* nature of cases like his.

Let's take a step back to learn how Osiel López Pérez came to a small town in Ohio to work. It turns out that he was following a long line of Indigenous Guatemalan migrants who began working at Case Farms as rejected refugees from the Guatemalan Civil War. It is now well documented that the Guatemalan military conducted a genocide campaign against the Indigenous Mayan population and over two hundred thousand were killed or disappeared. According to *The New Yorker*, "a report commissioned by the United Nations described instances of soldiers beating children 'against walls or throwing them alive into pits,' and covering people 'in petrol and burning them alive.'"[48] Among the towns affected was the village of Aguacatán, from where many Case Farms workers come. There, in 1981, "soldiers rounded up and shot twenty-two men. They then split their skulls and ate their brains, dumping the bodies into a ravine."[49] Despite these atrocities, the United States supported Guatemala's military, and the Reagan administration viewed those fleeing the violence as communist sympathizers who threatened national security. As a result, very few received asylum.

Under these conditions, the Maya who made it to Florida had limited options. So when there was an opportunity to bring them to work at Case Farms, many took the job. And this first group impressed the human resources manager, Norman Beecher, so much that he reported to Leon Fink in his book *The Maya of Morganton* that supervisors kept asking for more, prompting a return trip. Soon vans were running regularly between Indiantown and Morganton, bringing in new recruits.[50]

"I didn't want [Mexicans]," Beecher, who died in 2014, told Fink. "Mexicans will go back home at Christmastime. You're going to lose them for six weeks. And in the poultry business you can't afford that. You just can't do it. But Guatemalans can't go back home. They're here as political refugees. If they go back home, they get shot." Shelton approved hiring the immigrants, Beecher said, and when the plant was fully-staffed and production had doubled "he was tickled to death."[51]

Now, what does our global analysis reveal that we did not see before? I argue that we will see, at least, the following general differences. First, the global structures at play are revealed here (rather than simply domestic structures of U.S. law and immigration policy). Second, the targets and agents of global oppression are different. Third, the double-binds are formed by different structures and norms. And finally, the faces of global oppression experienced change. While I cannot go through a detailed defense of these claims, I will briefly expand on them to clarify my point.

First, new global structures, norms, policies, and practices enter the picture surrounding what happened to Osiel López Pérez. Specifically, the historically minded analysis of how Guatemalans from his village came to the United States for work exposes the role of the Cold War and U.S. foreign policy in his situation. The Cold War set up Guatemala to be in the sights of the United States in the first place because of the U.S. position that it would not allow communism to take root in the Western Hemisphere. This was first and most obviously evident when Jacobo Arbenz was elected on the promise of land reform and other reform initiatives. In 1954, the CIA (with support of the U.S. government) sponsored a coup to oust Arbenz. Ever since, the United States has supported military dictatorial regimes throughout Guatemala in the name of suppressing communism, despite the evidence of mass murder, death squads, and other threats to the Maya. As a result of this posture, the U.S. foreign policy characterized Mayans escaping the violence as terrorists and communists, which prevented them from being granted asylum.[52] Consequently, they were in a vulnerable position from which to sustain themselves. So the relevant structures change and new ones come into view when we focus on global analysis.

Second, when we explore global oppression we see that the targets and agents of the oppression change. In this assessment, the agents of global oppression include the United States, the U.S. government, and the Guatemalan government. And the targets of global oppression are Mayans and poor Guatemalans. Specifically, Osiel López Pérez was not randomly victimized or targeted simply as an undocumented Latino immigrant but also as a Guatemalan. That undocumented Guatemalan workers in particular were the targets was even stated by the human resources manager of Case Farms.[53] So Osiel López Pérez faced the exploitation, marginalization, and other forms of global oppression because of his national memberships.

Third, this broader analysis reveals the existence of new double-binds and the nature of these double binds. For the Maya, their choice was to stay in Guatemala and risk being murdered or to come to the United States without proper documentation. Once in the United States they could choose to return to the conditions of violence or stay and try to survive and work for companies like Case Farms. No matter what they did, they were vulnerable to various terrible consequences. Seeing López Pérez's case as simply another example of an undocumented migrant choosing between poverty and exploitative labor misses these other elements.

Finally, the faces of global oppression themselves are revealed as different when we take this approach. Exploring this via the lens of global oppression shows that exploitation, for example, is present in the transfer of the labor of Guatemalans to the United States and its economy, to the benefit of the United States, not simply a group of employees to a company. Moreover, this transfer of labor was systemic and intentionally connected to the conflicts in Guatemala to benefit business in the United States.

Similarly, we can now uncover the role of derivatization in this case. First, the United States derivatized Guatemala, specifically Mayans, in only being able to apprehend them through the lens of the United States and its needs, interests, and fears. All the United States could conceptualize was communism versus capitalism and could only read the Maya and other reformers' actions as communism, when in reality their actions were localized and basically unrelated to communism or the Cold War. Consequently, the United States could not apprehend the violence against the Maya as anything other than self-defense or responding to terrorists. And this meant that they could not offer refugee status to a group under attack. So the Maya and other Guatemalans were derivatized by the United States and victimized by its immigration policies—denying them protective status as a result.

Because of this systemic denial of protective status to Guatemalans, Osiel López Pérez was an "illegal immigrant." Because the United States has conceptualized immigrants from Central America, including Guatemala, as threatening and here for jobs U.S. citizens do not want, they cannot recognize their unique subjectivity; they cannot see their unique desires, needs, and fears. As a result, he faced exploitation, marginalization, and powerlessness.

While it is obvious to me that feminists would condemn most, if not all, of what was just discussed, the *global* nature of the oppression is missed by traditional feminist analyses focused on oppression. We would have missed, for example, the fact that Osiel López Pérez was not targeted solely as a member of social groups but also as a member of specific nations and transnational Indigenous communities. We also would have missed the fact that there are some specific wrongs going on here related to various global structures and parties in the United States (such as the military and U.S. Department of State) that made López Pérez vulnerable to this treatment. As such, addressing the issues he and others like him face not only requires changing things in the United States but also in U.S. foreign policy and how it interacts with immigration policy. The lens of global oppression, then, reveals new aspects of what happened to López Pérez and other Guatemalan immigrants that we previously did not see.

Of course, there is much more analysis required to defend these claims. What is important for our conversation is less the specific claims made in relation to Osiel López Pérez and more the fact that the lens of global oppression specifically adds important elements to our analyses of immigration. It reveals different structures, targets and agents, double-binds, and ways in which global oppression is experienced than the lens of oppression broadly construed. It demonstrates, for example, that not only are the Guatemalan migrants like López Pérez exploited through low wages and terrible working conditions in the United States but also that this exploitation was expressly part of a global set of structures with particular histories that came together to put Guatemalan refugees (and later immigrants) in double-binds. Clarifying the specific nature of global oppression, then, opens up an entire line of inquiry into the nature of what happens to immigrants, how that treatment relates to current immigration injustice, and what sorts of solutions would be appropriate.

GLOBAL OPPRESSION REVISITED

So what is global oppression all about? First, I want to reiterate that many of its characteristics are shared with oppression, generally speaking—it is structural and systemic, requires macroscopic analysis to uncover and identify, can be perpetuated intentionally or unintentionally, and does not target individuals as such. It also consists of numerous faces (exploitation, marginalization, powerlessness, cultural imperialism, violence, and derivatization), the presence of any one of which is sufficient to claim that global oppression is present in a given situation.

There are key distinctions that identify something as *global* oppression, however. First, the structures and systems that come together to place targets in a double-bind are specifically global in nature. This means that macroscopic analyses must include historical assessments of the relationship between affected nations, societies, and transnational collectivities and the global power dynamics that exist among them. Second, the targets and agents of global oppression are nations, national governments, societies, international organizations, and/or transnational communities. As such, one faces and perpetuates global oppression as a nation, society, transnational community, and international organization or a member of one of these bodies. Third, a nation, national government, society, transnational community or collective, and international organization can be both a victim and a perpetrator of global oppression, depending on context. Finally, given all of this, while the faces of *global* oppression are similar in name and idea, they differ from their counterparts in oppression in the nature of the global structures, double-binds, and who is in the cage and who builds it.

Given this, despite overlapping in many ways, oppression and global oppression are neither reducible to each other nor are they indistinguishable from each other. For one, an implication of my account is that *not* all oppression that crosses national or territorial boundaries constitutes *global* oppression. That is because to be *global* oppression, the oppression must be directed at nations, territories, and transnational communities and their members as such. If it is directed at social groups and their members without regard to the global order, laws, nationality, territory, and so forth, then it is oppression as feminists have traditionally conceived of it. Gender oppression is a prime example of oppression that crosses national and territorial boundaries and yet does not constitute global oppression. The reason is that women and gender nonconforming people are facing the oppression because of their gender identities, not because of anything specifically related to national membership, for example. So it is oppression that crosses national boundaries, but it is not global oppression.

And because the two concepts remain distinct, it is possible for someone to be a victim of and a perpetuator of both oppression and global oppression, depending on the context. Osiel López Pérez's experience again illustrates how this is the case. López Pérez was the victim of oppression in the United States as a Latino as well as simultaneously being a victim of global oppression as a Guatemalan immigrant who had to flee in the first place in part due to U.S. foreign policy in Guatemala. In fact, one could also note that he was a victim of oppression in his home country as a poor Indigenous teenager. So there are distinct types of oppression to which he is subject. Oppression and global oppression are not mutually exclusive.

As Frye once said, "and isn't it strange that any of us should have been confused and mystified about such a simple thing?"[54]

NOTES

1. Marilyn Frye, "Oppression," in *The Politics of Reality* (California: The Crossing Press, 1983), 1–16.

2. Of course, immigration is but one context where this is true. For the sake of focus, however, I am going to limit my examples and discussion to global oppression as it relates to this topic.

3. Frye, "Oppression," 2.

4. Ibid.

5. Ibid., 3.

6. Iris Marion Young, "The Five Faces of Oppression," in *Justice and the Politics of Difference* (Princeton: Princeton University Press, 1990).

7. Ibid., 53.

8. Ibid., 57.

9. Ibid.

10. Michael Grabell, "Exploitation at the Chicken Plant," *New Yorker*, May 8, 2017, https://www.newyorker.com/magazine/2017/05/08/exploitation-and-abuse-at -the-chicken-plant.

11. Reference from the film *El Norte*.

12. Grabell, "Exploitation at the Chicken Plant," 58.

13. Ibid., 58–59.

14. "Man Yells at Stranger for Speaking Spanish|CNN," YouTube Video, 1:35, *CNN*, May 23, 2017, https://www.youtube.com/watch?v=_a-NSz_CzIM; "Man Yells at People in Restaurant for Speaking Spanish || ViralHog," YouTube Video, 0:55, "ViralHog," May 17, 2018, https://www.youtube.com/watch?v=-wGOV2jGk6E; "Man Threatens to Call ICE on Servers Speaking Spanish," *NBC News*, May 17, 2018.

15. Dennis Baron, "Official American: English Only," *PBS*, August 6, 2014, https://www.pbs.org/speak/seatosea/officialamerican/englishonly/; Amy H. Liu and Anand Edward Sokhey, "When and Why Do U.S. States Makes English Their Official Language?" *Washington Post*, June 18, 2014, https://www.washingtonpost.com/ news/monkey-cage/wp/2014/06/18/when-and-why-do-u-s-states-make-english-their -official-language/?noredirect=on&utm_term=.d3937fb44928.

16. Grabell, "Exploitation at the Chicken Plant," 61.

17. Ibid., 61–62.

18. "Immigration and Border Policies," Incite!, accessed January 26, 2020, http:// www.incite-national.org/page/immigration-policing-border-violence.

19. I want to be clear that I am not suggesting that derivatization may not constitute a sixth face of oppression more generally—indeed, I think it does—but my focus is on expanding our understanding of global oppression, so I focus on that here.

20. Ann J. Cahill, *Overcoming Objectification: A Carnal Ethic* (New York: Routledge, 2012), 32.

21. Niraj Warikoo, "Dad Deported to Mexico after 30 Years in U.S.," *Detroit Free Press*, January 16, 2018, https://www.freep.com/story/news/local/michigan/wayne/2018/01/15/jorge-garcia-daca-deported-mexico-immigration/1033296001/.

22. I put this in quotes because entering the country without authorization is a misdemeanor charge, like a speeding ticket. And we would never say that someone who got a speeding ticket was a criminal who broke the law.

23. Carlos Sandoval García, *Otros Amenazantes: Los nicaragüenses y la formación de identidades nacionales en Costa Rica* (San José, Costa Rica: Editorial UCR, 2008).

24. See, for example, José Jorge Mendoza, *Moral and Political Philosophy of Immigration: Liberty, Security, and Equality* (Lanham, Boulder, New York, and London: Lexington Books, 2017).

25. Paul Ganster with David M. Lorey, *The U.S.-Mexican Border Today: Conflict and Cooperation in Historical Perspective*, third edition (Lanham, Boulder, New York, London: Rowman & Littlefield, 2016), 215; Kelly Lytle Hernández, *Migra! A History of the U.S. Border Patrol* (Berkeley, Los Angeles, and London: University of California Press, 2010).

26. Hernández, *Migra!*, 32–33.

27. Ibid., 35.

28. Ibid.

29. Ibid., 55.

30. Ibid., 89; Ganster and Lorey, *The U.S.-Mexican Border Today*, 215.

31. Hernández, *Migra!*, 105.

32. Ibid., 109–10.

33. Ganster and Lorey, *The U.S.-Mexican Border Today*, 215.

34. Hernández, *Migra!*, 153, 159.

35. Ibid., 201.

36. Ibid., 216.

37. Mae Ngai, *Impossible Subjects: Illegal Immigrants and the Making of Modern America* (Princeton, NJ: Princeton University Press, 2004), 261.

38. José Jorge Mendoza, "Illegal: White Supremacy and Immigration Status," in *The Ethics and Politics of Immigration: Core Issues and Emerging Trends*, ed. Alex Sager (New York and London: Rowman & Littlefield, 2016), 216.

39. Immigration Reform and Control Act, 1986.

40. Ganster and Lorey, *The U.S.-Mexican Border Today*, 218 and 220.

41. Mendoza, "Illegal," 217–18.

42. While Mexico's southern border with Guatemala began publicly in 2012, when President Obama's "border czar," Alan Bersin, announced that "the Guatemalan border with Chiapas is now our southern border," it was the crisis of unauthorized, unaccompanied Central American children entering the United States in July 2014

that was the true jump start to this policy, when Mexico's President Enrique Peña Nieto announced the plan with Guatemala's President Otto Pérez Molina at his side. Basically, this policy is about stopping Central American migrants from even reaching the U.S. border by stopping them at Mexico's southern border with Guatemala. According to Salvador Lacruz, a migrant advocate at Fray Matías de Córdova Human Rights Center in Tapachula, Chiapas said, "There has been the consolidation of the plan, and the establishment of a border that is the southern border of the United States. Mexico is doing the United States' dirty work."

43. An excellent essay on this topic is Anna Stilz, "Is There an Unqualified Right to Leave?" in *Migration in Political Theory: The Ethics of Movement and Membership,* eds. Sarah Fine and Lea Ypi (New York and Oxford: Oxford University Press, 2016).

44. For example, see Seyla Benhabib, *The Rights of Others: Aliens, Residents, and Citizens* (Cambridge and New York: Cambridge University Press, 2004).

45. For example, the Costa Rican Supreme Court ruled that it was unconstitutional for Costa Rica to sign a letter supporting U.S. intervention in Iraq during the Bush administration.

46. Grabell, "Exploitation at the Chicken Plant."

47. Ibid.

48. Ibid.

49. Ibid.

50. Ibid.

51. Ibid.

52. Ibid.

53. Ibid.

54. Frye, "Oppression," 16.

Chapter Two

Six Faces of Epistemic Oppression

On April 6, 2015, Raul Ernesto Morales-Ramos, a 44-year-old citizen of El Salvador, died at Palmdale Regional Medical Center in Palmdale, California, of organ failure, with signs of widespread cancer. He had entered immigration custody four years earlier in March 2011. Two independent medical experts, analyzing ICE's investigation for Human Rights Watch, agreed that he likely suffered from symptoms of cancer starting in 2013, but that the symptoms essentially went unaddressed for two years, until a month before he died.[1]

Throughout this time, Morales-Ramos repeatedly begged for care. In February 2015, he submitted a grievance in which he wrote, "To who receives this. I am letting you know that I am very sick and they don't want to care for me. The nurse only gave me ibuprofen and that only alleviates me for a few hours. Let me know if you can help me." In the three weeks leading up to his death, attorney Christina Fialho said her organization received multiple complaints from others detained at Adelanto "about a man who was suffering from diarrhea, severe abdominal pain and uncontrollable leakage of urine." Fialho reports: "When this man asked for a catheter, medical staff at Adelanto denied him."[2]

I stated in the introduction that I define immigration injustice as occurring when immigration policies, practices, norms, and enforcement create, reflect, perpetuate, or support oppression domestically and globally. In chapter 1, I presented a view of what constitutes oppression in both contexts, especially outlining the nature of global oppression. And based on those analyses, I am confident that Morales-Ramos's treatment and death clearly constitute immigration injustice—they reflect both global oppression and anti-Latinx oppression in the United States. But I think the oppression perpetuated and reflected in Morales-Ramos's case (and in the treatment or lack thereof of many others who are left to die in immigration detention centers)[3] goes beyond the social and political realm to the *epistemic*. In other words, the harms and abuses

Morales-Ramos and other immigrants are forced to endure are not simply political or social, they are also specifically epistemic in nature; they are experiencing epistemic oppression. Delineating what "epistemic oppression" is constitutes the primary purpose of this chapter.

KRISTIE DOTSON'S ACCOUNT OF EPISTEMIC OPPRESSION

Feminist theorists have been discussing epistemic injustice and oppression, both directly and indirectly, for years.[4] But Kristie Dotson was the first scholar who explicitly named epistemic oppression as such. She first took this up in "A Cautionary Tale: On Limiting Epistemic Oppression" in which she defines "epistemic oppression" as "epistemic exclusions afforded positions and communities that produce deficiencies in social knowledge."[5] Dotson elaborates by explaining that "epistemic exclusions" are "infringements on the epistemic agency of knowers that reduce her or his ability to participate in a given epistemic community."[6] Given this, epistemic oppression infringes on the ability of knowers to generate, validate, or contribute to knowledge production and dissemination in various communities of knowers. As a result, the knower has fewer epistemic resources from which to draw, struggles to belong to communities of knowers, and is often not afforded epistemic authority they have earned. Dotson explains that all forms of epistemic injustice constitute epistemic oppression because they all "involve some form of pervasive, harmful, epistemic exclusion."[7] And thus all theorists, including epistemologists, must concern themselves with its existence.

A few years later, Dotson continued her exploration into epistemic oppression in "Conceptualizing Epistemic Oppression." There she argues that theorists are reluctant to employ the term "epistemic oppression" and hypothesizes that the source of this reticence is rooted in an (incorrect) assumption that epistemic oppression is reducible to social and political oppression. Consequently, epistemologists, in part, wrongly think that there is nothing distinctly *epistemic* about "the catalyst for and maintenance of such oppression,"[8] and as a result there is no ontological distinction between epistemic oppression and social and political oppression. Given this, they mistakenly believe that epistemologists need not concern themselves with oppression.

The problem, argues Dotson, is that this assumption is false; there is something appropriately denoted as epistemic oppression that is not reducible to historical, social, and political factors. And she defines this epistemic oppression as "the persistent and unwarranted infringement on the ability to utilize persuasively shared epistemic resources that hinder one's contributions to knowledge production."[9] This distinctly *epistemic* oppression originates from epistemological systems and their epistemological resilience and thus cannot be addressed through changes in the historical, social, or political structures.[10] Epistemic oppression can only be altered by dealing with the epistemological systems themselves. Again, then, Dotson demonstrates the importance of thinking about epistemic oppression *epistemically* (and not just socially and politically).

Despite wholeheartedly agreeing with Dotson that we need to think more about epistemic oppression *epistemically*, I also think we must acknowledge that specifically epistemic oppression exists (or at least can exist) *even if it is somehow connected to similar forms of political and social oppression.* In other words, even areas that appear to be reducible are actually not because specifically *epistemic* oppression is present even in social and political oppression. While there *are* irreducible forms of epistemic oppression, in other words, it can also be apt to employ the term "epistemic oppression" in cases where the oppression is reducible to social and political structures. The question is not (or is not solely) how do we identify irreducible epistemic oppression but also how can we identify epistemic oppression in contexts of social and political oppression?

I believe that Iris Marion Young's now classic framework of the faces of oppression can help us here. Namely, understanding epistemic oppression as taking the form of (at least) six faces—exploitation, marginalization, powerlessness, cultural imperialism, systemic violence, and derivatization—will allow us to identify specifically epistemic oppression even if it is reducible or connected to social and political factors. I maintain that these are not simply the epistemic versions of the faces in question, though—epistemic exploitation, for example, is not simply the epistemic version of exploitation. To the contrary, the faces constitute particular sets of epistemic practices, norms, and institutions that cause or lead to distinctively epistemic harms in the various contexts and categories. As such, to use Dotson's language, there are at least six distinct persistent and unwarranted ways that a knower's ability to utilize persuasively shared epistemic resources that hinder their contribution to knowledge production and infringe upon the epistemic agency of knowers, reduce their ability to participate in a given epistemic community, and produce differences in social knowledge. For the remainder of this chapter, I will clarify each face of epistemic oppression using feminist social epistemology and examples from Latinx immigration experiences in the United States.

FACE 1: EPISTEMIC EXPLOITATION

Young refers to exploitation in the sociopolitical sphere as the systemic transfer of the labor of one social group to benefit another.[11] This systemic transfer of labor, however, is not simply in the economic, material, or social realm. As Nora Berenstain explains, there can also be a systematic transferring of epistemic labor from one social group to benefit another, which she calls "epistemic exploitation."

Epistemic exploitation occurs "when privileged persons demand an education or explanation from marginalized persons about the nature of the oppression they face."[12] In other words, in epistemic exploitation, rather than doing one's own epistemic knowledge gathering, those occupying dominant positions want the oppressed to do it for them. In epistemic oppression, then, the epistemic labor of members of marginalized groups is used by members of dominant groups to benefit themselves in various ways— allowing them to engage in epistemic projects of their own choosing, not expending epistemic energy learning about subjects out of their area, protecting their epistemic authority by appearing epistemically open, but still also protecting what Alison Bailey calls their epistemic home turf.[13] Often, if the marginalized person refuses, then they are condemned as uncooperative, selfish, not a team player, etc.

In those ways, epistemic exploitation is the systemic maintenance of epistemic structures that require members of marginalized groups to "do the unpaid and often unacknowledged work of providing information, resources, and evidence of oppression to privileged people who demand it,"[14] including the emotional and mental work of attending to the needs of those in dominant social groups who "just don't see it." And it does so "by centering the needs and desires of dominant groups and exploiting the emotional and cognitive labor of members of marginalized groups."[15] In the process, it protects the group's epistemic home turf and energy, while draining the epistemic resources of marginalized ones.

An example of epistemic exploitation is seen in the experience of one of my former students, Dani.[16] Dani was very public about their DACA status and was a well-known immigration rights activist both on and off campus. One day, Dani was in a political science course that included a unit on immigration. During the discussion, the professor (a self-identified conservative white male) continually referred to undocumented migrants as "illegal." At first, Dani simply raised their hand to ask the professor to stop using the term. The professor responded, "Well, that is a term that many political scientists use." When Dani continued to object, the professor replied that it was Dani's responsibility to explain why the term is offensive, after all, he "was not using the term that way." Dani obliged, carefully explaining the term's connections to underlying nationalism,[17] how it has been identified as a racial slur in the United States, and how it contributes to the criminalization of immigration. In response, a white student replied that "he didn't get the big deal" and the professor announced that he would be showing a documentary the next class that uses the word. Dani did not attend the remaining classes on the topic and refused to take another class with the professor (almost resulting in their inability to complete their major in political science).

Clearly, there are issues of oppression at play here—Dani was vulnerable because of their social group membership as Latinx and their DACA status and was placed into a double-bind of being epistemically exploited or facing consequences of refusing to do so. While there are social and political aspects to the issue, Dani's experience highlights the existence of epistemic exploitation specifically. First, the professor demanded an education from Dani rather than doing his own knowledge gathering. Consequently, he demanded that Dani's epistemic labor be systemically transferred to him. Similarly, the other members of the class did not have to expend epistemic energy learning about the issue—Dani did it for them.

Second, Dani was placed in the position to explain why the term "illegal" is offensive because of the epistemic laziness and pervasive (willful) ignorance of the professor. Dani had to explain the issue because the professor "just didn't get it." The professor of political science, after all, should have known the arguments against the term but did not. As a result, Dani's epistemic labor was transferred from a marginalized group to the dominant group in ways that benefitted the dominant group.

Third, Dani was epistemically harmed in various ways during this exchange. In forcing them to explain the issue, the professor was exploiting both Dani's cognitive and emotional labor, "centering the needs and desires of dominant groups,"[18] and implying that Dani's needs as a knower paled in comparison to their classmates' and professor's. This infringed on Dani's epistemic agency and prevented them from participating in the classroom community to produce knowledge. Dani also lost their ability to develop their epistemic capacities and produce even more knowledge. In essence, Dani was forced to "do the unpaid and often unacknowledged work of providing information, resources, and evidence of oppression to privileged people who demand it."[19] Given this, they were harmed specifically in their capacity as a knower.

FACE 2: EPISTEMIC MARGINALIZATION

Young defines marginalization as expelling a "whole category of people . . . from useful participation in social life."[20] Building on this, I characterize epistemic marginalization as effectively expelling a whole category of people from useful participation in the production and dissemination of knowledge.

Their positions are not considered in the construction of knowledge, their experiences are deemed irrelevant for knowledge acquisition or confirmation, and/or their knowledge is erased from the discourse.

Feminists have long pointed out that the Western philosophical tradition has excluded the entire group, WOMEN, from the group of knowers and potential knowers on the grounds that they are too emotional/not rational. Sally Haslanger, for example, explains that philosophy epistemically marginalizes women by operating on a schema that "presents it as hyper-rational, objective, masculine,"[21] while portraying women as emotional and subjective. Similarly, Kristie Dotson shows that the discipline of philosophy epistemically marginalizes groups via its "culture of justification,"[22] or the way it "requires the practice of making congruent one's own ideas, projects and . . . pedagogical choices with some 'traditional' conception of philosophical engagement."[23] The culture of justification, then, epistemically marginalizes entire groups by requiring them to make their claims cohere with (what are presumed to be) universally accepted philosophical tenets, despite the fact that many question the validity of those "accepted" claims.

Of course, epistemic exclusions go beyond the discipline of philosophy. Miranda Fricker describes another type of epistemic marginalization—hermeneutical marginalization—which occurs when entire groups or subgroups are prevented from participating in the generation of social meaning and understanding of their social experiences.[24] This marginalization is always socially coerced and prevents the hermeneutically marginalized from explaining their own experiences or contributing to the processes that explain them. Instead their experiences are identified and explained by others (dominant groups) or they are simply not acknowledged or validated at all.

Epistemic marginalization goes beyond being unable to generate knowledge; epistemic marginalization also refers to excluding categories of people from intellectual dialogue. As Cassandra Towney aptly phrases it, the epistemically marginalized have "lost the capacity to participate in epistemic relationships that require acknowledgment and reciprocity."[25] These exclusions make members of epistemically marginalized groups "unable to participate in cooperative epistemic interactions."[26] In this sense, as Towney explains, epistemic marginalization goes beyond being excluded as a knower to excluding whole categories of people to such a degree that they lose their place (or are denied a place to being with) in their epistemic communities.[27]

An example of epistemic marginalization in the U.S. immigration context can be seen in the form of "tone management," as described by Alison Bailey.[28] Tone management, at its core, refers to "the expectation that subordinated knowers, if they want to be heard, must calibrate the timber of their message, to fall within the audience's comfort zone."[29] This management, says Bailey, "weakens epistemic credibility by targeting, isolating, and attempting to manage the affective content (the speaker's *manner* of speaking) and the epistemic content (the *message*) in testimony."[30]

Bailey highlights two forms that tone management may take: tone policing and tone vigilance. Tone policing silences another by telling them to express themselves in a certain manner. If the speaker does not convey her message in a way acceptable to the hearer, then she is told that she cannot be engaged with. In the case of tone vigilance, however, the hearer is constantly monitoring the speaker's testimony for signs of anger or other unacceptable emotions that have been attributed to a social group (regardless of whether the speaker actually expresses them or not) and interprets the speaker through the emotions attributed to the group. Consequently, even when members of these social groups speak in a tone that is well within the speaker's comfort zone or what most people would consider "respectful" and "reasonable," they are often dismissed.

The idea is that in order to be invested with epistemic authority, one must deliver one's testimony within certain bounds and in accordance with certain norms. When groups and individuals do not conform to these standards, their epistemic authority is denied outright or their claims are dismissed as untrue or unimportant. As a result, these groups and individuals were prevented from participating in cooperative epistemic interactions (not simply political ones) about what the world is like and the truth of various claims about that world. Put differently, when groups are dismissed only because of their tone, they cannot help generate knowledge about how reality (in this case, immigration realities) is constructed and the facts about *what* is occurring in response to policy, and they are stripped of their place in their own epistemic communities. In this way, tone policing effectively marginalizes all who do not comply with what are taken as proper epistemic norms regarding how to generate and communicate information. As a result, they were rendered epistemically powerless, which is the third face of epistemic oppression.

FACE 3: EPISTEMIC POWERLESSNESS

Those who are powerless systematically, institutionally, and culturally lack power over various aspects of their lives.[31] Generally speaking, epistemic powerlessness refers to the lack of epistemic power and authority. While not explicitly discussing epistemic powerlessness, Cynthia Towney's analysis of the epistemic value of trust captures what I take to be the major elements of such powerlessness. The epistemically powerless are (often) epistemically marginalized and identified as lacking epistemic credibility. And as Towney points out, if one lacks credibility, then one lacks the power to influence others, *even if one is speaking the truth*.[32] The epistemically powerless agent's "assertions gain no purchase, they are overlooked [and] dismissed, as though she did not speak at all."[33] The epistemically powerless cannot defend their claims to know, have no discretion with respect to disclosure, cannot entrust another with what they know, and are excluded from cooperative interactions.[34]

The increasingly discussed phenomenon of "gaslighting" is a strong illustration of epistemic powerlessness. Rachel McKinnon explains that gaslighting refers to hearers telling speakers that that they are overreacting, being too sensitive, and/or misinterpreting events that happened to them. They may also simply deny that the speaker's contention is serious or warrants a response.[35] While there are many concerns with gaslighting, I am interested here in the fact that in casting doubt on the speaker's testimony, gaslighting renders the speaker epistemically powerless, which is part of what makes gaslighting epistemically harmful.

To see how this is the case, let us return to the definition of epistemic powerlessness. Again, epistemic powerlessness refers to the lack of epistemic influence and authority rooted in categorizing a group or its members as untrustworthy and, consequently, lacking in epistemic credibility. When someone is gaslighted, their epistemic credibility is undermined in ways that lead to the speaker's assertions being dismissed, overlooked, and without purchase. As a result, the disadvantaged speaker cannot adequately defend their claims and is denied epistemic authority, thus rendering them unable to entrust others with what they know and excluding them from cooperative interactions. In these ways, gaslighting is a tool to render the speaker epistemically powerlessness.

One place where we see epistemic powerlessness is in the detention of pregnant women by Immigration and Customs Enforcement (ICE). Between December 14, 2017, and April 7, 2018, 590 pregnant woman were booked into custody at immigration detention centers across the nation—where they were then denied sufficient medical care, like prenatal vitamins and regular OBGYN appointments, and physically abused.[36] One of these women, twenty-eight-year-old Rubia Mabel Morales, told BuzzFeed that when she was first taken into custody by the border patrol in December 2017, CBP officers pushed her to the ground and "threw [her] around." She told them again that she was pregnant but, she reported, "They didn't believe me, they said it wasn't important, that it wasn't their problem." According to Morales, "They said I didn't have any rights there and I told them I was asking for asylum because it was dangerous in my country . . . [when she continued to say she was pregnant and fleeing from danger] they said lies, lies, lies, that El Salvador was fine to live in."³⁷ Worse, when these and other accusations were brought to the attention of ICE and Homeland Security, then Secretary Kirstjen Nielsen told Congress that pregnant detainees receive prenatal care, separate housing, counseling, the attention of specialists, and are taken to appointments if they need to go somewhere else.³⁸ So Morales (and other women like her) was deemed epistemically untrustworthy by the ICE agent— both about the state of her home nation and the state of her body, and as a result she lacked the power to influence others about her circumstances *even though she was speaking the truth.* Her assertions gained no purchase, were overlooked, dismissed, as though she did not speak at all.³⁹ As a result, she could not entrust others with what she knew and was excluded from cooperative interactions.

Epistemic powerlessness is also on display in the case that started this chapter, that of Raul Morales. As we saw, Morales begged for care and repeatedly said that he was sick, only to have his responses dismissed and minimized. At one point, he was in excruciating pain from cancer and the facility gave him ibuprofen. When he asked for a catheter, he was denied. Similarly, other immigrants simply claimed that he was deeply ill, again only to have their claims dismissed and go unheeded. Even when their claims corroborated each other, they were not trusted. In these ways, the detention center staff gaslighted the immigrants' claims in ways that made them epistemically powerless; their assertions were dismissed, overlooked, as if they never spoke at all. Their claims gained no purchase because members of this group of immigrants lack epistemic authority.

Much of the lack of epistemic authority for these specific immigrants is rooted in the general fact that Latinx immigrants as a group have been deemed untrustworthy in the dominant epistemic imagination in the United States. Claims that they are fleeing violence, for example, are dismissed "lies to get into the country," as we saw in the case of Morales. This sentiment was echoed by Donald Trump, who said that Central American and Mexican migrants are not really fleeing danger but rather simply taught to say that so they can get into the United States more easily.⁴⁰ In not only gaslighting immigrant claims but then also categorizing them as dishonest and law breakers, the entire group is then stripped of epistemic credibility. The migrants, then, cannot contribute to the dialogue and knowledge about immigration issues *even when the truth.*

I want to emphasize here that, apart from the political harms of all of these issues, these are *epistemic* harms; they are not only being denied entry into a country, immigrants are being denied rightful epistemic authority about the conditions of their own existence, they are being denied recognition as trustworthy members of the epistemic community, and they are being placed in a position where they have no ability to defend their claims to know, have no discretion with respect to disclosure, cannot entrust another with what they know, and are excluded from cooperative interactions. Immigrants are being rendered epistemically powerless.

FACE 4: EPISTEMIC CULTURAL IMPERIALISM

Among other things, "cultural imperialism involves the universalization of a dominant group's experience and culture, and its establishment as the norm."[41] In situations of cultural imperialism, in other words, the dominant culture is equated with what is considered "normal"; all others are weird, odd deviations. Epistemic cultural imperialism, in particular, refers to the structures whereby the dominant group determines what constitutes knowledge, proper justification for knowledge claims, and who constitutes an appropriate knower. The dominant group universalizes their own epistemology as "the epistemology" and denotes alternative epistemologies as "backward," "crazy," or "primitive."

While not necessarily employing the term "epistemic cultural imperialism," numerous theorists, including feminist, critical race, and decolonial theorists, have described the phenomenon in relation to traditional Western systems of knowledge that present themselves as the only valid epistemic systems, displacing or demonizing all others as wrong, backward, or irrational. According to traditional Western epistemology, only justified, true beliefs that evade Gettier problems and can be proven via rational, logical discourse or Western empirical methodology (like the scientific method) can constitute knowledge. All other claims are denied such status and are instead relegated to mythology, confusions, superstitions, or old wives' tales. Under this system, knowledge can only be attained by the right sort of knower, namely one who is objective, dispassionate, and uninvested in the issue at hand; they must be a Cartesian knower—rational, ahistorical, objective, and detached from the object of study such that they can take a "G-d's eye view" and objectively assess the claims and the evidence. Paraphrasing Chief Justice of the United States John Roberts, a proper knower is someone who can just call the balls and strikes. Any subject who lacks these characteristics—for example, is perceived to be emotional, irrational, connected to a certain set of experiences and values, not formally educated, multiplicitous—cannot be a knower. In this way, epistemic cultural imperialism is connected to epistemic marginalization because members of certain social groups, communities, or nations cannot be "proper knowers" and thus are epistemically marginalized and cannot contribute to the discourse.

In asserting itself as the only legitimate epistemic system, epistemic cultural imperialism simultaneously delegitimizes an oppressed group's knowledge system. One way it does so is imposing a core hierarchy delineating human and nonhuman.[42] Lugones explains that the modern colonial logic dismisses those who resist the imposition of their logic as being backward and opposed to progress. Modern logic reduces nonmodern to premodern ways such that we read any attempt to preserve such norms as backward and conservative rather than resistant. So those theorists who present, for example, epistemologies of the South are not presenting new, innovative, resistant epistemic systems, they are simply trying to go back to a defeated, useless past. As a result, they are not proper knowers and both the proposed epistemology and the knower herself are dismissed.

Again, we see this play out in the lives of immigrants. In general, immigrants are denied epistemic authority to speak on immigration on the grounds that they are, in essence, not proper knowers; they lack objectivity and are too emotional or too invested in the topic to be given epistemic credibility. Worse, because they "broke the law" to enter the United States, they cannot be proper knowers; proper knowers after all, are law abiding.

Latinx immigrants also face epistemic cultural imperialism in the language they speak. Recently, for example, there have been public attacks on people speaking Spanish in public/demands that people speak English in their spaces.[43] While this trend expresses cultural imperialism in general, demanding that English be spoken in the United States is also a form of *epistemic* cultural imperialism specifically in that the public implies that in order to be given epistemic authority, one must speak English. We often hear that a teacher, for example, is less qualified if they speak English with an accent. ("They can't even speak English, why should I listen to them!?!") This occurs not only with Latinx immigrants but all immigrants who maintain their native tongues (arguably except for those from Europe). The idea, which infuses the lives of so many first- and second-generation immigrants, is that their native language is the "old country," it is part of the past, and English is the future. In fact, many immigrants do not see a point in having their children and grandchildren speak their native languages.

While some of this is about social acceptance and assimilation, there is also an epistemic component—the knowledge that matters is what English yields. What you would learn in the native tongue is not knowledge—it is backward, old-fashioned stories and myths. Or those with whom you could communicate in the native tongue are not seen as proper epistemic sources (or, at least, not as epistemically important as English-speaking ones). In this way, the language one speaks is associated with knowledge and being a proper knower. And Spanish is not a sign of either in the United States. As a result, epistemic cultural imperialism justifies exclusionary immigration laws for some but not others and the epistemic marginalization of these groups on the grounds that they lack epistemic credibility ("they don't have the right knowledge anyway so we can exclude their contributions") and the social and political marginalization of Latinx immigrants.

FACE 5: EPISTEMIC VIOLENCE

When facing systemic violence, "members of some groups live with the knowledge that they must fear random, unprovoked attacks on their persons or property, which have no motive but to damage, humiliate, or destroy the person."[44] And this violence occurs because one is a member of a social group and is, to some extent, supported by societal norms, practices, and institutions. Clearly this account focuses on physical and emotional violence, but members of nations, social groups, and communities are also subject to systematic epistemic violence. And this epistemic violence, like its social and political counterparts, is supported by societal norms, practices, and institutions.

Kristie Dotson defines "epistemic violence" as

> a failure of an audience to communicatively reciprocate, either intentionally or unintentionally, in linguistic exchanges owing to pernicious ignorance. Pernicious ignorance should be understood to refer to any reliable ignorance that, in a given context, harms another person (or set of persons). Reliable ignorance is ignorance that is consistent or follows from a predictable epistemic gap in cognitive resources.[45]

In other words, this type of systemic violence refers to members of dominant social groups failing to engage in a reciprocal communication with marginalized groups as a result of pernicious ignorance that results from predictable gaps in epistemic resources and that harms the speaker(s). And this is permitted by systems of knowledge that deny epistemic authority to some groups while conferring it to others. Given this, I would add that often epistemic violence occurs because of the speaker's and hearer's social group memberships or nationalities. In other words, the agents and targets of epistemic violence are not random individuals—they are often members of specific social groups. As a result, members of social groups or nations live with the knowledge that that their ideas will often not get uptake (or even be engaged)—intended or not—in ways that are both unprovoked and harmful to both the speaker and the groups to which they are a part.

As Dotson explains, the attacks of epistemic violence take at least two forms—testimonial quieting and testimonial smothering. Testimonial quieting occurs when an audience fails to identify a speaker as a genuine knower.[46] In other words, someone's testimony is quieted when she is refused epistemic authority; she is not seen as someone who could produce or convey authoritative knowledge. Again, I would add that the reason they are denied their rightfully earned epistemic authority is because of their social group or national membership (for example, women are too emotional to reason). As a result, their testimony goes unheard or unengaged; the speaker is not taken seriously by the hearer.

The second form epistemic violence takes is testimonial smothering. Testimonial smothering occurs when the speaker perceives the immediate audience as unwilling or unable to gain the appropriate uptake of proffered testimony, and consequently they do not speak. Or they do speak but only on topics or in ways that the hearer will validate or understand. As Dotson puts it, "Testimonial smothering, ultimately, is the truncating of one's own testimony in order to insure that the testimony contains only content for which one's audience demonstrates testimonial competence."[47] Put differently, the speaker silences themselves because they perceive the audience as unable or unwilling to hear their testimony. This type of epistemic violence is often found with the other faces in that it leads to, reflects, and reinforces epistemic marginalization, powerlessness, cultural imperialism, and derivatization.

Here too we see numerous cases of epistemic violence committed against immigrants. We can immediately note testimonial quieting in the Trump administration and its supporters to protests of the zero-tolerance policy. Defenders of policy refused to see the immigrants and their children affected as epistemic authorities and refused to engage them in a reciprocal conversation or serve as a genuine audience to their claims out of pernicious (and willful) ignorance. They simply refused to engage. One supporter said, for example, "You know, I'm sick of these bleeding-heart liberals, career Democrats like Pelosi . . . complaining about these immigrants. What have they done for 30 years? You know, tell me. What have they done? It's why we have these problems. All of a sudden they come on and they're so heartfelt. It makes me sick. People need to obey the law."[48] In this case, the speaker refuses to engage because he thinks that they are too liberal and emotional. Similarly, conservative commentator Tucker Carlson refuses to engage on the grounds that people are not really interested in the issue. He said, "You think any of these people really care about family separation? . . . No matter what they tell you, this is not about helping children. . . . Their goal is to change your country forever—and they are succeeding, by the way."[49] Attorney General Jeff Sessions expressed similar sentiments recently, saying,

> The rhetoric we hear from the other side on this issue—as on so many others—has become radicalized. We hear views on television today that are on the lunatic fringe. And what is perhaps more galling is the hypocrisy. These same people live in gated communities many of them and are featured at events where you have to have an ID even to even come in and hear them speak—they like a little security around themselves. And if you try to scale the fence, believe me, they'll be only too happy to have you arrested and separated from your children, I would like to see that.[50]

So Sessions refuses to listen to the protesters' points by denying the genuineness of their anger and, as a result, of their claims.

We have also seen evidence that immigrants are smothering their testimony about their experiences and thus face epistemic violence in another way. Increasingly, for example, immigrants report being too fearful of being deported themselves to come forward to authorities when they are victims of crimes or workplace violations.[51] Or in a classroom setting or work environment, sensing that they are dealing with a hostile audience, immigrants will smother their testimony. Returning to the example of Dani, because the professor gave no uptake to their testimony about the oppressive nature of the term "illegal," Dani chose not to attend classes where immigration was discussed and did not feel that they were able to participate in class discussions going forward because their previous testimony was dismissed and they were not granted epistemic authority others enjoyed (thus causing another harm of cheating them out of the educational opportunities they are paying for). So they smothered their testimony.

FACE 6: EPISTEMIC DERIVATIZATION

To derivatize someone is to fail to recognize them as a distinct being, as a mere extension of another. As Ann Cahill explains, "To derivatize something is to portray, render, understand, or approach a being solely or primarily as the reflection, projection, or expression of another being's identity, desires, fears, etc. The derivatized subject becomes reducible in all relevant ways to the derivatizing subject's existence."[52] The derivatized subject is one who is seen or treated as a being who is reducible to another; she is simply a projection of another's will, desires, identity, and fears.

I propose that the sixth face of epistemic oppression is epistemic derivatization. The epistemically derivatized are not treated as epistemic subjects in their own right. Their knowledge and perspectives are portrayed, rendered, understood, and approached as being solely or primarily reflections, projections, or expressions of the epistemic agents' identities, desires, and fears. To the extent that they are consulted, it is only about matters deemed important to the dominant agents. Moreover, they are denied any epistemic existence apart from the dominant agent; their projects are appropriated by dominant groups, not acknowledged, or discredited as not being knowledge at all (instead they are superstition, mythology, or relics of the past).

Gaile Pohlhaus Jr. explains the nature of epistemic derivatization in more detail in her essay "Discerning the Primary Epistemic Harm in Cases of Testimonial Injustice."[53] There Pohlhaus suggests that the derivative epistemic relationship be conceived of in terms of the subject/other (rather than subject-object) framework. In this relation, says Pohlhaus, the epistemic "other" serves to recognize and maintain the understanding of the world as it is experienced from dominant subjectivities, but they do not receive reciprocal epistemic support for their own experiences and understanding of the world.[54] So the recognition only goes in one direction—the epistemic other recognizes the dominant subjectivities but not the reverse. In these cases, the derivatized "other's capacities as a subject are reduced to attending only to that which stems from the perpetuator's subjectivity, so that anything the victim might try to express that exceeds the range of the perpetuator's subjectivity is actively prohibited and/or left unrecognized by the perpetuator."[55] In other words, the epistemically derivatized's subject can only be seen as epistemically credible when supporting the perpetuator's worldview; she cannot express or be seen as a knower about anything that goes beyond the perpetuator's understanding.

In the context of immigration, we can see multiple examples of epistemic derivatization. Donald Trump, for example, respects the knowledge of Reverend Samuel Rodriguez about DACA (who agreed to support his calls for funding a border wall)[56] because his views cohere with Trump's worldview, but he denies that miserable conditions exist for children in detention centers because it goes beyond what he is willing to accept. And this is the case about immigrant testimony about abusive conditions in detention centers. For example, while Rafael and Kimberly Martinez, Honduran asylum seekers, reported to *The Guardian* that "the conditions were horrible, everything was filthy and there was no air circulating. . . . It's as though they wanted to drain every positive feeling out of us,"[57] Donald Trump claimed that "the treatment of detainees could not be better"[58] because that is all his epistemic apparatus will allow him to acknowledge. This is despite the fact that there are numerous reports detailing abuse at the hands of ICE.[59] Despite this litany of evidence, however, these experiences are all denied by those who support more severe immigration restrictions. A Customs and Border Protection (CBP) spokeswoman said, "The alleged incidents do not equate to what we know to be common practice at our facilities. We treat those in our custody with dignity and respect."[60] She even questioned whether the "hieleras"—the icebox facilities referred to by the detainees—were in fact run by its sister agency ICE, despite ICE actually affirming that they do.[61] Immigrants and others who document their stories are treated as epistemic derivatives of the dominant group and are not accorded epistemic authority unless they reinforce the epistemic structures of those in power. As such, they are epistemically harmed because they are not recognized as knowers in their own right; they are not recognized as being epistemic subjects who can generate knowledge that goes beyond the derivatizer's epistemic resources.

RELATIONSHIPS AMONG THE FACES

Broadly speaking, all of the faces highlight unique ways in which epistemic oppression is expressed and how epistemic institutions and practices cause harm. The fact that they can be distinguished in their own right should not obscure the fact that the faces of epistemic oppression are also often interrelated. For example, Dani's case demonstrates how epistemic exploitation can lead to epistemic violence in the form of *both* testimonial quieting (the professor refuses to engage with them) and testimonial smothering (in that Dani feels they cannot engage in any more discussions on immigration) as well as being epistemic marginalization and derivatization (Dani cannot add anything to the professor's knowledge base). Before concluding, then, I want to briefly highlight a couple of ways the faces relate to each other.

The first relationship I want to highlight is that between epistemic cultural imperialism, which is often carried out or maintained via epistemic exploitation and violence. Aníbal Quijano's account of the colonial project of epistemic cultural imperialism illustrates this relationship well. According to Quijano, beginning in 1492, Spanish conquerors formed relationships of power with the Indigenous peoples based on ethnic and epistemic norms that identified the former as superior to the latter. "This matrix of power did not only entail militarily subjugating the indigenous peoples and dominating them by force (colonialism); it also attempted to radically change their traditional knowledge of the world, to adopt the cognitive horizon of the dominator as their own (coloniality)."[62] In other words, colonial power was

not limited to Europe's military or economic domination but was also fundamentally epistemological; it was about convincing the Indigenous groups to
accept Eurocentric knowledge as natural and normal so that they would not
impede colonial power. As Quijano explains,

> The repression was imposed, above all, on the ways of knowing, producing
> knowledge, producing perspectives, images, and systems of images, symbols,
> modes of signification; . . . the colonizers also imposed a mystified image of
> their own models of production of knowledge and meaning.[63]

In other words, an essential element of the colonial project was for the European epistemology to come to be seen as natural, neutral, normal, and universal. But because the Indigenous peoples had their own epistemologies, tactics
had to be employed to discredit, repress, and eliminate any vestige of Indigenous epistemologies. This could not be done exclusively via military and
other physical domination; the process had to have epistemic components.

To achieve successful epistemic cultural imperialism, numerous strategies
were deployed. First, colonial logic "expropriated those cultural discoveries
of the colonized peoples that were most apt for developing capitalism to the
profit of the European center."[64] In other words, they stole the cultural insights
of conquered peoples and used them to the economic and cultural benefit of
Europe; they engaged in epistemic exploitation. Second, "they repressed as
much as possible the colonized forms of knowledge production, models of
the production of meaning, symbolic universe, and models of expression of
objectification and subjectivity."[65] As much as they could, the colonizers sup-
pressed epistemic and ontological systems of the colonized. They repressed
spiritual expression, imposed conversion to Christianity, required speaking
Spanish, mocked Indigenous cosmologies, etc. In other words, they committed epistemic violence; the Europeans quieted the testimonies of Indigenous
people and engaged in tactics that forced Indigenous peoples to smother their
testimony. Of course, this could not be done completely so "forms of knowledge [that] were not completely eliminated . . . were at most deprived of their
ideological legitimacy."[66] So whatever forms of knowledge were associated
with traditional Indigenous ideas (or simply not modern, colonial ones) were
portrayed as superstition, myth, or simply the past. So epistemic exploitation,
epistemic cultural imperialism, and epistemic violence are interconnected.

We can also see various connections around epistemic powerlessness. When
a group is epistemically marginalized, they are also often rendered epistemically powerless. When people are systemically excluded from the community
of knowers, then they are no longer able to contribute to that community of
knowers. Similarly, when a group's knowledge is erased from the discourse,
their members are often interpreted as lacking credibility (after all, if they had

credibility then they would not have been marginalized). And as Towney elucidated, if one lacks credibility, then one lacks the power to influence others, *even if one is speaking the truth.*[67] As a result, the speaker is denied epistemic authority and cannot entrust others with what she knows. Often epistemic marginalization and epistemic powerlessness go hand in hand.

Epistemic powerlessness and marginalization are also very connected to epistemic derivatization, as can be seen if we return to gaslighting. Recall that gaslighting involves a hearer casting doubt on the claims of a speaker. Sometimes this doubt is clearly expressed and sometimes it is subtle. In either case, I would suggest that, at least some of the time, the hearer casts doubt on the speaker's claims because they do not conform to the hearer's perceptions and experiences. So because the speaker's claims do not match the hearer's perception of the world, they must be false. In this way, then, gaslighting treats a speaker as an epistemic derivative. This, then, can have the effect of rendering them epistemically powerless; they will lack credibility to influence others even when they are speaking the truth, their assertions gain no purchase when they conflict with or challenge the epistemic picture of the hearer, and they are overlooked when their assertions do not conform to the picture the hearer subscribes to.

I could keep going, but I have made my point—the faces interrelate and reinforce each other at the same time that they are distinct. All of the faces convey unique ways in which epistemic oppression is experienced and how epistemic systems and practices are harmful. The presence of one or many indicates that epistemic oppression is operative in that context.

CONCLUDING THOUGHTS

Sadly, since Raul Ernesto Morales-Ramos's death, many more have followed. As of June 2019, twenty-four immigrants have died in ICE custody since Donald Trump took office.[68] Since then, seven more have died, including Samuelino Pitchout Mavinga.[69] Every time news of another death emerges, we condemn it. But what has been largely ignored in the political discussion is how these deaths result not only from social and political oppression but also from *epistemic* oppression. In part, I think Dotson has it right—some mistakenly think that a uniquely epistemic oppression does not exist (since such oppression is reducible to others). Thankfully, Dotson demonstrated that this is false—there is something that is specifically *epistemic oppression.*

Still, there is another piece of the puzzle. The other part of the explanation, I think, is that we lack a robust understanding of what epistemic oppression is and specifically how it can manifest in relation to social and political factors. In that regard, we lack an account of how we can identify something as distinctly *epistemic* oppression when it is connected to social and political oppression. This chapter has tried to make progress in remedying that. Specifically, I have tried to provide a framework that can be used to support those who claim that they are experiencing epistemic oppression and to reject those who refuse to recognize those claims. Hopefully, I have succeeded to some degree such that we can hear the claims of immigrants, recognize and respect their status as knowers, and confront the *epistemic* oppression they face.

NOTES

1. Mitch Blunt, *Systemic Indifference: Dangerous and Substandard Care in US Immigration Detention* (Human Rights Watch, 2017).

2. Kate Linthicum, "Salvadoran Immigrant Held at Adelanto ICE Facility Dies," *Los Angeles Times*, April 7, 2015, https://www.latimes.com/local/lanow/la-me-ln-detainee-death-20150407-story.html.

3. Allison B. Wolf, "Dying in Detention as an Example of Oppression," *APA Newsletter on Hispanic/Latino Issues in Philosophy* 19, no. 1 (Fall 2019): 2–8; Wolf, "Dying in Detention: Where Are the Bioethicists?" in *Applying Nonideal Theory to Bioethics: Living and Dying in a Nonideal World*, eds. Elizabeth Victor and Laura Guidry-Grimes (Springer, forthcoming).

4. See, for example, Miranda Fricker, *Epistemic Injustice: Power and Ethics of Knowing* (New York and London: Oxford University Press, 2009); José Medina, *Epistemologies of Resistance: Gender and Racial Oppression, Epistemic Injustice, and Resistant Imaginations* (London and New York: Oxford University Press, 2011); Rachel McKinnon, "Allies Behaving Badly: Gaslighting as Epistemic Injustice," in *Routledge Handbook on Epistemic Injustice*, eds. Gaile Pohlhaus Jr., Ian James Kidd, and Jose Medina (New York: Routledge, 2017); Nora Berenstain, "Epistemic Exploitation," *Ergo: An Open Access Journal of Philosophy* 3 (2016): 569–90; Kristie Dotson, "A Cautionary Tale: On Limiting Epistemic Oppression," *Frontiers: A Journal of Women Studies* 33, no. 1 (2012): 24–47; Dotson, "Conceptualizing Epistemic Oppression," *Social Epistemology* 28, no. 2 (2014): 115–38; Gaile Pohlhaus Jr., "Discerning the Primary Epistemic Harm in Cases of Testimonial Injustice," *Social Epistemology: A Journal of Knowledge, Culture and Policy* 28, no. 2 (2014): 99–114; Alison Bailey, "On Anger, Silence, and Epistemic Injustice," *Royal Institute of Philosophy Supplements* 84 (November 2018): 93–115, https://doi.org/10.1017/S1358246118000565.

5. Dotson, "A Cautionary Tale," 24.

6. Ibid., 24.

7. Ibid., 36.

8. Dotson, "Conceptualizing Epistemic Oppression," 116.

9. Ibid.

10. Ibid.

11. Iris Marion Young, *Justice and the Politics of Difference* (Princeton, NJ: Princeton University Press, 1990), 49.

12. Berenstain, "Epistemic Exploitation."

13. Alison Bailey, "Tracking Privilege—Preserving Epistemic Pushback in Feminist and Critical Race Philosophy Classes," *Hypatia* 32, no. 4 (Fall 2017): 876–92, https:doi/pdf/10.1111/hypa.12354; Bailey, "The Unlevel Knowing Field: An Engagement with Dotson's Third-Order Epistemic Oppression," *Social Epistemology Review and Reply Collective*, 3, no. 10 (2014): 62–68.

14. Ibid.

15. Ibid.

16. I have changed "Dani's" name to protect their privacy.

17. For an excellent discussion of the connection between "illegal" and white nationalism, see Mendoza, "Illegal: White Supremacy and Immigration Status," in *The Ethics and Politics of Immigration: Core Issues and Emerging Trends*, ed. Alex Sager (New York and London: Rowman & Littlefield, 2016).

18. Mendoza, "Illegal."

19. Ibid.

20. Young, *Justice and the Politics of Difference*, 53.

21. Sally Haslanger, "Changing the Ideology and Culture of Philosophy: Not by Reason (Alone)," *Hypatia* 23, no. 2 (2008): 210–23, https://doi.org/10.1111/j.15272001.2008.tb01195.x.

22. Kristie Dotson, "How Is This Paper Philosophy?" *Comparative Philosophy* 3, no. 1 (2012): 3–29.

23. Ibid., 6.

24. Fricker, *Epistemic,* 153–54.

25. Cynthia Towney, "Trust and the Curse of Cassandra: An Exploration of the Value of Trust," *Philosophy in the Contemporary World* 10, no. 2 (Fall–Winter 2003): 107.

26. Ibid., 106.

27. Ibid., 108.

28. Bailey, "On Anger, Silence, and Epistemic Injustice."

29. Ibid., 97.

30. Ibid.

31. Young, *Justice and the Politics of Difference*, 57.

32. Towney, "Trust and the Curse of Cassandra."

33. Ibid., 105.

34. Ibid., 108.

35. McKinnon, "Allies Behaving Badly"

36. Ema O'Connor and Nidhi Prakash, "Pregnant Women Say They Miscarried in Immigration Detention and Didn't Get the Care They Needed," *BuzzFeed*, July 9, 2018, https://www.buzzfeednews.com/article/emaoconnor/pregnant-migrant-women-miscarriage-cpb-ice-detention-trump; Madeleine Gatto, "Pregnant Women Are Being Abused and Neglected in Immigration Detention Centers," *Ms.*, July 13, 2018, http://msmagazine.com/blog/2018/07/13/pregnant-women-abused-neglected-immigration-detention-centers/.

37. O'Connor and Prakash, "Pregnant Women"; Harriet Sinclair, "Pregnant Women Detained by ICE Miscarried and Did Not Get Medical Care, Report Claims,"

Newsweek, July 10, 2018, https://www.newsweek.com/pregnant-women-detained -ice-miscarried-babies-and-didnt-get-medical-care-1015676.

38. Ibid.

39. Ibid., 105.

40. Emma Roller, "Trump Implies Asylum Seekers Are Liars, So It's Not Hard to See Where This Goes Next," *Splinter*, June 21, 2018, https://splinternews.com/trump -implies-asylum-seekers-are-liars-so-its-not-hard-1827016969.

41. Young, *Justice and the Politics of Difference*, 58–59.

42. María Lugones, "Toward a Decolonial Feminism," *Hypatia* 25, no. 4 (Fall 2010): 743.

43. "Man Yells at Stranger for Speaking Spanish|CNN," YouTube Video, 1:35, *CNN*, May 23, 2017, https://www.youtube.com/watch?v=_a-NSz_CzIM; "Man Yells at People in Restaurant for Speaking Spanish ‖ ViralHog," YouTube Video, 0:55, "ViralHog," May 17, 2018, https://www.youtube.com/watch?v=-wGOV2jGk6E; "Man Threatens to Call ICE on Servers Speaking Spanish," *NBC News*, May 17, 2018.

44. Young, *Justice and the Politics of Difference*, 61.

45. Kristie Dotson, "Tracking Epistemic Violence, Tracking Practices of Silencing," *Hypatia* 26, no. 2 (Spring 2011): 238.

46. Ibid., 242.

47. Ibid., 244.

48. Rush Limbaugh, "Without Zero Tolerance America Will Cease to Be," *The Rush Limbaugh Show*, June 21, 2018, https://www.rushlimbaugh.com/daily/2018/06/21/ without-zero-tolerance-our-culture-will-be-erased/.

49. Michelle Lou, "Tucker Carlson: Keeping Immigrant Families Together Threatens 'Your Country,'" *Huffington Post*, June 19, 2018, https://www.huffingtonpost. com/entry/tucker-carlson-immigration-separation_us_5b28f904e4b05d6c16c7536e.

50. Emily Tillett, "Jeff Sessions Mocks Liberals on 'Lunatic Fringe' over Family Separation," *CBS News*, June 27, 2018, https://www.cbsnews.com/news/jeff -sessions-mocks-liberals-on-lunatic-fringe-over-family-separation/.

51. Tom Dart, "Fearing Deportation, Undocumented Immigrants Wary of Reporting Crimes," *The Guardian*, March 23, 2017, https://www.theguardian .com/us-news/2017/mar/23/undocumented-immigrants-wary-report-crimes -deportation?CMP=share_btn_link.

52. Ann J. Cahill, *Overcoming Objectification: A Carnal Ethic* (New York: Routledge, 2012), 32.

53. Pohlhaus Jr., "Discerning the Primary Epistemic Harm in Cases of Testimonial Injustice," 99–114.

54. Ibid., 105–106.

55. Ibid.

56. Laurie Goodstein, "I Know I'll Be Criticized: The Latino Evangelical Who Advises Trump on Immigration," *New York Times*, March 27, 2018, https://www .nytimes.com/2018/03/27/us/evangelical-dreamers-rodriguez.html.

57. Andrew Gumbel, "'They were laughing at us': Immigrants Tell of Cruelty, Illness and Filth in US Detention," *The Guardian*, September 12, 2018, https://www .theguardian.com/us-news/2018/sep/12/us-immigration-detention-facilities.

58. Yamily Habib, "Violence and Abuse: The Daily Life of Immigrants in Detention Centers," *Al Día*, July 20, 2018, http://aldianews.com/articles/politics/immigra tion/violence-and-abuse-daily-life-immigrants-detention-centers/53396.

59. Alice Speri, "Detained, then Violated," *The Intercept*, April 11, 2018, https:// theintercept.com/2018/04/11/immigration-detention-sexual-abuse-ice-dhs/

60. Habib, "Violence and Abuse."

61. Ibid.

62. Santiago Castro-Gómez, "(Post)Coloniality for Dummies: Latin American Perspectives on Modernity, Coloniality, and the Geopolitics of Knowledge," in *Coloniality at Large: Latin America and the Postcolonial Debate*, eds. Mabel Moraña, Enrique Dussell, and Carlos A. Jáuregui (Durham and London: Duke University Press, 2008), 281.

63. Aníbal Quijano, "Colonialidad y Modernidad/Racionalidad," in *Los Conquistadores: 1492*, eds. Robin Blackburn and Heraclio Bonilla, as cited by Castro-Gómez, "(Post)Coloniality for Dummies," 281.

64. Ibid., 189.

65. Ibid.

66. Castro- Gómez, "(Post)Coloniality for Dummies," 282.

67. Towney, "Trust and the Curse of Cassandra."

68. Hannah Rappleye and Lisa Riordan Seville, "24 Immigrants Have Died in ICE Custody During the Trump Administration," *NBC News*, June 9, 2019, https://www .nbcnews.com/politics/immigration/24-immigrants-have-died-ice-custody-during -trump-administration-n1015291.

69. American Immigration Lawyers Association, "Deaths at Adult Detention Centers," accessed January 9, 2020, https://www.aila.org/infonet/deaths-at-adult -detention-centers.

PART II

Chapter Three

DACA, Raids, and Deportation

The Immigration Injustices of Focusing on "Legality" in U.S. Deportation Policy

> I want people to know that if they come into the United States illegally, they're getting out.
>
> —Donald Trump

While Donald Trump's statement now reflects the official views of the U.S. government and many of its people, this is not always how the United States viewed undocumented Mexican and Central American immigrants. In fact, the category of "illegal immigrant" itself is a recent creation.

Our attitudes toward specific undocumented immigrants, those from Mexico and Central America, have seen some of the most dramatic changes over the past century. Our southern border with Mexico was not patrolled at all until the end of the nineteenth century. When this changed, for example in 1917 and 1924 when the first immigration control laws were passed, Mexican citizens were exempted from regulation.[1] And when the border was patrolled during most of the twentieth century, the border patrol and Immigration and Naturalization Services did not focus on detention or deportation; their job was to *regulate* migration, not to *punish* it.[2] But then this began to change in the mid-1990s.

The 1965 Immigration and Naturalization Act converted an open border between Mexico and the United States into a regulated one. In less than twenty-four hours, Mexicans who had been crossing the border for generations to work in the United States and then returned home to Mexico when the job was complete suddenly became "illegal."[3] And this was the intent. As historian Mae Ngai highlights, the 1965 act imposed a 20,000-person annual cap on Mexican immigrants, which "recast Mexican migration as 'illegal.' When one considers that in the early 1960s annual 'legal' Mexican migration

comprised some 200,000 braceros and 35,000 regular admissions for permanent residency,"[4] it is clear that an intention of the 1965 act was to render
normal migration from Mexico "illegal." And from then on, the category
of "illegal immigrant" became part of the U.S. imaginary and connected to
Mexican immigration.

Twenty years later, however, the big push began to connect immigration
from Mexico and Central America to criminality. In 1986, the Immigration
Reform and Control Act was passed, requiring employers to verify the immigration status of their employees, prohibiting them from hiring undocumented
immigrants, and expanding border security and enforcement.[5] It also expanded
the population eligible for deportation in U.S. law and reinforced the connection between deportation and "illegal" behavior.[6] Then in 1988, the Anti-Drug
Abuse Act created provisions for deporting noncitizens who commit aggravated felonies,[7] reinforcing further the connection between "illegality" and
irregular immigration. In 1996, however, the game really changed when the
Illegal Immigration Reform and Immigrant Responsibility Act targeted criminal aliens as a major enforcement priority and expanded the list of aggravated
felonies for which one could be deported to include petty theft, minor drug
offenses, and DUIs.[8] This solidified associations of "illegal immigrant" with
actual criminality—it is not really about the "crime" of crossing the border
without papers, it is that people who cross without papers are criminals.

Now we are seeing a whole host of efforts to continue this pattern of increasing deportations, including increasing the use of immigration raids and
trying to end the Deferred Action for Childhood Arrivals program (DACA).
And the rationale that consistently justifies these moves is "they came here
illegally." But this begs the question: Is entering a country without permission
sufficient justification to make people eligible for deportation? Exploring this
question is the primary focus of this chapter.

Specifically, in this chapter, I explore two Trump administration efforts to
increase deportations—increasing raids and ending DACA—to interrogate
the longstanding rationale offered by those who defend deportation programs
on the grounds that the immigrants came "illegally." I will argue that such
rationale is philosophically and morally flawed for at least four reasons. First,
"illegality," or whether a person entered the country through authorized channels, is not be the relevant moral concern for assessing the validity of deportations. Second, focusing on "illegality" is immoral because it dehumanizes
undocumented immigrants. Third, appealing to the "illegality" or "legality"
of how an immigrant came to the country is immoral because it reflects and
perpetuates racism and white supremacy. And fourth, appealing to "illegality" reifies and enforces colonial logics that derivativize undocumented immigrants and perpetrate global oppression. So justifying these programs to

increase deportation on the grounds that the immigrants are "illegally" in the country is flawed and immoral logic. And basing any policy on such grounds reflects and perpetuates oppression and thus commits immigration injustice. I will now elaborate on these points in more depth by highlighting two Trump administration initiatives to increase deportation—increased immigration raids and ending DACA.

IMMIGRATION RAIDS

Immigration raids are not unprecedented in modern U.S. history. In 2008, George W. Bush ordered a raid at a kosher meat-packing plant in Postville, Iowa, for example, where almost four hundred people were arrested.[9] But these raids have not been commonplace. In fact, according to Migration Policy Institute lawyer and policy analyst Muzaffar Chishti, Bush only ordered the Postville raid in an effort to "nudge congressional Republicans into supporting immigration reform by showing them how inhumane enforcement would be without an agreement."[10] And even though Barack Obama deported hundreds of thousands of undocumented immigrants, his administration ordered ICE *not* to conduct sweeping raids.[11] This changed with the election of Donald Trump.

Donald Trump came to power on a platform that touted tough immigration enforcement and promised increasing deportations of undocumented immigrants through all possible measures, including increasing immigration raids. And he has stayed focused on trying to keep that process. In February 2017, for example, ICE agents spread across the country and arrested over 680 people.[12] Immigration raids of workplaces increased by 400 percent in 2018,[13] including two in June 2018—one of Corso's Flower and Garden Center (arresting more than 100 workers)[14] and another of Fresh Mark meat supplier in Salem, Ohio (arresting 146 largely Guatemalan workers).[15] In July 2019, Donald Trump announced raids across the country targeting 2,000 undocumented migrants (only thirty-five were actually arrested). In August 2019, agents raided a Mississippi poultry plant in what may be the largest worksite enforcement action ever to have occurred in a single state.[16] And there is no end in sight as the White House has ordered ICE to identify more targets for raids.[17]

ENDING DACA

Increasing immigration raids is not the only way that the Trump administration is making more undocumented immigrants vulnerable to deportation. It is also trying to terminate the DACA program, created by President Barack Obama to shield undocumented immigrants with no criminal record brought to the United States as children, who are studying, have completed a degree, or have served in the military from deportation.[18] Later, the program was expanded to include parents of U.S. citizens and lawful permanent residents (provided they have passed required background checks), spouses of lawful permanent residents, and the sons and daughters of U.S. citizens.[19] As of June 30, 2019, U.S. Citizenship and Immigration Services reports 660,880 individuals who receive DACA protection.[20]

In early September 2017, however, former Attorney General Jeff Sessions announced that the Trump administration would begin ending the DACA program and would fully terminate it six months later to give Congress time to pass legislation.[21] These actions, however, were put on hold (meaning the program must continue) when the Supreme Court ruled against the Administration. Still, the Trump Administration is currently exploring other ways to end the program.

Before going further, one may question my choice to include DACA as part of the Trump administration efforts to increase deportations. After all, the administration has said that it does not want to deport Dreamers, it just wants Congress, rather than the Executive Branch, to pass legislation to protect them. Still, given that years have passed without action on this issue, I think it is disingenuous to deny that exposing Dreamers and their families to deportation is the *effect* of ending DACA. Moreover, given the countless options the Trump administration has to protect this group, in combination with these other efforts on immigration, ending DACA is clearly part of the strategy to increase deportations.

THE TRUMP ADMINISTRATION'S
REASONING FOR THESE ACTIONS

Here I am not concerned with whether ending DACA or conducting immigration raids is legally justifiable. Instead I am concerned with the underlying reason to *want* to undertake these efforts, specifically the idea that deporting undocumented immigrants, regardless of circumstances or time in the country, is justified because they are in the United States "illegally." To not deport them, it is argued, threatens the rule of law and the integrity of the U.S. immigration system by encouraging more people to enter through illicit channels. As Sessions explained when he announced the plan to end DACA, "To have a lawful system of immigration that serves the national interest, we cannot admit everyone who would like to come here. . . . Therefore, the nation must set and enforce a limit on how many immigrants we admit each year and that means all cannot be accepted." He continued: "And without more action, we could see illegality rise again rather than be eliminated."[22] In other words, DACA must end because Dreamers (or their parents) broke the law when they came to the United States without documents. And if we permit some to break the law without consequences, then this will lead down a slippery slope of increased undocumented immigration and illegal behavior that the United States cannot permit.

This line of reasoning is common in these discussions. When defending the August 2019 Mississippi raid, acting ICE director Matthew Albence said, "Raids are part of normal ICE operations that seek to enforce U.S. immigration law."[23] And in expressing his anger that national leaders helped thwart the success of the July 2019 raids, he said, "I don't know of any other population where people are telling them how to avoid arrest as a result of illegal activity."[24] Similarly, defending the deportation of José Garcia, an undocumented immigrant from Mexico who worked and lived in the United States for thirty years with his wife and children (all U.S. citizens), Detroit ICE spokesman Khaalid Walls said, "ICE does not exempt classes or categories of removable aliens from potential enforcement. All of those in violation of the immigration laws may be subject to immigration arrest, detention and, if found removable by final order, removal from the United States."[25] Even Donald Trump himself has said, "I say they came in illegally, and we're bringing them out legally,"[26] meaning that it is perfectly justified to deport anyone who came to the United States through unauthorized channels. In fact, many actions related to immigration—increased raids and enforcement of the nations' interior; deporting long-term undocumented residents with families, jobs, and no criminal record; and separating families at the border—have all focused on this line of thought: being in the country "illegally" is sufficient reason for deportation.

There are countless reasons to decry these efforts. We can decry them on the grounds that increasing deportations in these ways will negatively impact institutions of higher education[27] and access to health care and "perpetuate inequities and lack of diversity within our physician workforce."[28] Or we can condemn these actions on the grounds that they are immoral,[29] cowardly,[30] heartless,[31] "inhumane,"[32] and tearing families apart.[33] While I am sympathetic to all of these stances, here I advance arguments that these efforts to increase deportations are wrong because their justification—that people are in the country "illegally" and so they must be deported—is deeply flawed on multiple grounds. Therefore any efforts taken on these illegitimate grounds constitute immigration injustices. I will now detail why this is the case.

PROBLEM 1: "ILLEGALITY" IS NOT THE ISSUE

My first critique of the rationale is that it wrongly focuses on "legality" rather than more morally relevant factors. Joseph Carens advances a version of this argument in *Ethics of Immigration* where he essentially argues that one does not earn the right to stay in a country via legal processes but rather via time spent in the community. As such, Carens says that "the longer one stays, the more one becomes a member. The shorter the stay, the weaker the claim."[34] In light of this, entering the country without papers is not the operative factor; time is what counts.

To see what Carens is highlighting, let's look at a few examples of DACA recipients who would be threatened if the program were terminated. First, we have Michelle Valladarez, who came to the United States from Honduras when she was nine; she is now twenty-five. From age fourteen, she remembers wanting to join the Air Force.[35] Now she wants to both do this and study psychology so that she "can provide better care for veterans with PTSD."[36] For Carens, the fact that she entered the country "illegally" is irrelevant compared to the fact that she has spent sixteen years in the United States and clearly wants to contribute to giving the nation a brighter future. What matters is the time she has spent here and the ways that she is clearly integrated into U.S. society.

Similarly, Dulce Garcia was brought to the United States when she was four; she is now thirty-five and living in San Diego. She lived her life like all of her friends, including studying hard and applying to colleges. But she said, "One day, I had received several acceptance letters from different universities. I walked into my counselor's office and he said, 'You're an illegal immigrant. You're not even going to go to community college. Forget the universities.' And it just . . . crushed me."[37] Again, Carens would say that deporting someone after thirty-one years of living in a country, who has community ties and aspirations, only because of their legal status, is morally misguided.

So Carens would deny the government has any moral right to deport Michelle, Dulce, or any of the hundreds of thousands of DACA recipients or other longtime undocumented immigrants residing in the United States. As he explains, "The moral right of states to apprehend and deport irregular migrants erodes with the passage of time. As irregular migrants become more and more settled, their membership in society grows in moral importance, and the fact that they have settled without authorization becomes correspondingly less relevant."[38] It does not matter how someone came to the United States; the morally relevant factor is time. Consequently, deporting people on the basis of their legal status is unjust.

In her book *Socially Undocumented: Identity and Immigration Justice*, Amy Reed-Sandoval goes beyond what Carens is arguing to highlight another reason that legal status is not the salient concern. To the contrary, what matters is how immigrants act and how they are treated. When this is explored, it becomes clear that being documented or undocumented goes well beyond one's legal status, and failing to notice this leads us to obscure many other immigration justice issues. Specifically, Reed-Sandoval argues that one can be *socially undocumented* yet *legally* documented and vice versa. According to Reed-Sandoval, being *socially* undocumented means that

1. one is "perceived to be undocumented on the mere basis of their appearance—not on the basis of any fair and egalitarian confirmation of legally undocumented status. To be presumed to be undocumented is to be presumed to be 'an illegal' in the U.S" and
2. one is subjected to "demeaning immigration-related constraints" or "illegalizing forces" on that very basis.[39]

So one can be treated as documented even if one lacks legal status and vice versa, which leads to other injustices. And these other injustices ought be our focus. Consequently, deporting people based on legal status alone perpetuates obscuring other immigration justice concerns that are more relevant.

PROBLEM 2: FOCUSING ON "ILLEGALITY" IS DEHUMANIZING

A second reason to reject the idea that it is defensible to deport people on the grounds that they are in the country "illegally" is presented by Carlos Alberto Sánchez. In his 2014 essay "'Illegal' Immigrants: Law, Fantasy, and Guts," Sánchez says appealing to legal status and referring to undocumented immigrants as "illegal" is fundamentally flawed because it simultaneously dehumanizes irregular immigrants and allows for their exploitation. As Sánchez explains, the term "'illegal' is reserved for those who are perceived to have no place in our ordered civilized world; a world in which we even include rapists and murderers in by referring to them as 'criminals,' but never as 'illegals.'"[40] In calling people "illegal," we are marking them as beyond the bounds of the state.[41] This then renders this population vulnerable to exploitation because in ejecting the "illegal" immigrant body from the realm of civilized society (which is governed by rights), we turn it into an object through a variety of legislative and other processes.

Turning the "illegal" immigrant body into an object is achieved through specific processes. First, says Sánchez, we turn the "illegal" immigrant into

> a strange otherness that aims to take away what "we" have, who labors in the intentional pursuit of replacing "American culture" with her own, degenerate, culture, and who schemes and plots a way to terrorize us all. Through a simultaneous process of deconstruction, however, this "illegal" is stripped of rights, humanity, and intention.[42]

The first step, in other words, is to dehumanize "illegal" immigrants by turning them into a threatening other. But we have a problem—we still need the "illegal" immigrant body to labor for us, and thus we cannot *actually* expel them. So rather than eject them from our territory, we turn them into an object we can use. In other words, says Sánchez, once we have stripped them of their humanity, we then turn "the 'illegal' immigrant [into] a thing or a piece of equipment; the 'illegal' immigrant must assume a certain role in that social economy, namely the role of equipment necessary for the maintenance of a lifestyle."[43] He continues: "the body of the illegal immigrant is objectified so as to complement other household appliances; it becomes an extension of the vacuum cleaner, the lawn mower, or the hoe."[44] As such, it is both dehumanized and simultaneously converted into exploitable labor.

When we read the efforts to end DACA through the lens of Sánchez's analysis, its injustices become more apparent. This is especially evident when we take the "illegality" justification together with the administration's claim that we need to let Congress, rather than the executive, act to protect Dreamers. Allow me to explain. First, the administration is trying to strip "legal" status from Dreamers by ending DACA. And they are doing so on the grounds that their parents (or other relatives who brought them to the United States) did so "illegally." As such, they are turning them into "illegal immigrants" once again (as they were before DACA). Once returned to this status, they have been ejected from the "civilized order," no longer able to receive protection. But, says the administration, don't worry because Congress will pass a law to make sure that this does not happen. The problem is that Congress has never actually done anything to protect this group and there is no empirical evidence to suggest that they will act any time soon. Here is the thing, though: nobody actually wants to deport the Dreamers. After all, apart from the poor optics, the electoral consequences, and the logistical impossibility of actually doing so, Dreamers are a group of U.S.-educated, motivated, hard-working young people who U.S. tax dollars have benefitted. We do not want to lose access to that talent or our investment. So in reality, ending DACA will force them to remain out of status but not yet deported, which will then turn them into an exploitable workforce.

I argue the increased immigration raids represent a similar phenomenon—they are about terrorizing undocumented immigrants in order to reinforce their status as being "outside society." And there is evidence that this is precisely what is occurring. *CNN*, for example, reported that in a Tennessee public school district, more than five hundred kids were absent the day after ICE swept through the meatpacking district where many of their parents work.[45] People are not going to church in Texas.[46] In California, a social worker described seeing a sign taped to a family's front door at a child's eye level bearing the warning: *No abra la puerta* (Do not open the door).[47] And the Urban Institute reports that immigrant families are "increasingly avoiding routine activities, such as interacting with teachers or school officials, health care providers, and the police, which poses risks for their well-being and the communities in which they live."[48] Almost 8 percent avoided public places, like parks and libraries; about 6 percent avoided talking to doctors or teachers.[49] The raids are having their intended effect of ejecting undocumented immigrants from public society.

The fact that these raids are, indeed, about expelling undocumented immigrants from civil society is further supported by other facts on the ground. First, almost no employers have actually been arrested for violating the law and hiring undocumented migrants, which suggests that the administration is not really concerned with curtailing the labor force of undocumented migrants or practices of hiring them. Second, many of these raids do not yield valid arrests or actual deportations. The July 2019 raid, for example, only yielded thirty-five arrests (recall that 2,000 undocumented immigrants were targeted). In the August 2019 raid, over three hundred migrants were later released with notices to appear, the precise thing that the government says cannot be allowed.[50] Third, again, Congress is making no efforts to address the issue. This all suggests that these raids are meant to reduce undocumented immigrants to "illegal" beings to justify their expulsion from society yet keep them in a constant state of fear so that they will be compliant members of the workforce.

Exploring these actions through Sánchez's analysis, then, reveals a more insidious problem in these logics, namely that appealing to both people's legal status and to a legal process that we know will not fix the problem paves the way for undocumented immigrants to be made vulnerable to violence, abuse, and exploitation. In light of all of this, the administration's reasoning crumbles because it is not really about enforcing laws but rather about converting these immigrants into an exploitable workforce, which furthers oppression and injustice. And so the reasoning that we can deport undocumented immigrants because they came to the United States "illegally" should be rejected because it enables dehumanization and exploitation rather than highlighting a legitimate moral concern.

PROBLEM 3: "ILLEGALITY," RACISM,
AND WHITE SUPREMACY

While Sánchez's analysis is not focused on explicitly connecting "illegality" to racism, it is clear that this is also involved. To help see why, I turn to Grant Silva and José Jorge Mendoza. In his 2015 essay "Embodying a 'New' Color Line: Racism, Anti-Immigrant Sentiment and Racial Identities in the 'Postracial' Era,"[51] Silva maintains that we should see anti-immigrant and anti-foreigner sentiment as both fundamentally racist and as being deployed to protect the connection between whiteness and being a "true American." In this way, "illegal" is a racial trope that cannot morally justify any policy.[52]

Immediately some will object that those who want to increase deportations via these measures are not against immigration per se, they are only against "illegal" immigration;[53] their problem is not with people coming to the United States but rather "with people not waiting in line."[54] This echoes Jeff Sessions's claim that he wants to enforce the nation's immigration laws and end *illegal* immigration, not end immigration altogether. The problem with this line of argument, says Silva, is that it willfully ignores how many of our white ancestors entered the country under a quote system that privileged immigration from Europe. And, I would add, it willfully ignores that there was no such category as an "illegal immigrant" in the United States at the time most white people's ancestors came from Europe. Emphasizing "law and lawfulness,"[55] then, both conflates U.S. immigration eras and reflects a historical vantage point that makes white normativity the basis for American national identity. Therefore justifying deporting any group on the grounds of their legal status (or lack thereof) is also about reinforcing white normativity and the idea that being "American" is synonymous with being white and should be rejected.

Allow me to elaborate. It is not just the case that the United States regulating immigration is a relatively recent event primarily geared at Asian, Mexican, and Central American immigrants but also that, as countless scholars have documented,[56] until very recently, the law stated that to enter the United States and become a citizen, one had to be white.[57] Given this, intended or not, the U.S. standards of "lawful" immigration serve to exclude nonwhites. So when someone says they favor preserving "legal" immigration, advertently or not, they are favoring the immigration of white Europeans to the United States to the exclusion of immigrants of color or ignoring how the law is biased in favor of admitting white immigrants (and always has been). In these ways, as Silva explains, "illegal" operates as a "racial dog whistle."[58]

In light of Silva's analysis, it becomes apparent that justifying deportation efforts like ending DACA and increasing immigration raids on the grounds that they are in the country "unlawfully" reinforces this legacy of white normativity and—intended or not—promotes a racist immigration structure. In this context, the justification of "illegality" serves as a racial dog whistle meant to signal other whites that nonwhites are trying to encroach on "their" nation. In the face of such a threat, the (white) nation must respond lest they lose control.

I submit this is precisely what we see in Jeff Sessions's appeals to the need to enforce immigration laws because not doing so (by allowing DACA to stand or failing to do everything possible to hunt down undocumented people and deporting them) could lead to "illegality" rising again. Because ending DACA is part of the larger sets of policies aimed at curbing immigration from Mexico and Central America (some of which we are exploring in other chapters of this book), it clear that Sessions is saying that if we make an exception for the Dreamers, for example, by allowing DACA to stand, then we risk returning to the "bad old days" when Mexicans could come to the United States as they pleased. And we cannot let that happen. In this way, Sessions is deploying racial dog whistles to white people that ending DACA is required to protect "their" nation and that failing to do so could lead them down a path to be overrun by Latinx people. Thus appeals to "illegality" are disingenuous ways to cover up and justify the racism underlying the moves to end DACA and increase deportations of undocumented immigrants through public and intimidating raids.

Again, someone might object that I (and Silva) am injecting race where it does not exist. People just want folks to follow the law and not be rewarded (with being able to stay in the country) if they do not, this objector would declare. The problem with this response, though, is that race is always part of the immigration discussion in the United States. Always. And when people in the United States hear "illegal immigrant," they know exactly who is being referenced: Latinx (and sometimes Asian) people; they never associate "illegal immigrant" with a white person. In fact, Gregory Rodriguez's reporting showed that "most 'Americans' do not think twice about the legal status of white immigrants."[59] Far from simply referring to someone who "broke the law," then, "illegal" does indeed have specific, racialized meanings that designate *nonwhite status*.[60] As such, it is fundamentally a racist term and arguing that we can increase deportation because people came into the country "illegally" perpetuates racism in the United States.

Still, some will remain unsatisfied and continue to argue that "illegal" is not inherently connected to racism. In an effort to test this claim, José Jorge Mendoza surveys U.S. law and the literature on whiteness. In doing so, he discovers another piece of the puzzle, namely that whiteness is a social construct around race, ethnicity, *and* nationality. He explains, "*Whiteness* is thought to be analogous to a braid of three interwoven strands: the racial strand (e.g. science, biology, or phenotypes), the ethnic strand (e.g. culture, customs, or heritage), and the national strand (e.g. territory, sovereignty, and citizenship."[61] Part of the nationality strand is the deep legal history in U.S. immigration and citizenship law we alluded to earlier that enshrined the connection between *whiteness* and U.S. citizenship. And here is where we find the connections between illegality and white supremacy (and thus racism).

Once we understand that *whiteness* is also connected to nationality, says Mendoza, we can see that even when legislation is not racist or ethnocentrist, it is still nationalistic. And even a cursory survey of U.S. immigration law shows that, in the United States, nationalism and whiteness are inherently connected. For example, the Naturalization Act of 1790 codified into law that only white people could become U.S. citizens.[62] Beyond expressly establishing whiteness as a requirement for U.S. citizenship, though, immigration regulations and laws can either confer or strip *whiteness* from a group. This is perfectly exemplified in the case of *U.S. v. Thind* in 1923.

In this case, Bhaget Singh Thind was declared "not a white person" because he was born in India.[63] The reason this case is so significant, though, is that Thind had enlisted in the U.S. Army during World War I and then applied for U.S. citizenship, which received. Later, his citizenship was revoked and Thind appealed on the grounds that he was a member of the high caste in India and a member of the Caucasian race. While the U.S. Court of Appeals agreed that he was a member of the Caucasian race, it rejected his claim on two grounds:

1. "Free white persons," as used in [the 1790 Act], are words of common speech, to be interpreted in accordance with the understanding of the common man, synonymous with the word "Caucasian."
2. The action of Congress in excluding from admission to this country all natives of Asia within designated limits including all of India, is evidence of a like attitude toward naturalization of Asians within those limits.[64]

In other words, despite being a member of the Caucasian race, Thind was not what the common person would consider white. And beyond this, Congress had forbidden Asians to receive citizenship. Therefore his petition was denied, and, in the process, it became clear that the law can both confer and strip away whiteness from entire groups of people based on racialized and white supremacist understandings of who constitutes a citizen. In this way, the law can create a group of perpetual foreigners,[65] or those "who reside within a nation-state—sometimes for multiple generations [sometimes including] natural born U.S. citizens—but because of their race, ethnicity, or nationality are constantly treated or misrecognized by as not full or real members of the state."[66] So regardless of whether the restrictions intend to be racist or ethnocentric, they nonetheless perpetuate white supremacy via a nationalist vision. And in this way, "illegal" is deeply connected to white supremacy, despite claims to the contrary.

When we combine Silva's and Mendoza's insights, we arrive at a third reason to reject claims that it is acceptable to engage in these deportation actions because those affected came "illegally" to the United States and/or to protect the integrity of our nation's immigration laws. Specifically, such arguments serve as racist dog whistles and reflect and perpetuate racism and white supremacy in the United States. As such, to accept them perpetuates oppression within the United States against immigrants and Latinx (and other nonwhite) populations, which, on my account, constitutes immigration injustice.

DACA, DEPORTATION RAIDS, LEGALITY, AND GLOBAL OPPRESSION

I think that Carens, Reed-Sandoval, Sánchez, Silva, and Mendoza have clearly exposed serious flaws in the claim that the United States is justified in ending DACA and conducting more raids to increase deportation on the grounds that these immigrants entered and reside in the United States "illegally." At minimum, this justification fails because it (1) ignores other, more relevant, concerns; (2) dehumanizes Latino/a/x immigrants and makes them vulnerable to exploitation; and (3) is a racist, white supremacist dog whistle that perpetuates oppression in the United States. But I do not think the injustice stops here. In what remains, I will demonstrate how the reasoning focusing on "illegality" must also be rejected because it creates, reflects, and perpetuates global oppression by derivatizing undocumented immigrants and promoting and trying to reify colonialist logic and thus immigration injustice.

Seeing how justifications around "illegality" reflect and further global oppression requires returning to Carlos Sánchez's arguments. Recall that Sánchez argues against the idea of "illegality" on the grounds that it dehumanizes undocumented migrants and turns them essentially into exploitable tools. While I agree with much of what Sánchez says, I think he miscategorizes a core part of the problem (or at least misses another aspect of it). The "illegal" immigrant is not dehumanized and turned into an object, she is derivatized and turned into a specific type of subject—the colonized subject. What I want to say here is that "illegal" does not dehumanize undocumented migrants the way that Sánchez suggests because, on this logic, colonized beings they were never fully "human" to begin with; to the contrary, calling undocumented immigrants "illegal" and then using that status to justify their treatment is about derivatizing undocumented immigrants by reducing them to mere extensions of what U.S. citizens need them to be by making undocumented immigrants into colonized subjects in the racialized modern colonial gender system.

According to this system, the world is divided between human and nonhuman, where only Christian, white, heterosexual people were placed in the category human. Anibal Quijano shows that part of the colonial project divided the peoples of the world up by "races" and denoted that "by 'nature' there exist superior and inferior races."[67] Unsurprisingly, on this logic, Europeans were identified as the superior race and Indigenous populations as the inferior one. As inferior races, they were not civilized, rational, and thus by extension could not be considered full human beings.

But this system is not simply racialized, it is also gendered. As María Lugones has explained, while colonial logic initially imposed a core hierarchy delineating human and nonhuman,[68] this division

> was accompanied by other dichotomous hierarchical distinctions, among them between men and women. This distinction became a mark of the human and a mark of civilization. Only the civilized are men or women.[69]

As such, the Indigenous peoples were not classified as human but rather as some other species of animal, one that was "uncontrollable, sexual, and wild."[70] On this ontology, bourgeois white Europeans were civilized (that is, fully human) and thus could be assigned a gender while "the behaviors of the colonized and their personalities/souls were judged as bestial and thus non-gendered, promiscuous, grotesquely sexual, and sinful."[71] So the colonial dichotomy relegated nonwhites to some nonhuman, exploitable, ontological state.

I mention all of this because I submit that calling undocumented immigrants "illegal" harkens back to this logic. In designating nonwhite undocumented migrants (as Sánchez shows) "illegal," society expels them from civil society and thus the human species. As a result, and here is where I differ from Sánchez, the "illegal" immigrant is *not* dehumanized (they were never human in the first place on this logic) but rather is relegated "to their rightful place" outside of society. In other words, calling them "illegal" is meant to reinscribe their status as colonized beings that simply serve our ends rather than full human beings with their own ends. And once they have been assigned that status, we can derivatize them as mere extensions of ourselves and exploit them as we see fit.

Now we can see why appealing to the "illegality" of undocumented immigrants is an important and necessary step to justify these efforts to increase deportation in the face of those who oppose such measures. Those who support DACA and condemn immigration raids do so on the grounds that that Dreamers and other undocumented immigrants deserve our compassion and our respect. After all, Dreamers were brought to the United States as children and other undocumented immigrants just came here to have better lives. So those promoting these actions to increase deportations need to show that their opponents are mistaken—that their ontology is flawed. To do that, they call undocumented immigrants "illegal."

In calling undocumented immigrants "illegal," proponents of these deportations efforts are trying to return these irregular immigrants to their ontological status under the modern colonial gender system, which maintains that, as nonwhites, undocumented immigrants are uncivilized and are inherently *incapable* of reason, following the law, or engaging in full human relationships. And how do they show that? By suggesting that civilized and reasonable people follow the law, protect their children, and migrate through proper channels. Because undocumented immigrants failed to do that, it confirms their irrationality and uncivilized nature. But because they are uncivilized and irrational, these immigrants lack the needed qualities for being a desirable citizen—being white and law abiding. Consequently, their presence threatens our ability to maintain "our" civilization. So we must banish them for our own protection. As such, increasing raids and ending DACA so we can deport more "illegals" is justified. When seen in this light, appealing to "illegality" is about creating policies to execute and enforce colonial, racist logic and perpetrating immigration injustice by turning the undocumented immigrant into a derivatized subject—into a colonized being.

But when we bring the ideas of the racialized modern colonial gender system into view, we see that there is more going on here; proponents of increased deportation efforts are not calling undocumented immigrants "illegal" to return them just to colonized beings but rather into gendered colonized beings. The male undocumented immigrant must be removed because he is what Carlos Sandoval refers to as a "threatening other"; he physically threatens our society—as a violent gang member (more specifically in the current discourse as an MS-13 gang member) who rapes (our?) women and has no fear, respect, or desire to follow the law. All he wants to do is literally and metaphorically kill our (nice white?) children—either by turning them into violent, raping gang members or by getting them off of their "proper" paths of going to college and to church, not taking drugs, and being outstanding citizens. The only way to deal with such a menace is to deport him by subjecting him to state-sanctioned violence by police and ICE agents.

The "illegal" female migrant, on the other hand, is conceived of differently. She threatens civilized order and its norms of family and sexuality by being promiscuous and willing to abandon her family in her native country. So she must be put in her place of subordination through sexual violence (by white men) and degrading and exploitative work conditions. To ensure the subordination is working, you deny her the ability to control her body and reproduction by refusing to provide birth control, access to reproductive health care, or abortion services (as is occurring in ICE detention facilities). And you place her under constant threat of deportation, for example, by making public immigration raids on workplaces. This constant fear will then make them riper for exploitation and more vulnerable to abuse. In this way, increased deportation efforts maintain specifically gendered violence.[72] Denoting female undocumented immigrants as "illegal," then, does not simply justify bad deportation policy, it turns them into a colonized subject with no rights or protection, thus making them vulnerable to our will.

When we turn our attention to the ways in which colonial logic and the modern colonial gender system are operative in the context of immigration, then, it becomes clear that the justification for these increased deportation efforts reflect and further oppressive systems. And so it is easy to see why this may appear to be dehumanizing—because it is, just not in the ways that Sánchez suggests. The "illegal" immigrant is reduced to a specific kind of colonized subject, one that, I suggest, is a mere derivative of how the dominant white population wishes to view them. On this logic, the goal is not simply to maintain an exploitable workforce but to maintain the racialized modern colonial gender system that preserves the colonial order that maintains the power of the United States. As such, the justification for ending DACA, ordering massive immigration raids, and supporting increased deportation of undocumented immigrants reflects and perpetuates global oppression and is unjust.

CONCLUDING REMARKS

Appealing to an immigrant's legal status to justify ending DACA or defend increase efforts to deport undocumented immigrants perpetuates a long line of immigration injustices against Mexican and Central American immigrants. Michelle and Dulce did not have legal permission to be in the country and neither did their parents. Nor did the hundreds of people deported as a result of being caught up in immigration raids across the country. But that does not justify ending DACA or deporting hard-working people. First, the way that someone entered the receiving nation is not morally relevant; what matters is the time they have spent in that nation. Second, appealing to "legality" is not about promoting the rule of law but rather about imposing and reinforcing racial, white supremacist, and colonial ideologies that maintain white hegemony. It is also, intended or not, about reinforcing colonial ontologies about who is and is not a full human being or, at the very least, qualified to be a member of society and receive its protections. As such, it reflects and perpetuates oppression within the country and globally.

All of these arguments come together to reveal the illegitimacy of the rationale to end DACA and increase deportation efforts via raids simply because of the immigrant's legal status. And any immigration policy, practice, law, system, or norm based on this flawed rationale will reflect and promote domestic and global oppression and thus will be unjust. In light of the above, regardless of what the Trump administration demands or the Supreme Court decides, ending DACA or increasing raids to expand deportations of undocumented immigrants must be condemned. Rather than trying to deport them, we need to defend Michelle's, Dulce's, and the millions of undocumented immigrants' full humanity and rightful place in our society.

NOTES

1. Paul Ganster with David M. Lorey, *The U.S.-Mexican Border Today: Conflict and Cooperation in Historical Perspective*, third edition (Lanham, Boulder, New York, London: Rowman & Littlefield, 2016), 215; Kelly Lytle Hernández, *Migra! A History of the U.S. Border Patrol* (Berkeley, Los Angeles, and London: University of California Press, 2010).

2. Patrisia Macías-Rojas, *From Deportation to Prison: The Politics of Immigration Enforcement in Post-Civil Rights America* (New York: New York University Press, 2016), 17.

3. Ibid., 216.

4. Mae Ngai, *Impossible Subjects: Illegal Immigrants and the Making of Modern America* (Princeton, NJ: Princeton University Press, 2004), 261.

5. Immigration Reform and Control Act, 1986.

6. Macías-Rojas, *From Deportation to Prison*, 59.

7. Ibid.

8. Ibid., 61.

9. "What Do Donald Trump's Immigration Raids Accomplish?" *The Economist*, August 22, 2019, https://www.economist.com/united-states/2019/08/22/what-do-donald-trumps-immigration-raids-accomplish.

10. Ibid.

11. Ibid.

12. Dara Lind, "The First Immigration Raids of the Trump Era, Explained," *Vox*, February 14, 2017, https://www.vox.com/policy-and-politics/2017/2/14/14596640/immigration-ice-raids.

13. Clark Mindock, "US Workplace Immigration Raids Surge 400% in 2018," *Independent*, December 12, 2018, https://www.independent.co.uk/news/world/americas/

us-politics/ice-immigration-workplace-migrants-undocumented-immigrants-raids
-trump-obama-2018-a8678746.html.

14. Samantha Schmidt, "'Utter Chaos': ICE Arrests 114 Workers in Immigration Raid at Ohio Gardening Company," *Washington Post*, June 9, 2018, https://www
.washingtonpost.com/news/morning-mix/wp/2018/06/06/utter-chaos-ice-arrests
-114-workers-in-immigration-raid-at-ohio-gardening-company/.

15. Kristine Phillips, "ICE Arrests Nearly 150 Meat Plant Workers in Latest Immigration Raid in Ohio," *Washington Post*, June 20, 2018, https://www.washingtonpost
.com/news/post-nation/wp/2018/06/20/ice-arrests-nearly-150-meat-plant-workers-in
-latest-immigration-raid-in-ohio/.

16. Miriam Jordan, "ICE Arrests Hundreds in Mississippi Raids Targeting Immigrant Workers," *New York Times*, August 7, 2019, https://www.nytimes.com/
2019/08/07/us/ice-raids-mississippi.html.

17. Edward Helmore, "More Major US Immigration Raids Likely Despite Outcry," *The Guardian*, August 10, 2019, https://www.theguardian.com/us-news/2019/
aug/10/ice-raids-us-immigration-workplaces.

18. U.S. Citizenship and Immigration Services, "Consideration of Deferred Action for Childhood Arrivals (DACA)," accessed January 28, 2020, https://www.uscis
.gov/archive/consideration-deferred-action-childhood-arrivals-daca.

19. U.S. Citizenship and Immigration Services, "2014 Executive Actions on Immigration," accessed January 28, 2020, https://www.uscis.gov/archive/2014-execu
tive-actions-immigration.

20. U.S. Citizenship and Immigration Services, "Approximate DACA Recipients as of June 30, 2019," accessed January 28, 2020, https://www.uscis.gov/sites/default/
files/USCIS/Resources/Reports%20and%20Studies/Immigration%20Forms%20
Data/Static_files/DACA_Population_Receipts_since_Injunction_Jun_30_2019.pdf.

21. Jacob Pramuk, "Trump Administration Ending DACA Program, Which Protected 800,000 Children of Immigrants," *CNBC*, September 5, 2017, https://www
.cnbc.com/2017/09/05/trump-administration-is-ending-daca-immigration-program
-ag-sessions-says.html.

22. Jeff Sessions, "Statement to End DACA," *PBS Newshour*, September 5, 2017, https://www.pbs.org/newshour/politics/read-sessions-full-remarks-daca.

23. Matthew Albence cited by Abigail Hauslohner, "ICE Agents Raid Mississippi Work Sites, Arrest 680 People in Largest-Scale Single State Immigration Enforcement Action in U.S. History," *Washington Post*, August 7, 2019, https://www.washing
tonpost.com/immigration/ice-agents-raid-miss-work-sites-arrest-680-people-in-larg
est-single-state-immigration-enforcement-action-in-us-history/2019/08/07/801d5cfe
-b94e-11e9-b3b4-2bb69e8c4e39_story.html.

24. Matthew Albence cited by Miriam Jordan, "More than 2000 Migrants Were Targeted in Raids. 35 Were Arrested," *New York Times*, July 23, 2019, https://www
.nytimes.com/2019/07/23/us/ice-raids-apprehensions.html.

25. Khaalid Walls cited by Niraj Warikoo, "ICE Defends Deportation of Garcia to Mexico," *Detroit Free Press*, January 17, 2018, https://www.freep.com/story/
news/2018/01/17/immigration-customs-enforcement-ice-jorge-garcia-mexican-im
migrant-deported/1039806001/.

26. Caitlin Dickerson and Zolan Kanno-Youngs, "Thousands Are Targeted as ICE Prepares to Raid Undocumented Migrant Families," *New York Times*, July 7, 2019, https://www.nytimes.com/2019/07/11/us/politics/ice-families-deport.html?smid=nytcore-ios-share.

27. Nicolas Tapi-Fuselier and Jemimah L. Young, "Texas Community Colleges Respond to the Threatened End of DACA: A Document Analysis," *Community College Journal of Research and Practice* 43, no. 10–11 (2019): 807–11, doi-org.ezproxy.uniandes.edu.co:8443/10.1080/10668926.1600605.

28. Danish Zaidi and Mark Kuczewski, "Ending DACA Has Pragmatic and Ethical Implications for U.S. Health Care," *Hastings Center Report* 47, no. 6 (2017): 14–15, https://doi.org/10.1002/hast.780.

29. Ilya Somin, "The Case for Keeping DACA," *New York Times*, September 4, 2017, https://www.washingtonpost.com/news/volokh-conspiracy/wp/2017/09/04/the-case-for-daca/.

30. Jennifer Rubin, "Ending DACA Would Be Trump's Most Evil Act," *Washington Post*, September 4, 2017, https://www.washingtonpost.com/blogs/right-turn/wp/2017/09/04/trump-ending-daca-would-be-cruelty-wrapped-in-a-web-of-lies/; Micheal Shear and Julie Hirschfeld Davis, "Trump Moves to End DACA and Calls on Congress to Act," *New York Times*, September 5, 2017, https://www.nytimes.com/2017/09/05/us/politics/trump-daca-dreamers-immigration.html; Vanessa Romo, Martina Stewart, and Brian Naylor, "Trump Ends DACA, Calls on Congress to Act," *National Public Radio*, September 5, 2017, https://www.nytimes.com/2017/09/05/us/politics/trump-daca-dreamers-immigration.html.

31. Pramuk, "Trump Administration Ending DACA Program"; Julia Conley, "Immigrant Groups Mobilize to Combat Trump Administration's Plan to End DACA," *Common Dreams News*, September 4, 2017, https://www.commondreams.org/news/2017/09/04/immigrant-groups-mobilize-combat-trumps-cruel-and-heartless-plan-end-daca.

32. Nancy Pelosi cited by Kate Sullivan and Devin Cole, "Democrats, including Nancy Pelosi and Joe Biden, Slam ICE Raids," *CNN*, July 14, 2019, https://edition.cnn.com/2019/07/14/politics/ice-raids-democrats-reactions-2020-presidential-nominees/index.html.

33. Nancy Pelosi, in Sullivan and Cole, "Democrats Slam ICE Raids."

34. Joseph Carens, *Ethics of Immigration* (New York: Oxford University Press, 2017), 104.

35. Michelle Valladarez, "We Can't Go Back to the Shadows: Six Dreamers Tell Their Stories," *Mother Jones*, September 26, 2018, https://www.motherjones.com/politics/2018/09/we-cant-go-back-to-the-shadows-six-dreamers-tell-their-stories/.

36. Valladarez, "We Can't Go Back to the Shadows."

37. Dulce Garcia, "We Can't Go Back to the Shadows: Six Dreamers Tell Their Stories," *Mother Jones*, September 26, 2018, https://www.motherjones.com/politics/2018/09/we-cant-go-back-to-the-shadows-six-dreamers-tell-their-stories/.

38. Carens, *Ethics of Immigration*, 150.

39. Amy Reed-Sandoval, *Socially Undocumented: Identity and Immigration Justice* (New York: Oxford University Press, 2020), intro.

40. Carlos Alberto Sánchez, "'Illegal' Immigrants: Law, Fantasy, and Guts," *Philosophy in the Contemporary World* 21, no. 2 (Spring 2014): 4.

41. Ibid.

42. Ibid., 3.

43. Ibid., 3 and 5.

44. Ibid., 5.

45. Catherine E. Shoichet, "ICE Raided a Meatpacking Plant. More than 500 Kids Missed School the Next Day," *CNN*, April 12, 2018 https://edition.cnn.com/2018/04/12/us/tennessee-immigration-raid-schools-impact/index.html; Sarah Holder, "The Real Intention Behind the Recent ICE Raids Is Intimidation," *Pacific Standard*, July 30, 2019, https://psmag.com/social-justice/the-real-intention-behind-the-recent-ice-raids-is-intimidation.

46. Ibid.

47. Ibid.

48. Hamutal Bernstein, Dulce Gonzalez, Michael Karpman, and Stephen Zuckerman, "Adults in Immigrant Families Report Avoiding Routine Activities Because of Immigration Concerns," *Urban Institute*, July 24, 2019, https://www.urban.org/research/publication/adults-immigrant-families-report-avoiding-routine-activities-because-immigration-concerns.

49. Ibid.

50. "ICE Raids: 300 People Released Amid Outrage over Mississippi Arrests," *BBC News*, August 9, 2019, https://www.bbc.com/news/world-us-canada-49283157.

51. Grant J. Silva, "Embodying a 'New' Color Line: Racism, Anti-Immigrant Sentiment and Racial Identities in the 'Postracial' Era," *Knowledge Cultures* 3, no. 1 (2015): 65–90.

52. Ibid., 65.

53. Ibid., 68.

54. Ibid.

55. Ibid., 69.

56. See, for example, Ngai, *Impossible Subjects*; Matthew Frye Jacobson, *Whiteness of a Different Color: European Immigrants and the Alchemy of Race* (Cambridge, MA: Harvard University Press, 1999); David Roediger, *Working Towards Whiteness: How America's Immigrants Became White* (New York: Basic Books, 2005).

57. Silva, "Embodying a 'New' Color Line," 67.

58. Ibid., 74.

59. Gregory Rodriguez, "Illegal? Better If You're Irish," *Los Angeles Times*, April 8, 2007, www.latimes.com/la-op-rodriguez8apr08-column.html.

60. Silva, "Embodying a 'New' Color Line," 75.

61. José Jorge Mendoza, "Illegal: White Supremacy and Immigration Status," in *The Ethics and Politics of Immigration: Core Issues and Emerging Trends*, ed. Alex Sager (New York and London: Rowman & Littlefield, 2016), 202.

62. Naturalization Act of 1790, https://www.mountvernon.org/education/primary-sources-2/article/naturalization-acts-of-1790-and-1795/.

63. United States v. Bhagat Singh Thind, 261 U.S. 204 (1923).

64. United States v. Bhagat Singh Thind (1923).

65. Mendoza, "Illegal," 219.

66. Ibid., 207.

67. Aníbal Quijano, "Colonialidad y Modernidad/Racionalidad," in *Los Conquistadores: 1492 y la población indígena de las Américas*, ed. Robin Blackburn and Heraclio Bonilla (Tercer Mundo Editores, 1992), 280.

68. María Lugones, "Toward a Decolonial Feminism," *Hypatia* 25, no. 4 (Fall 2010): 743.

69. Ibid, *743*.

70. Ibid.

71. Ibid.

72. Randall Akee, "Outdated Immigration Laws Increase Violence Toward Women," *Brookings Institute*, May 20, 2019, https://www.brookings.edu/opinions/outdated-immigration-laws-increase-violence-toward-women/.

Chapter Four

"Cruelty" Doesn't Capture It

An Exploration of the Trump Administration's Family Separation Policy as Global Oppression

On April 6, 2018, then U.S. Attorney General Jeff Sessions announced a "Zero-Tolerance Policy" directing federal prosecutors to arrest and detain all who cross the southern border of the United States without documents.[1] Because U.S. law prohibits minors from being detained with adults, the Zero-Tolerance Policy contains within it a "Family Separation Policy," such that if a detained adult has a child or children with them, then the children are taken, placed in the custody of the Office of Refugee Resettlement, and separated from their family. As Sessions explained, "We do not want to separate children from their parents. . . . We do not want adults to bring children into this country unlawfully, placing them at risk. But we do have a policy of prosecuting adults who flout our laws to come here illegally instead of waiting their turn or claiming asylum at any port of entry."[2]

This policy did not come out of nowhere; the Trump administration had been considering separating children from their parents as a way of deterring Central American migration to the United States for over a year.[3] Thirteen days after Trump was inaugurated, the asylum chief for the U.S. Citizenship and Immigration Service, John Lafferty, announced that the Department of Homeland Security was developing a plan for separating women and children crossing into the United States "to deter *mothers* from migrating to the United States with their children."[4] Then in an interview with *CNN*, former head of the Department of Homeland Security, John Kelly, responded to a question of whether the U.S. government was considering separating children from their parents at the border: "Yes I'm considering, in order to deter more movement along this terribly dangerous network. I am considering exactly that."[5] And the separations began. In April 2018, the Office of Refugee Resettlement reported that over 700 families were separated since October 2017, including over 100 children under the age of four.[6] Reuters reported that over 1,800 families had been separated at the border since February 2017.[7] Originally, the Department of Homeland Security confirmed that since the policy was officially implemented, 1,995 children were separated from 1,940 adults who were referred for prosecution at the U.S.-Mexico border from April 19 through May 31, 2018.[8] However, court documents released by the American Civil Liberties Union show that the number is actually 5,500.[9] All in all, the House Oversight Committee's investigation into the Family Separation Policy released in July 2019 found that during the ten months the policy was officially operative,

- at least eighteen infants and toddlers under two years old were taken away from their parents at the border and kept apart for time periods ranging from twenty days to half a year;
- at least 241 separated children were kept in border patrol facilities longer than the seventy-two hours permitted by law;
- many separated children were kept in government custody far longer than previously known—at least 679 were held for forty-six to seventy-five days, more than fifty were held for six months to a year, and more than twenty-five were held for more than a year;
- even after being reunited with their parents, hundreds of separated children continued to be detained for months in family detention facilities—far longer than the twenty-day limit under the *Flores* case;
- more than 400 children were moved to multiple CBP facilities, more than eighty children were moved to multiple ORR facilities, and at least five children were moved to multiple ICE facilities—including to one, Port Isabel, after the administration claimed that "no children will be housed at the facility . . . even for short periods"; and
- at least ten separated children were sent to the "tent city" in Tornillo, Texas, the notorious emergency influx facility near El Paso, before the CEO of the facility's parent company refused to continue operations as a result of the administration's pressure to expand capacity despite delays in releasing children.[10]

Under the growing and intense domestic and international pressure, on June 20, 2018, Donald Trump signed an executive order supposedly ending the policy. Despite this, families continue to be separated, many have yet to be reunited, and various efforts continue to formally reinstate policies that separate children from their families. More specifically, at least thirty children separated under the policy have yet to be reunited with their families, despite court orders demanding their reunification.[11] As of early September 2019, over 1,000 children had been separated from their families since

Trump's executive order.[12] And not only are there no plans to remedy things,[13] the Trump administration continues to think the policy was a great success for deterring Central American migrants, as it introduced proposals to suspend the *Flores* settlement[14] (which requires that children be released from detention after twenty days and, while in detention, receive a certain standard of care),[15] and created a new "binary choice" policy that tells Central American parents to decide to separate from their children or keep the family together in detention until their day in immigration court.[16]

The outcry against all of these policies has been widespread. While the condemnations have taken many forms, one of the most common has been to denounce the policies as "cruel." The Center for the Study of Social Policy, for example, released a memo titled "Zero Tolerance Immigration Policy Is a Cruel and Immoral Human Rights Violation."[17] Conservative commentator Geraldo Rivera told Sean Hannity on his very pro-Trump Fox News show, "This is cruelty as policy."[18] Former First Lady Laura Bush published an op-ed in the *Washington Post* stating, "This zero-tolerance policy is cruel. It is immoral."[19] Chris Matthews declared that the policy is "cruel" on the June 18, 2018, edition of *Hardball*.[20] Senator Jeff Merkley refers to the family separation policy as "the Most Cruel Law," in his book *America Is Better Than This: Trump's War Against Migrant Families*.[21] Similar language has been invoked by *The Atlantic*, *The Conversation*, *The Chicago Tribune*, Amnesty International, and the country of Mexico, just to name a few.[22] Although I see why critics refer to the policy as "cruel," I suggest that "cruelty" is not the most apt term to capture the nature of the injustice in these family separation policies. The problem, I argue, is not that the policy is cruel, but rather that it viciously reflects, promotes, and perpetuates global oppression.

CRUELTY AND ITS LIMITS

I understand why many argue that the family separation policy is cruel—to many of its critics, there just seems to be such a depth of immorality and pain embedded in the policy that the common terms of our everyday moral and political discourse seem woefully inadequate. The problem is that "cruelty" also fails us, as becomes clear when we examine the nature of "cruelty."

In "Three Faces of Cruelty: Towards a Comparative Sociology of Violence," Randall Collins identifies three types of cruelty throughout human history: ferocious cruelty, callous cruelty, and aesthetic cruelty.[23] Ferocious cruelty refers to what Collins calls "overt brutality"; it is cruelty that takes the forms of awful and extreme violence, such as torture, mutilation, peremptory executions, human sacrifices, and ritual war hunts.[24] The second type of cruelty, what Collins calls "callous cruelty," is, as he puts it, "cruelty without passion: the kind of hardship of violence people may inflict on others without a special intent to hurt."[25] In this type of cruelty, Collins says, the target "is simply an instrument or an obstacle, and his [*sic*] suffering is merely an incidental (usually ignored) feature of some other intention."[26] And in callous cruelty there is very limited contact between the agent who is executing the action and the victim as the cruelty is actually carried out via bureaucratic structures that "cut off the possibility of personal empathy."[27] As such, Collins reports that in callous cruelty,

> Both the means and the ends of bureaucratic action deal not with the individual person and his subjective feelings, but with segmented elements of individual lives. . . . Thus, even the application of violence is carried our segmentally; the bureaucrat does not invest his personality and his subjective status in the dominance relationship that results, and the identity and feelings of the victim are not a concern.[28]

Finally, Collins identifies a third type of cruelty, aesthetic cruelty. This type of cruelty primarily refers to "cruelty turned on oneself,"[29] for example, in the form of deprivation of food or other pleasures in the name of religion or the quest to find spiritual enlightenment.[30] It is about treating oneself cruelly to attain some other good.

This brings us to the question: Do any of these three types of cruelty capture what is so egregious about the family separation policy? I do not think so. First, because the cruelty is inflicted on others and not oneself, aesthetic cruelty is not an apt description. Second, because widespread physical torture, mutilation, or execution is not part of the policy, ferocious cruelty does not seem to be a suitable description of what is wrong with the policy.

The case is less clear with callous cruelty. After all, as a policy, it does seem to inflict "cruelty without passion," and its cruelty does seem to be delivered via a bureaucratic structure and institutions that cut off the possibility of personal empathy. Despite this, I contend that it too fails to describe the policy or what is wrong with it. First, despite appearances, the family separation policy does not, in all reality, impose cruelty without passion; as I discuss elsewhere, there is a great deal of passion involved from those who advocate for it, and there is a clear intent on the part of the policy's advocates to hurt migrants.[31] Second, it is neither the case that the migrant is "simply an instrument or an obstacle" nor that her suffering is a "merely incidental (usually ignored)" feature of the policy. To the contrary, migrant suffering is core to the policy because it is their extreme level of suffering that leads to the deterrence. So the policy is not accurately characterized as a form or expression of callous cruelty.

Still, I do not want to be too hasty. After all, although Collins explores what many would call cruel acts throughout history, he does not seek to offer a philosophical or prescriptive account of how we should define cruelty. So I will turn to Max Scheler's, Carlos Alberto Sánchez's, and Etienne Balibar's discussions of cruelty to help us better understanding what "cruelty" is and why it is not the concept we seek.

To say that something is "cruel" is to say that it is evil, intentional, and immoral. We refer to individuals' actions that intend to cause extreme, unde-served pain and suffering to others as "cruel." As Carlos Alberto Sánchez puts it in the context of his discussion of brutality and violence in narco-culture, cruelty is a concept that references "*subjective* violence tied to individual psychology"[32] and does not apply to culture, systems, and structures. Refer-encing Max Scheler's 1913 phenomenological account on cruelty detailed in *The Nature of Sympathy*, Sánchez explains that cruelty is phenomenologically the opposite of caring and loving; it is the opposite of *being-with* others in sympathy.[33] As Scheler explains,

> The cruel man owes his awareness of the pain or sorrow he causes entirely to a capacity for visualizing feeling! His joy lies in "torturing" and in the agony of his victim. As he feels, vicariously, the increasing pain or suffering of his victim, so his own primary pleasure and enjoyment at the other's pain also increases. Cruelty consists not at all in the cruel man's being simply "insensi-tive" to other people's suffering . . . it is chiefly found in pathological cases . . . where it arises as a result of the patient's exclusive preoccupation in his own feelings, which altogether prevents him from giving emotional accep-tance to the experience of other people.[34]

Cruelty, then, according to Scheler, is not simply a lack of caring or of "being mean," it involves the individual agent taking pleasure in the suffer-ing of others, in inflicting the very suffering that the victim is experiencing. Etienne Balibar picks up on this point as well by suggesting that part of the nature of cruelty is that it "has to derive from itself, and obtain from those who wield it, *jouissance* ('enjoyment')[35]—it derives pleasure from the suffer-ing of others."[36]

In connecting cruelty to the deriving of pleasure from the victim's suffer-ing caused by the agents themselves, Sánchez notes that Scheler's definition "firmly locates cruelty within the subjective realm of the intentional sub-ject—that is, cruelty is internal to subjective dispositions and intentionally directed toward the suffering of others."[37] As such, cruelty inherently refers to conscious the actions of *individuals* that inflict suffering on other individuals and the fact that the agent takes pleasure in both inflicting the suffering and in watching the victim suffer at their hand. To focus on cruelty, then, is to speak of individual moral failure rather than systemic failings.

There also seems to be an aspect of cruelty that includes the idea of *excess*—there is an excessive amount of injustice, immorality, violence, etc. in cruel acts. And Balibar tries to capture this, arguing that cruelty refers to "forms of extreme violence, either intentional or systemic, physical or moral . . . that appear to be worse than death."[38] While I do not think that human beings who lack any knowledge of the nature of death can claim something is worse or better than it, I do think that Balibar is right in highlighting that cruelty refers to things that go beyond; cruelty encompasses what we commonly consider excess layers of violence, pain, malice, denigration, and intent.

Now that we have an expanded understanding of cruelty, does the concept seem to be a better fit for describing what is so wrong with the family separation policy? I still do not think so. First, as we have said, cruelty is fundamentally about subjective violence caused by and inflicted upon individuals as such. It refers to individual moral failings. And while we can identify individual politicians, border patrol officers, judges, and detention facility employees who have been cruel and/or displayed deep individual moral failures as they create and implement this policy, that is not really the issue; the issue is the policy and larger institutions and structures that enact, reinforce, and promote it. This leads to a second reason I reject "cruelty" as the operative moral concept to describe the wrongs of this policy, namely that because cruelty occurs between individuals, there is no such thing as a "cruel" policy, system, practice, or structure. So "cruelty" is not apt for capturing the injustice of an immigration system or policy, such as the one under discussion.

Our third reason that "cruelty" is not the concept we seek comes from Sánchez's discussion of narco-culture. There he reminds us that a crucial aspect of cruelty is that the cruel actor takes pleasure not only in watching others suffer but also in actually inflicting that suffering. As Scheler says, "His joy lies in 'torturing' and in the agony of his victim."[39] In light of this, Sánchez reminds us that for "cruelty" to be the most apt term, the policy would include demonstrations of individuals taking pleasure in inflicting suffering upon specific others, in this case Central American immigrants.[40] Some say this is precisely what is occurring. A headline from *The Atlantic*, for example, reads: "The Cruelty Is the Point: President Trump and His Supporters Find Community by Rejoicing in the Suffering of Those They Hate and Fear."[41] But this is not really in line with the definition, in which the cruel agent takes pleasure in directly inflicting the suffering because while these supporters may take pleasure in watching Central American migrants suffer, they do *not* directly inflict that suffering upon them. Still, some argue individuals, like presidential advisor Stephen Miller, are taking great pleasure in inflicting suffering on these migrants, and Miller, as an architect of the policy, is directly involved in inflicting it. Miller aside, however, if it were true that there were public expressions of joy, we would see them. But this is not what is happening. To the contrary, most administration officials, including Miller, go to great pains in public to appear to *not* be taking pleasure in the migrants' suffering. For example, from the beginning, the Trump administration worked hard to counter the idea that separating children from their parents would harm them, instead suggesting that the policy would actually *help* children.[42] Before the official policy started, for example, John Kelly said that the policy would be good for children because the United States has "tremendous experience in dealing with unaccompanied minors."[43] And recently Trump himself said, "I didn't like the sight or the feeling of families being separated."[44] All of these things seem to suggest that there is no public joy in causing suffering, regardless of what individual motivations may be.

Again, however, some may want to claim that individuals creating and carrying out the policy are indeed taking pleasure in causing migrants to suffer and so remain unconvinced that "cruelty" is not the core aspect of aspect what makes the policy wrong. But even if they are right and people like Miller, Kelly, Sessions, or Trump do take personal pleasure from this, we must not confuse them as individuals with the fact that we are assessing a policy and its effects, not the individuals themselves. In other words, even if they or others involved in the policy can be found to be cruel under the framework presented, the issue with which we are concerned is whether *the policy* is cruel. And while cruelty can be systemized, it is inherently *subjective*. As such, as Sánchez notes, "talking about an 'ultra-objective' cruelty doesn't make much sense";[45] the idea of a system, policy, practice, or norm being cruel simply doesn't fit the definition. Sánchez summarizes the point as such:

> Scheler's distinction forces us to reserve the designation "cruel" to individual *persons*, that is, to individuals who enjoy torturing and enjoying the pain they cause others. This points to an inaccuracy in designating systems, societies, weather patterns, etc. as "cruel," since it assumes that these things can enjoy or take pleasure in the pain of others. To say, then, that a policy is cruel, is a misnomer. We need a different lens through which to view the situation. I suggest that lens is global oppression.[46]

FAMILY SEPARATION POLICY AS GLOBAL OPPRESSION

Rather than "cruelty," I propose that we should condemn the Trump administration's family separation policy as unjust because it creates, perpetuates, and reflects global oppression. First, this policy is part of a systemic, structural effort on the part of the Trump administration to place Central American migrants and their families in metaphorical and literal cages to deter and prevent them from entering the United States. The policy is *not* the product of some views of random individuals' actions, nor is it the result of a few bad actors misapplying the policy or applying it based on their personal problematic viewpoints. To the contrary, the policy results from a deliberate set of actions by the U.S. government to place immigrants from Central America into a double-bind to either deter future migrants and/or punish those who come for "not respecting our laws." As such, the policy is not accidental, random, or avoidable, nor are its effects; the suffering is central to the policy itself (as that is the source of the deterrence). As Senator Merkely said, "Child separation didn't happen due to random actions of rogue agents. It happened because of deliberate action by the Trump Administration."[47] And this deliberate, systemic effort is based on the idea that "if you hurt families, particularly the children, it would discourage victims of war, famine, and persecution from seeking refuge in the United States."[48]

And we know this is the case from the administration's own comments on this issue. Remember, John Lafferty explicitly stated that it was being developed specifically "to deter mothers from migrating to the United States with their children."[49] This sentiment was then repeated by John Kelly when he was Donald Trump's chief of staff when he said, "A big name of the game is deterrence."[50] He continued: "The children will be taken care of—put into foster care or whatever—but the big point is they elected to come illegally into the United States."[51] After the policy was implemented (and supposedly ended), Donald Trump told a crowd in Virginia, "We have people trying to come in like never before. . . . If they feel there will be separation, then they won't come."[52] And these are just some of the numerous administration officials who explicitly stated that the policy was expressly created to create suffering so great on Central American families that it would deter them from migrating to the United States. So this policy was neither random, accidental, avoidable, nor some isolated product of a few people. To the contrary, it is part of a deliberate and systemic effort to specifically use children to place immigrants from Central America into double-binds—face horrors at home or face horrors in the United States—to deter them from coming or punishing them if they do.

It is also important to emphasize that these policies and practices are specifically targeting these migrants because of their particular nationality; they are in these double-binds *simply because they are migrating from Central America.*[53] Put differently, when parents, children, and family members ask why they are trapped in a cage by this policy, the answer is because of the nation where they hold citizenship. It is not because they migrated, because many people migrate without facing these consequences. It is not because they "broke the law" because many, including those who enter the United States without permission, do not have their children taken from them. These migrants are not in the position they are in because of their individual actions but rather because they are from Central America. In fact, we know this to be true because of who the policy applies to and because administration officials have stated this outright. John Kelly, for example, said, "Let me start by saying I would do almost anything to *deter the people from Central America* to getting on this very, very dangerous network that brings them up through Mexico to the United States."[54] Again, the family separation policy is not randomly affecting various migrants but rather is aimed at Central American migrants in particular.

The policy does not target all Central American migrants equally, though; there is a clear gendered aspect to it. First, while Central American immigration has increased, it was not deemed a "crisis" until families, that is, women and children, began to arrive in large numbers. Historically, most migrants from Mexico and Central America have been men looking for work. But this has been changing as more women migrate. So now we are not simply experiencing large influxes of Central Americans, we are experiencing influxes of Central American women and children. And *that* is what many say must be stopped. And this is supported by the fact that, as we saw earlier, the policy was originally constructed to deter *mothers* from migrating to the United States with their children.[55] So the policy was aimed in gender-specific ways from the start.

Second, the family separation policy is having a disproportionate effect on women—directly and indirectly. Directly, the policy targeted children, which meant it would disproportionately affect women because they are disproportionately more likely to bring a child to the United States. Central American men have only recently begun to come with children, and with more women fleeing violence, they are not going to leave their children behind if they are threatened. Beyond this, the policy disproportionately places women at risk from not only high levels of violence in their societies but also gender-specific violence. While some women migrate because there is a wide gender gap in terms of economic earnings and opportunity in Central America, most flee because of high levels of violence and homicide specifically directed at women in the Northern Triangle nations. According to an Amnesty International report, between 2007 and 2012, for example, El Salvador, Honduras, and Guatemala had the highest annual female homicide rate (femicide) in the world.[56] More recently, the femicide rate in Guatemala is more than three times the global average; in El Salvador, it is nearly six times; and in Honduras, it is almost twelve times the global average, one of the most dangerous places for women in the world.[57] So in creating policies separating children at the border specifically to deter their mothers from coming, the policy targets women and places them at increased risk for gender-specific violence.

Indirectly, the policy is also disproportionately affecting women. For example, children do not necessarily understand what is happening to them and, even if they do understand it at an intellectual level, they do not really get it emotionally. So many think that their mothers failed to protect them or that they abandoned them. One sixteen-year-old girl was in tears, for example, as she told UCLA professor Leisy Abrego, "My life has been pure suffering without [my mother]. One never really understands why a mother would abandon you."[58] So while the policy separated the children, the moms are being blamed, which will have lasting damage to relationships and mental health.

When we put all of these elements together, then, it becomes clear that the family separation policy is part of a larger immigration system that places Central American migrants into double-binds only because of their national origins and, often, their gender. And this is the policy's intent. When we explore specific manifestations of global oppression in the policy in the form of powerlessness, derivatization, and systemic violence, it becomes even more evident that the policy is wrong because it reflects, creates, and perpetuates global oppression.

Powerlessness

Political and epistemic powerlessness are prominently manifest in the family separation policy. Recall that powerlessness as a face of global oppression refers to systemic lack of control over various aspects of one's life due to one's national or communal membership.[59] The family separation policy robs parents and family members of decision-making power over their own lives (that is, where they want to live), over who will care for their children, and over where their children will reside. As such, it inherently involves rendering Central American migrants powerless.

Now some may object here that because the migrants decided to come to the United States, they made their decision and now are simply facing the consequences. So it is not fair of me to simply say that powerlessness results from the policy. Moreover, as we saw before, the new version of this policy— the binary choice policy—allows parents to decide whether to separate from their children or keep their children with them in detention. So again, the policy preserves migrants' decision-making abilities.

I caution against falling into this trap; neither the family separation policy nor the binary choice policy give parents or family members genuine decision-making power. At best, they gives them to ability to decide *from among the bad options that the U.S. government has predetermined for them*, which is coercion, not choice. Marilyn Frye explained this phenomenon in her piece "In and Out of Harm's Way: Arrogance and Love." There she explains that coercion is fundamentally about manipulating the oppressed's option:

> To coerce someone into doing something, one has to manipulate the situation so that the world as perceived by the victim presents the victim with a range of options the least unattractive of which (or the most attractive of which) in the judgment of the victim is the act one wants the victim to do. Given the centrality of the victim's perception and judgment, the plotting coercer might manipulate the physical environment but usually would proceed, at least in part, by manipulating the intended victim's perception and judgment through various kinds of influence and deception.[60]

I suggest that this is precisely what is going on with the family separation policy and its more recent instantiations. At first, the family separation policy was expressly enacted to deter migrants from coming. The idea was precisely this: the U.S. government arranged the potential options to be so horrible that the migrant would choose what the U.S. government wanted, namely, not to come. When that did not work (that is, in the original family separation policy), they created new policies (detaining entire families in wretched conditions, migrant protection protocols, raids, and the binary choice policy, etc.) to create horrific options so that migrants would either not come or face severe consequences. But to say that the migrants had decision-making power under these circumstances is absurd; their options have been manipulated by the U.S. government. We have given them a Sophie's choice, not actual autonomy. As such, the policies render them powerless.

The policy also renders Central American migrants epistemically powerless. Again, epistemic powerlessness refers to the lack of epistemic power, authority, and credibility that makes it such that the speaker cannot defend her claims to know, has no discretion with respect to disclosure, cannot entrust another with what she knows, and is excluded from cooperative interactions.[61] This policy renders Central American migrants epistemically powerless by stripping away their epistemic credibility and authority. Migrants who describe their experiences with the policy are simply not believed, even when there is clear evidence (like video and audio) supporting their claims. Popular conservative commentator and talk show host Laura Ingraham, for example, said after the release of the audio tapes and photos of children kept in cages at immigration detention centers that immigrant children were being housed "in what are basically summer camps."[62] Similarly, Fox News host Ann Coulter said these photos and videos were fake and not the images of migrants children bur rather child actors, thus denying them epistemic credibility. And because they deny epistemic credibility to immigrants and their advocates, the commentators are rendering the victims of the policy epistemically powerless; they cannot defend their assertions, influence the flow of knowledge on the issue, or participate in the production of knowledge about the policy.

Derivitization

Global oppression also manifests in the family separation policy in the fact of derivatization of Central American migrants. Again, derivatization occurs when the subject is not seen or treated as a being in his own right; he is simply a projection of another's will, desires, identity, and fears. I suggest that the family separation policy reduces Central American asylum seekers, refugees, and undocumented immigrants to "illegals" and "law breakers" rather than understanding them as complex human beings with many social identities; the policy strips Central American migrants of their own unique subjectivities. All that matters is that they "broke the law"—they are simply in the country "illegally." They are mere extensions of their migration status. As such, their full humanity and identity as a subject are denied/erased by the policy (as we discussed in chapter 3).

Specifically related to this policy, we can see derivatization, for example, in the way the policy's supporters respond to the migrants. According to the policy's supporters, Central American migrants are not fully actualized human beings but rather are mere extensions of the will, fears, and desires of a certain U.S. citizen—one who is fearful of immigrants and sees them as "threatening others"[63] who do deserve our condemnation and not our compassion or empathy. They are simply law breakers who deserve punishment. For example, one supporter of the policy said, "These people that we have coming across the border illegally are breaking the rules. *I have no feelings for them at all.*"[64] Another said, "I think people need to stop constantly bringing up the poor children, the poor children. The parents are the problems. They're the ones coming in illegally."[65] Both comments reflect the way the migrants have been stripped of their unique humanity and subjectivity by being reduced to the perception of the supporter.

The derivatization manifest in the policy is both racialized and unsurprising if we take recent research seriously. In general, the vast majority of these migrants are people of color, and white people tend to diminish the suffering and pain felt by people of color. For example, a post–Hurricane Katrina study by Cuddy, Rock, and Norton found that people think that members of racial groups other than their own suffered less than members of their own racial group. This is born out in the family separation policy such that most of its supporters are white and thus do not see migrants of color as experiencing a full gamut of human emotions—they only experience the emotions that the perceiver attributes to them. And this is supported in research specific to immigration attitudes. Nour Kteily and Emile Bruneau found that, in general, in the United States there are "high levels of prejudice and dehumanization toward Mexican immigrants."[66] And holding these anti-Mexican prejudices is correlated with support for anti-immigrant policies, like the family separation policy. Kteily and Bruneau observe that

> blatant dehumanization of Mexican immigrants was uniquely associated with more support for the anti-immigration statements and policies, controlling for levels of political conservatism and prejudice. Thus, individuals who dehumanized Mexican immigrants to a greater extent were more likely to cast them in threatening terms, withhold sympathy from them, and support measures designed to send and keep them out, such as surveillance, detention, expulsion, and building a wall between the United States and Mexico.[67]

Beyond this, the study found a correlation specifically between these racialized attitudes and support for Donald Trump specifically, reporting, "those who dehumanized Mexican immigrants to a greater extent were significantly more likely to endorse firm measures (many taken directly from Donald Trump's actual campaign platform) to restrict immigration, such as tightening border control and the detention and expulsion of existing illegal immigrants. Moreover, our findings suggest that support for the Republican candidates, particularly for Donald Trump, is associated with blatant dehumanization of Mexican immigrants."[68] As journalist German Lopez summarized it, "There's a basic concept behind this: Once someone can relate to the person who's suffering, it becomes much easier to empathize. But since the majority of the public and policymakers in America are white, this line of research suggests that Americans are simply less likely to care for suffering Latinx families."[69] And that is the point; this policy portrays Central American immigrants as Other—they are not like us, they will change our culture, they must be stopped to protect the United States and its way of life. But why are they not like us? Because of their race and national origins. These sentiments are not directed at Irish undocumented migrants, for example. In fact, many use the term "Mexican" immigrant as a derogatory placeholder for the Central American migrants specifically to invoke a long history between the United States and Mexico to further derivatize the migrant as an extension of the U.S. imaginary.[70] So the racial dynamics at play do not simply reference things occurring within the United States but also *between* the nations of the United States, Mexico, Guatemala, El Salvador, and Honduras and how the U.S. imaginary has characterized members of these nations as violent, dangerous, misogynistic, and threats to the U.S. way of life, in ways similar to how we characterize the nations themselves. And this allows for a derivatization that is not abstract or random but rather is specifically constructed to reduce Central American migrants as mere extensions of a racialized and nationalized U.S. imaginary that we explored in detail in chapter 3.

Before leaving this part of the discussion, I want to highlight one more aspect of derivatization going on in this policy. As we have seen, numerous administration officials defend the family separation policy on the grounds that it successfully deters Central Americans from entering the United States in the first place. While some may interpret this as treating the migrants as mere means in the Kantian sense, I suggest that it is more accurate to see this reasoning as further demonstrating the derivatization of migrants, especially the children. Central American children being detained at the border cannot serve as deterrents if they are simply reduced to objects or things. If they were mere objects, then they would not properly function as a deterrent—after all, nobody is going to not come to the United States out of fear of losing some sort of material possession. However, if parents fear losing their children, that could, in theory, serve as a deterrent. That means that they must be specific types of subjects (namely children) to have the desired effects of deterrence. So it is more accurate to say that the children of these migrants are being derivatized; they are being reduced to a mere extension and projection of the will, desires, identity, and fears of the Trump administration and its supporters.

Systemic Violence

I think the most egregious way that global oppression manifests itself in this policy is via systemic violence. Recall that systemic violence refers to violence to which one is vulnerable because one is a member of a particular nation. This vulnerability means that members of these nations constantly know that they must fear violence, even if they do not experience it directly. The family separation policy advocates and condones systemic violence against Central American migrants in numerous ways.

Let's begin by being crystal clear that the act of forcibly taking children from their parents *is* structural, systemic, and institutionally supported violence against Central American migrants. Specifically, it is institutionally supported kidnapping by the U.S. government of migrant children. In fact, according to a group of experts convened by the UN, "Detention of children is punitive, severely hampers their development, and in some cases may amount to torture."[71] So executing the policy requires carrying out state-sponsored structural violence directed at members of specific nations *only because they are members of that nation.*

Beyond this, these migrants and their children have been victims of abuse and violence by U.S. agents.[72] One report detailed 1,224 reports of abuse at the hands of ICE.[73] And this is not an outlier. The Office of the Inspector General of the United States released a report that also detailed abuses and human rights violations at the hands of ICE, stating, "Overall, we identified problems that undermine the protection of detainees' rights, their humane treatment, and the provision of a safe and healthy environment."[74]

The abuse just described does not stop at adults; it is now documented that ICE and U.S. customs and border patrol are emotionally, physically, and sexually abusing children, including mentally ill children, in their custody. According to detailed allegations, "adult staff members had harassed and assaulted children, including fondling and kissing minors, watching them as they showered, and raping them. They also included cases of suspected abuse of children by other minors."[75] The American Civil Liberties Union further reports based on Freedom of Information Act documents, "hundreds of cases of alleged abuse said to have occurred between 2009 and 2014."[76] Their documents show that customs and border patrol officials

- punched a child's head three times;
- kicked a child in the ribs;
- used a stun gun on a boy, causing him to fall to the ground, shaking, with his eyes rolling back in his head;
- ran over a seventeen year old with a patrol vehicle and then punched him several times;
- verbally abused detained children, calling them dogs and "other ugly things";
- denied detained children permission to stand or move freely for days and threatened children who stood up with transfer to solitary confinement in a small, freezing room;
- denied a pregnant minor medical attention when she reported pain, which preceded a stillbirth;
- subjected a sixteen-year-old girl to a search in which they "forcefully spread her legs and touched her private parts so hard that she screamed";
- left a four-pound premature baby and her minor mother in an overcrowded and dirty cell full of sick people, against medical advice; and
- threw out a child's birth certificate and threatened him with sexual abuse by an adult male detainee.[77]

In June 2019, more reports of deplorable conditions and abuses against children emerged. As various observers have reported,

> The children separated from their parents—both in the last year and those yet to be reunited with their parents from before the "end" of family separation—have been placed in unspeakable environments, characterized by a complete loss of human dignity. They reportedly lack basic hygiene products like toothbrushes

and soap in many cases, and are often covered in lice. Lights are sometimes left on all night (a known form of torture) and the temperature is regularly kept so cold that individuals refer to these facilities as "hieleras," meaning "ice boxes."[78]

According to a recent Inspector General's Report, there is dangerous over-crowding in detention centers along the Texas-Mexico border.[79] And the conditions failed to meet minimal standards. The report states, "For example, children at three of the five Border Patrol facilities we visited had no access to showers."[80] It continued: "While all facilities had infant formula, diapers, baby wipes and juice and snacks for children, we observed two facilities had not provided children access to hot meals . . . until the week we arrived."[81] Lawyers who visited one facility observed that "a 2-year-old boy wants to be held all the time," and so a few girls as young as ten are trying to take care of him. "The report also stated that the child had wet his pants but had no diapers and was wearing a mucus-smeared shirt. The Clint facility, where some children are held, was built for 106 people but was holding seven times as many children."[82] Pediatrician Sara Goza told *CNN* that she did not observe a single pediatrician on site and that "the first thing that hit me when we walked in the door was the smell. It was the smell of sweat, urine and feces. No amount of time spent in these facilities is safe for children."[83] Doctor Dolly Lucio Sevier summed it up in a court declaration about border patrol holding facilities in Clint and McAllen, Texas, saying, "The conditions within which they are held could be compared to torture facilities . . . extreme cold temperatures, lights on 24 hours a day, no adequate access to medical care, basic sanitation, water, or adequate food."[84]

Again, these examples are not simply random acts committed by rogue agents or a few bad apples. To the contrary, they are institutionally and structurally supported by U.S. immigration policies that separate children from their parents and detain them, a failure of coordination by Homeland Security, ICE, and border patrol, an administration that directs resources to enforcement rather than the care of immigrants and their children. And this has a long history. Historian Deborah Kang highlights that for almost one hundred years, Congress has exercised very little oversight over the nation's immigration agencies.[85] And now when they do, the administration ridicules them or does not cooperate. So nothing is done. In 2017, for example, the then secretary of Homeland Security said that Congress should "shut up" rather than criticize ICE for abuses.[86] This violence is not random, avoidable, or accidental but rather is systemic and supported by U.S. immigration policy and the U.S. government.

The family separation policy also perpetuates systemic violence in the form of reproductive injustice.[87] Kamila Price defines reproductive justice as "the complete physical, mental, spiritual, political, economic, and social well-being of women and girls, and will be achieved when women and girls have the economic, social and political power and resources to make healthy decisions about our bodies, sexuality and reproduction for ourselves, our families and our communities in all areas of our lives."[88] Ross and Solinger interpret this to mean that "at the heart of reproductive justice is this claim: all fertile persons and persons who reproduce and become parents require a safe and dignified context," for realizing those rights.[89] Given this, Loretta Ross says that reproductive justice includes "(1) the right to have a child; (2) the right not to have a child; and (3) the right to parent the children we have, as well as to control our birthing options, such as midwifery."[90] In forcibly taking children from their parents, the family separation policy constitutes systemic violence in the form of reproductive injustice by failing to allow parents the ability to "parent their children in a safe environment"[91] and by prohibiting parents from parenting their own children or deciding who parents them in their absence. And according to Leandra Hinojosa Hernández, this constitutes a form of gendered reproductive violence because "pregnant women are detained with no legal rules in place to ensure proper access to health care; women are caged and later forcibly separated from their children with no guarantee of family reunification; and women who seek to locate their children are provided with no resources—or are provided with incongruent information to help them locate their children."[92] So there are multiple levels of systemic violence in the family separation policy.

Before concluding, I want to expressly note the epistemic violence in this policy in the form of testimonial quieting. Again, testimonial quieting occurs when a person's testimony does not receive the uptake it deserves because the hearer will not serve as a willing audience to listen to the speaker's claims. Most generally, the administration has committed testimonial quieting by failing to provide a genuine audience to listen to the countless expert reports or migrant experiences. This is in addition to seeing how the policy's supporters will not even listen to migrant claims of why they fled to the United States or what happened to their children, despite there being over 4,500 accusations of sexual abuse by children separated from their parents, the administration claims that "'the vast majority' proved to be unfounded,"[93] despite being presented with evidence to the contrary.

Moreover, many refuse to listen precisely because they think the immigrants' nationality disqualifies them from serving as trustworthy sources of knowledge at all. Charles Mills refers to this phenomena as "epistemic norming of space."[94] In essence, the idea here is that we map who can serve as genuine knowers and producers of knowledge geographically. For example, we epistemically norm North America and Western Europe as knowledge-generating spaces and, by extension, their citizens as proper knowers. By contrast, we deny that Africa, parts of Asia, and most of Central America can be spaces that produce knowledge. And by extension, we deny that those who come from those spaces can be trusted to provide knowledge.

Now, of course, I do not argue that any of this is conscious or at the forefront of any of these instances of testimonial quieting. But we would be remiss and naïve to fail to recognize that who we believe and who we do not is raced, gendered, and influenced by geography. And I think this is happening in immigration discussions—the testimony of Central Americans is met with skepticism because Central Americans are seen as untrustworthy because they are not from a space that we consider to be knowledge producing. In fact, the opposite it true; they are from dangerous places that are nefarious and criminal, and so are they. Consequently, Central American migrants are not knowers who provide information to be taken seriously about the family separation policy. But this leads to testimonial quieting and a lack of willingness to engage, let alone listen.

In all of these exchanges, it is clear that epistemic violence is manifesting in the creation, implementation, and justification of the family separation policy and the debate around it. Again, this is part of the *global* oppression in the policy because the reason that these migrants are facing epistemic violence is precisely because they come from Central America. They are not given epistemic authority because they come from places and spaces deemed "uncredible" and "untrustworthy" like Guatemala and El Salvador. Worse, the reasons for this distrust are specifically rooted in U.S. actions in the region that portrayed these nations and their people as communists, rebels, drug dealers, and gang members. Again, this is systemic and directed at the members of these nations specifically.

CONCLUSION

In February 2019, eight immigrant families filed a lawsuit against the U.S. government for "inexplicable cruelty" and lasting trauma.[95] I support them. There is no question that the U.S. government and its agencies exhibited (and continue to exhibit) an astonishing lack of basic morality in the process toward Central American migrants expressed in the family separation policies and the victims should be compensated and recognized.

Still, focusing on cruelty does not actually reveal the type or depth of the injustices of the policies. This is not about some immoral individuals who enjoy causing specific immigrants suffering (though some such people clearly exist), it is about systemic injustice via immigration policy and upheld by U.S. government institutions. When we stop using the lens of cruelty and start applying the feminist lens of global oppression to the issue, however, we can get a more expansive and accurate view of what is so wrong with these family separation policies. The family separation policy is a systemic effort to deter Central American migrants specifically from coming to the United States by making the process so awful that folks will deem it better to stay in their home nations than to come to the United States. And they do so by rendering migrants powerless, treating them as derivatives, and by carrying out systemic violence against them, all because they are Central American. In other words, the family separation policy is wrong because it reflects, perpetuates, and creates global oppression, and it must be resisted. It will not be enough, though, to simply fire some bad actors or even to have an election (though both could help). Instead we need to find ways to empower migrants, treat them as full human beings, and make sure that they are safe in the United States. And the first step is to call family separation what it is: global oppression.

NOTES

1. Lydia Wheeler and Raphael Bernal, "Sessions Orders 'Zero Tolerance' Policy at Southwest Border," *The Hill*, April 2, 2018, http://thehill.com/regulation/administration/381991-sessions-orders-zero-tolerance-policy-at-southwest-border.

2. Jeff Sessions, "Speech to the National Sheriffs' Association," *Department of Justice*, June 18, 2018, https://www.justice.gov/opa/speech/attorney-general-sessions-delivers-remarks-national-sheriffs-association-annual.

3. Joshua Barajas, "How Trump's Family Separation Policy Has Become What It Is Today," *PBS Newshour*, June 14, 2018, https://www.pbs.org/newshour/nation/how-trumps-family-separation-policy-has-become-what-it-is-today.

4. Julia Edwards Ainsley, "Exclusive: Trump Administration Considering Separating Women, Children at Mexican Border," *Reuters*, March 3, 2017, https://www.reuters.com/article/us-usa-immigration-children-idUSKBN16A2ES; emphasis added.

5. Daniella Diaz, "Kelly: DHS Is Considering Separating Undocumented Children from Their Parents at the Border," *CNN*, March 7, 2017, https://www.cnn.com/2017/03/06/politics/john-kelly-separating-children-from-parents-immigration-border/index.html.

6. Caitlyn Dickerson, "Hundreds of Immigrant Children Have Been Taken From Parents at U.S. Border," *New York Times*, April 20, 2018, https://www.nytimes.com/2018/04/20/us/immigrant-children-separation-ice.html.

7. Mica Rosenberg, "Exclusive: Nearly 1,800 Families Separated at U.S.-Mexico Border in 17 Months through February," *Reuters*, June 8, 2018, https://www.reuters.com/article/us-usa-immigration-children-exclusive/exclusive-nearly-1800-families-separated-at-us-mexico-border-in-17-months-through-february-idUSKCN1J42UE.

8. Barajas, "How Trump's Family Separation Policy Has Become What It Is Today."

9. Jasmine Alguilera, "Everything to Know About the Status of Family Separation," *Time*, September 21, 2019, https://time.com/5678313/trump-administration-family-separation-lawsuits/.

10. U.S. House of Representatives Staff, "Child Separations from the Trump Administration," *Committee on Oversight and Reform U.S. House of Representatives*, July 2019, oversight.house.gov.

11. Ibid.

12. Alguilera, "Everything to Know About the Status of Family Separation"; Nila Bala and Arthur Rizer, "Trump's Family Separation Policy Never Ended. Here's Why," *NBC News*, July 1, 2019, https://www.nbcnews.com/think/opinion/ trump-s-family-separation-policy-never-really-ended-why-ncna1025376; Lomi Kriel and Dug Begley, "Trump Administration Still Separating Hundreds of Migrant Children at the Border Through Often Questionable Claims of Danger," *Houston Chronicle*, June 22, 2019, https://www.houstonchronicle.com/news/houston-texas/ houston/article/Trump-administration-still-separating-hundreds-of-14029494.php; Miriam Jordan and Caitlyn Dickerson, "U.S. Continues to Separate Migrant Families Despite Rollback of Policy," *New York Times*, March 9, 2019, https://www.nytimes .com/2019/03/09/us/migrant-family-separations-border.html; Rick Gervis and Alan Gomez, "Trump Administration Has Separated Hundreds of Children from Their Migrant Families Since 2018," *USA Today*, May 2, 2019, https://www.usatoday .com/story/news/nation/2019/05/02/border-family-separations-trump-administration -border-patrol/3563990002/.

13. Bala and Rizer, "Trump's Family Separation Policy Never Ended."

14. Gretchen Frazee, "Why Trump Wants to Detain Immigrant Children Longer," *PBS Newshour*, August 21, 2019, https://www.pbs.org/newshour/nation/why-trump -wants-to-detain-immigrant-children-longer; Molly O'Toole and Molly Hennesy-Fiske, "Trump Administration Plans to End Limits on Child Detention," *Los Angeles Times*, August 21, 2019, https://www.latimes.com/politics/story/2019-08-21/trump -child-detention-limits-flores-agreement.

15. Though this plan was recently rejected by a federal judge. Miriam Jordan, "Judge Blocks Trump Administration Plan to Detain Migrant Children," *The New York Times*, September 27, 2019, https://www.nytimes.com/2019/09/27/us/migrant -children-flores-court.html.

16. John Burnett and Mara Liasson, "Trump Administration Mulls Tougher Immigration Policies Amid DHS Shake-UP," *National Public Radio*, April 9, 2019. https:// www.npr.org/2019/04/09/711446892/trump-administration-mulls-tougher-immigra tion-policies-amid-dhs-shake-up.

17. "Zero Tolerance Immigration Policy Is a Cruel and Immoral Human Rights Violation," Center for the Study of Social Policy, June 19, 2018, https://www.cssp .org/media-center/press-releases/zero-tolerance-immigration-policy-is-a-cruel-and -immoral-human-rights-violation.

18. Pat Ralph, "Rivera Rips Trump's Zero-Tolerance Policy in Sean Hannity Interview that Went Off the Rails," *Business Insider*, June 20, 2018, https://www.businessin-sider.com/geraldo-rivera-rips-trump-zero-tolerance-policy-on-fox-news-hannity-2018-6.

19. Laura Bush, "Laura Bush: Separating Children from Their Parents at the Border 'Breaks My Heart,'" *Washington Post*, June 17, 2018, https://www.wash ingtonpost.com/opinions/laura-bush-separating-children-from-their-parents-at-the -border-breaks-my-heart/2018/06/17/f2df517a-7287-11e8-9780-b1dd6a09b549_ story.html?noredirect=on&utm_term=.df7882ab2112.

20. "USA: Policy of Separating Children from Parents Is Nothing Short of Torture," Amnesty International, June 18, 2018, https://www.amnesty.org/en/latest/ news/2018/06/usa-family-separation-torture/; Chris Matthews, "Matthews: Trump's Family Separation Policy Is Cruel," *NBC News*, June 18, 2018, https://www

.nbcnews.com/dateline/video/matthews-trump-s-family-separation-policy-is
-cruel-1258664515965.

21. Jeff Merkley, *America Is Better than This: Trump's War Against Migrant Families* (New York and Boston: Twelve, 2019), prologue.

22. Quinta Jurecic, "A Choice Between Cruelty and Mercy," *The Atlantic*, June 18, 2018, https://www.theatlantic.com/politics/archive/2018/06/border-policies
-antigone/563126/; Jeffrey Davis, "US 'Zero-Tolerance' Immigration Policy Still Violating Fundamental Human Rights Laws," *The Conversation*, June 27, 2018, https://theconversation.com/us-zero-tolerance-immigration-policy-still-violating
-fundamental-human-rights-laws-98615; Patrick J. McDonnell, "Mexico Blasts U.S. Family Separation Policy as 'Violation of Human Rights," *Los Angeles Times*, June 19, 2018, http://www.latimes.com/world/mexico-americas/la-fg-mexico-family
-separation-20180619-story.html.

23. Randall Collins, "Three Faces of Cruelty: Towards a Comparative Sociology of Violence," *Theory and Society* 1, no. 4 (Winter 1974): 415–40.

24. Ibid., 419–23.

25. Ibid., 432.

26. Ibid.

27. Ibid.

28. Ibid., 433.

29. Ibid., 432.

30. Ibid., 419, 434–36.

31. Allison B. Wolf, "'Quit trying to make us feel teary-eyed for the children!' Constructions of Emotion, Anger, and Immigration Injustice," Colloquio: Emociones en las Ciencias Sociales, La Universidad de los Andes, Bogotá, Colombia, August 28, 2018.

32. Carlos Alberto Sánchez, "On Brutality: Or, Toward a Philosophy of Excessive Violence," *A Sense of Brutality: Philosophy and Narco Culture* (Amherst, MA: Amherst College Press, 2020, forthcoming).

33. Ibid., 125.

34. Max Scheler, *The Nature of Sympathy*, revised edition (New York: Transaction Publishers, 2008), 15.

35. Etienne Balibar, "Outlines of a Topography of Cruelty: Citizenship and Civility in the Era of Global Violence," *Constellations* 8, no. 1 (2001): 15.

36. Etienne Balibar, *Politics and the Other Scene* (New York: Verso Books, 2012): 135–36.

37. Sánchez, "On Brutality," 126.

38. Balibar, "Outlines of a Topography of Cruelty," 15.

39. Scheler, *The Nature of Sympathy*, 125.

40. Sánchez, "On Brutality," 129.

41. Adam Serwer, "The Cruelty Is the Point: President Trump and His Supporters Find Community by Rejoicing in the Suffering of Those They Hate and Fear," *The Atlantic*, October 3, 2018.

42. Merkely, *America Is Better than This*, 23.

43. John Kelly, "Full Interview with DHS Secretary John Kelly," Interview by Wolf Blitzer, *The Situation Room, CNN,* March 6, 2017, video, 9:39, https://edition

.cnn.com/videos/politics/2017/03/06/john-kelly-dhs-trump-travel-ban-wiretap-tsr
-intv-full.cnn.

44. Ryan Bort, "Trump Wants to Bring Back 'Large-Scale' Family Separations" *Rolling Stone*, April 8, 2019, https://www.rollingstone.com/politics/politics-news/mexico-border-family-separation-homeland-security-trump-819195/.

45. Sánchez, "On Brutality," 131.

46. Sánchez, "On Brutality: Or, Toward a Philosophy of Excessive Violence," 113

47. Merkely, *America Is Better than This*, 41.

48. Ibid., 23.

49. Ainsley, "Exclusive."

50. John Kelly, "White House Chief of Staff John Kelly's Interview with NPR," interviewed by John Burnett, *National Public Radio*, May 11, 2018, https://www.npr.org/2018/05/11/610116389/transcript-white-house-chief-of-staff-john-kellys-interview-with-npr.

51. Kelly, "White House Chief of Staff John Kelly's Interview with NPR."

52. Donald Trump cited in Toluse Olorunnipa, Tamara Thueringer, and Jennifer Epstein, "President Trump Says Family Separations May Deter Illegal Immigration," *Time*, October 14, 2018, https://time.com/5424225/trump-family-separation-illegal-immigration/.

53. Philip Bump, "Here are the Administration Officials Who Have Said that the Family Separation Policy Is Means as a Deterrent," *Washington Post*, June 19, 2018, https://www.washingtonpost.com/news/politics/wp/2018/06/19/here-are-the-administration-officials-who-have-said-that-family-separation-is-meant-as-a-deterrent/.

54. John Kelly, cited in Bump, "Administration Officials."

55. Ainsley, "Exclusive."

56. "Fleeing for Our Lives," Amnesty International, https://www.amnestyusa.org/fleeing-for-our-lives-central-american-migrant-crisis/.

57. Azam Ahmed, "Women Are Fleeing Death at Home. The U.S. Wants to Keep Them Out," *New York Times*, August 18, 2019, https://www.nytimes.com/2019/08/18/world/americas/guatemala-violence-women-asylum.html.

58. Natalie Escobar, "Family Separation Isn't New," *The Atlantic*, August 14, 2018, https://www.theatlantic.com/family/archive/2018/08/us-immigration-policy-has-traumatized-children-for-nearly-100-years/567479/.

59. See chapter 3 of this book.

60. Marilyn Frye, "In and Out of Harm's Way: Arrogance and Love," in *Politics of Reality* (California: Crossing Press, 1983), 56–57.

61. Ibid., 108.

62. Willa Frej, "Laura Ingraham Compares Child Immigrant Detention Centers to Summer Camps," *HuffPost*, June 19, 2018, https://www.huffingtonpost.com/entry/laura-ingraham-immigrant-summer-camp_us_5b28b769e4b0f0b9e9a4840c.

63. Carlos Sandoval García, *Otros Amenazantes: Los nicaragüenses y la formación de identidades nacionales en Costa Rica* (San José, Costa Rica: Editorial UCR, 2008).

64. Martin Savage, Tristan Smith, and Emanuella Grinberg, "What Trump Supporters Think of Family Separations at the Border," *CNN*, June 20, 2018, https://www.cnn.com/2018/06/19/us/trump-voters-family-separation/index.html.

65. Ibid.

66. Nour Kteily and Emile Bruneau, "Backlash: The Politics and Real-World Consequences of Minority Group Dehumanization," *Personality and Social Psychology Bulletin* 43, no. 1 (2017): 90.

67. Ibid.

68. Ibid., 91.

69. German Lopez, "The Research on Race Explains Trump's Family Separation Policies," *Vox*, June 19, 2018, https://www.vox.com/identities/2018/6/19/17478970/trump-family-separation-immigration-policy-racism.

70. Ibid.

71. Clark Mindock, "UN Says Trump Separation of Migrant Children with Parents 'May Amount to Torture,' in Damning Condemnation," *Independent*, June 22, 2018, https://www.independent.co.uk/news/world/americas/us-politics/un-trump-children-family-torture-separation-border-mexico-border-ice-detention-a8411676.html.

72. Nomann Merchant, "Immigrant Kids Seen Held in Fenced Cages at Border Facility," *Associated Press*, June 18, 2018, https://www.apnews.com/6e04c6ee01dd46669eddba9d3333f6d5/Immigrant-kids-seen-held-in-fenced-cages-at-border-facility; David Graham, "Are Children Being Kept in 'Cages' at the Border?" *The Atlantic*, June 18, 2018, https://www.theatlantic.com/politics/archive/2018/06/ceci-nest-pas-une-cage/563072; Salvador Rizzo, "Jeff Merkley's Claims about Immigrant Children in 'Cages,' Access to a Texas Shelter," *Washington Post*, June 6, 2018, https://www.washingtonpost.com/news/fact-checker/wp/2018/06/06/does-the-u-s-keep-immigrant-children-in-cages/?utm_term=.04050bf69e66.

73. Alice Speri, "Detained, then Violated," *The Intercept*, April 11, 2018, https://theintercept.com/2018/04/11/immigration-detention-sexual-abuse-ice-dhs/.

74. "Concerns About ICE Detainee Treatment and Care at Detention Facilities," Inspector General of the Department of Homeland Security, December 11, 2017, https://www.oig.dhs.gov/sites/default/files/assets/2017-12/OIG-18-32-Dec17.pdf.

75. Matthew Haag, "Thousands of Immigrant Children Said They Were Sexually Abused in U.S. Detention Centers, Report Says," *New York Times*, February 27, 2019, https://www.nytimes.com/2019/02/27/us/immigrant-children-sexual-abuse.html.

76. "ACLU Obtains Documents Showing Widespread Abuse of Child Immigrants in U.S. Custody," American Civil Liberties Union. May 22, 2018, https://www.aclu.org/news/aclu-obtains-documents-showing-widespread-abuse-child-immigrants-us-custody; Richard Gonzalez, "ACLU Report: Detained Immigrant Children Subjected to Widespread Abuse by Officials," *National Public Radio*, May 23, 2018, https://www.npr.org/sections/thetwo-way/2018/05/23/613907893/aclu-report-detained-immigrant-children-subjected-to-widespread-abuse-by-officia; David M. Perry, "ICE Keeps Raiding Hospitals and Mistreating Disabled Children," *Pacific Standard*, January 15, 2018, https://psmag.com/social-justice/ice-keeps-raiding-hospitals-and-harming-disabled-children.

77. ACLU, "ACLU Obtains Documents Showing Widespread Abuse."

78. Bala and Rizer, "Trump's Family Separation Policy Never Ended."

79. Office of the Inspector General, "Management Alert—DHS Needs to Address Dangerous Overcrowding and Prolonged Detention of Children and Adults in the Rio Grande Valley," Department of Homeland Security, July 2, 2019.

80. Ibid.

81. Ibid.

82. Bala and Rizer, "Trump's Family Separation Policy Never Ended."

83. Elizabeth Cohen, "Pediatricians Share Migrant Children's Disturbing Drawings of the Time in US Custody," *CNN*, July 4, 2019, https://edition.cnn.com/2019/07/03/health/migrant-drawings-cbp-children/index.html.

84. James Sergent, Elinor Aspegren, Elizabeth Lawrence, and Olivia Sanchez, "Chilling First-Hand Reports of Migrant Detention Centers Highlight Smell of 'Urine, Feces,' Overcrowded Conditions," *USA Today*, July 17, 2019, https://www.usatoday.com/in-depth/news/politics/elections/2019/07/16/migrant-detention-centers-described-2019-us-government-accounts/1694638001/.

85. Deborah Kang, "15 Years After Its Creation, Critics Want to Abolish ICE," interview by Meghna Chakrabarti, *Here and Now*, NPR, June 25, 2018, http://www.wbur.org/hereandnow/2018/06/25/immigration-abolish-ice.

86. Devlin Barrett, "DHS Secretary Kelly Says Congressional Critics Should 'Shut Up' or Change Laws," *Washington Post*, April 18, 2017, https://www.washingtonpost.com/world/national-security/dhs-secretary-kelly-says-congressional-critics-should-shut-up-or-change-laws/2017/04/18/8a2a92b6-2454-11e7-b503-9d616bd5a305_story.html?utm_term=.c4f79cec3d4c; Stephen Dinan, "Secretary Kelly Tells DHS Critics to 'Shut Up,' Let Agents Do Their Jobs," *Washington Times*, April 18, 2017, https://www.washingtontimes.com/news/2017/apr/18/dhs-chief-critics-shut-up-let-agents-do-their-jobs/.

87. Leandra Hinojosa Hernández, "Feminist Approaches to Border Studies and Gender Violence: Family Separation as Reproductive Injustice," *Women's Studies in Communication* 42, no. 2 (2019): 131.

88. Kimala Price, "What Is Reproductive Justice? How Women of Color Activists Are Redefining the Pro-Choice Paradigm," *Meridians: Feminism, Race, Transnationalism* 10, no. 2 (2010): 42–65; SisterSong: Women of Color Reproductive Justice Collective, accessed January 18, 2013, http://sistersong.net/reproductive_justice.html.

89. Loretta Ross and Rickie Solinger, *Reproductive Justice: An Introduction* (Los Angeles: University of California Press, 2017).

90. Ibid., 14.

91. Hinojosa Hernández, "Feminist Approaches to Border Studies and Gender Violence," 131.

92. Ibid., 133.

93. John Burnett and Richard Gonzalez, "Thousands of Migrant Children Reported Sexual Abuse While in Custody," *National Public Radio*, February 26, 2019.

94. Charles Mills, "Part 2," in *The Racial Contract* (New York: Cornell University Press, 1999).

95. Lauren Aratani and Agencies, "'Inexplicable Cruelty': US Government Sued over Family Separations at Border," *The Guardian*, February 12, 2019, https://www.theguardian.com/us-news/2019/feb/11/immigrant-families-sue-us-government-over-family-separation.

Chapter Five

Exporting U.S. Immigration Policy

As I write this, the United States is currently enacting or continuing various policies and plans to export its immigration policy to Mexico and the nations of Central America. Here are just a few of those policies.

PLAN FRONTERA SUR

This plan was announced during the Obama administration. While the plan itself came from Mexico, there is no doubt that the United States was deeply influential in its creation, content, and financing.[1] In essence, it requires Mexico to increase efforts to stop Central American migrants *before* they reach the U.S. southern border and in exchange the United States will provide significant financial and logistical support. As part of the plan, the United States and Mexico have trained more border patrol forces and increased border security at twelve points of entry throughout southern Mexico to review people's documents, detain them, and deport them back to Central America.[2] The plan also establishes "three bands of security" throughout the Mexican state of Chiapas, including sending at least three hundred border patrol agents (from other parts of Mexico) to the country's south, increasing policing of trains and hostels used by migrants, and establishing checkpoints throughout the country.[3] To ensure the program's stability long term, the United States has pledged to give Mexico at least $100 million and has provided hundreds of millions more in training and border technology.[4]

MIGRANT PROTECTION PROTOCOLS
(AKA THE REMAIN IN MEXICO POLICY)

Before this policy was put into place, U.S. asylum law required erring on the side of caution in that the United States did not want to risk sending someone back to situations where they would be tortured or killed.[5] In other words, U.S. asylum law followed the principle of refoulment and thus allowed most asylum seekers to pass their initial screening and enter the United States while they waited for their asylum hearing.[6] The Trump administration changed this starting on January 28, 2019. On that day, the U.S. Customs and Border Patrol enacted the Migrant Protection Protocols (MPP) (more commonly known as the "Remain in Mexico" policy). According to these protocols,

> Certain foreign individuals entering or seeking admission to the U.S. from Mexico—illegally or without proper documentation—may be returned to Mexico and wait outside of the U.S. for the duration of their immigration proceedings, where Mexico will provide them with all appropriate humanitarian protections for the duration of their stay.[7]

In other words, customs and border patrol agents can decide to send migrants entering the United States on its southern border to Mexico until their case is heard in court. And under this new policy, asylum seekers will only get an initial interview with an asylum officer if they explicitly state that they fear for their safety *in Mexico* (as opposed to the usual protocol of explaining why they fear for their safety in their home countries).[8] The order does not apply to unaccompanied minors, those in the process of expedited removal, those with credible fears of facing persecution or torture in Mexico, or Mexican citizens.[9]

The U.S. government argues this policy is necessary to respond to a national security and humanitarian crisis on the southern border and that it "will help restore a safe and orderly immigration process, decrease the number of those taking advantage of the immigration system, and the ability of smugglers and traffickers to prey on vulnerable populations, and reduce threats to life, national security, and public safety, while ensuring that vulnerable populations receive the protections they need."[10] Moreover, says the U.S. Department of Homeland Security, "The MPP will provide a safer and more orderly process that will discourage individuals from attempting illegal entry and making false claims to stay in the U.S., and allow more resources to be dedicated to individuals who legitimately qualify for asylum."[11]

Even though the United States says it is helping Mexico deal with the migrants, this is questionable. Yes, the United States sends $5 million to Mexico to house migrants while they wait, but this money only goes to official Mexican government shelters and only provides for 8,000 migrants.[12] But as of November 2019, the United States has sent over 57,000 people (including about 16,000 children) back to Mexico and over 21,000 are waiting to be processed.[13]

TARIFFS

In late May 2019, Donald Trump abruptly threatened to raise tariffs on Mexican goods in response to what he called "Mexico's passive cooperation in allowing this mass incursion."[14] Specifically, Trump said,

> On June 10th, the United States will impose a 5% Tariff on all goods coming into our Country from Mexico, until such time as illegal migrants coming through Mexico, and into our Country, STOP. . . . The Tariff will gradually increase until the Illegal Immigration problem is remedied . . . at which time the Tariffs will be removed. Details from the White House to follow.

In essence, the United States threatened to impose 5 percent tariffs on all goods entering the United States from Mexico and steadily increase that amount to 25 percent unless and until the Mexican government meets U.S. demands for increased Mexican assistance in preventing Central American migrants from reaching and entering the United States. Because Mexico agreed to deploy 6,000 Mexican troops to its southern border with Guatemala as part of Plan Frontera Sur, to expand the Migrant Protection Protocols, and agreed to work to dismantle human smuggling rings,[15] these tariffs did not go into effect. But on June 10, 2019, Trump renewed his threats to impose tariffs if Mexico does not implement these strategies to U.S. satisfaction.[16]

CUTTING AID AND SAFE THIRD COUNTRY AGREEMENTS

The United States is now demanding that Guatemala, Honduras, and El Salvador (the nations from where these immigrants are fleeing) act to curb the flow of immigrants. First, on March 31, 2019, the United States cut $500 million in aid to these nations[17] on the grounds that they were not stopping migrant caravans.[18] According to the administration, they will only release aid once the United States is convinced these nations do more to stop their citizens from leaving, thus making future aid conditional on Guatemala, Honduras, and El Salvador violating migrants' human right to exit.[19] Second, the United States is demanding action from these nations, pressuring them to sign "safe third country" agreements. These agreements essentially mean that refugees from other nations can ask for asylum in these countries before applying in the United States and these nations will process such requests. On July 26, 2019, the United States created such an agreement with Guatemala, and on September 20, 2019, the administration announced that it would seek a similar agreement with El Salvador.[20] Signing these agreements is required in order for these nations to start receiving U.S. aid again.[21] It is not clear this will occur, however, because of opposition within each nation.

I maintain that all of the policies just outlined reflect, perpetuate, and create global oppression against Mexico, the Central American nations of the Northern Triangle, and their people. Generally, they form a system of immigration policies that place these nations and their citizens into harmful double-binds *only* because of their national identity and the geographic location of these countries in relation to the United States. So in this chapter I will argue these policies are wrong.

EXPORTING IMMIGRATION POLICY AS GLOBAL OPPRESSION AGAINST CENTRAL AMERICAN MIGRANTS

These policies—together and separately—create, reflect, and perpetuate global oppression. First, they oppress the Central American migrants themselves. Second, they create, reflect, and further the global oppression of the nations of Mexico, Guatemala, El Salvador, and Honduras. I will begin by focusing on the former and then turn to the latter.

I want to begin by highlighting how the policies just reviewed, individually and together, create, reflect, and perpetuate global oppression against the Central American migrants as a group. First, we must be clear that these policies were not randomly or accidentally created, nor are they avoidable. To the contrary, they were systematically constructed, in part to create suffering and prevent Central Americans from migrating to the United States.[22] As one U.S. asylum officer put it with respect to MPP, "This policy seemed designed to send tons of people back to Mexico."[23] And as is true of all oppressive systems, they accomplish this task by creating many instances that cause this group extreme suffering and by placing these people into double-binds.

First, these policies are specifically aimed at creating suffering for Central American migrants. Plan Frontera Sur, for example, is expressly about using raids and checkpoints to make the journey for Central Americans through Mexico so difficult that the migrants live in constant fear and suffering. Similarly, the MPP send people back to Mexico where they have no potable water or proper sanitation (one report said that there are five toilets for 2,500 migrants).[24] As a result, they are repeatedly contracting communicable diseases like infectious diarrhea and pink eye. And, again, this is not accidental or avoidable—the policy is specifically designed to reduce the number of Central Americans admitted into the United States by making things so bad that they just give up and go back to their home countries (which is exactly what is happening).[25] As such, these are policies that create suffering for these migrants only because of their nationality, migration status, and U.S. policy goals.

Still, we see this most prominently in how these policies put these migrants into dangerous double-binds by making them vulnerable to systemic violence as citizens of Central American nations. Generally speaking, all of the policies outlined at the chapter's outset come together to ensure that there is no safe place for those from the Northern Triangle to go—they suffer in their own nations, on the journey to the United States and Mexico, in Mexico, and in the United States. For example, a United Nations High Commissioner for Refugees Report indicates that "a surging tide of violence [is] sweeping across El Salvador, Guatemala, and Honduras [that] forces thousands of women, men, and children to leave their homes every month."[26] More specifically, "Honduras ranks first, El Salvador fifth, Guatemala sixth for rates of homicide globally. Furthermore, El Salvador, Guatemala, and Honduras rank first, third, and seventh, respectively, for rates of female homicides globally."[27] These rates of violence show that many migrants (especially women) face violence at home. And now these policies create high levels of violence when they leave as well, be it from Mexican authorities, gangs, smugglers, or U.S. border agents. As such, they create a double-bind for migrants to either face the violence in their home countries or face violence in the journey to the United States. And this is intentional—the idea is to deter migration by making it so onerous and dangerous that many will not even attempt it. In fact, right before he announced cutting off aid to Central America, Donald Trump stated that the United States was creating tougher policies to deter migrants because migrants think it is too easy to come to the United States.[28] This is similar to the logic we saw in chapter 4 when the administration decided to separate Central American families to make it too painful for them to come. So it is clear that making conditions worse by these policies is not accidental or random but rather part of an express effort to create an immigration process so awful that Central American migrants specifically will decide not to make the journey.

Beyond using violence to try to deter Central American immigrants, the specific policies under review also place them in direct danger of violence. Let us begin with Plan Frontera Sur and the MPP. An explicit part of Plan Frontera Sur is for the United States to train Mexican officials in tactics that promote violent raids on Central American migrants. And it is now well documented that Mexican officials consistently commit human rights crimes against these migrants in order to keep them from reaching the U.S. border so as to comply with Plan Frontera Sur.[29] In requiring increased checkpoints and training for conducting border raids, the plan itself makes Central American migrants specifically vulnerable to violence. And we see this even more dramatically and directly with the Remain in Mexico policy.[30]

When the United States sends Central American migrants back to Mexico, they face violence from Mexican gangs, corrupt officials, and, increasingly, from local residents *because they are immigrants*.[31] Countless migrants in Mexico are becoming victims of kidnappings, robberies, sexual assault, and murder.[32] This is so prevalent that one woman asked if they would give out condoms so she could ask her rapist to wear one the *next* time she is raped.[33] And the U.S. policy is knowingly placing them in this kind of danger. One asylum officer, Ursela, said that she interviewed a woman who told her she was afraid that if she was sent back to Mexico, she would be raped. But Ursela was obligated to send her back (despite evidence supporting her claim and the fact that Ursela believed her) because the policy requires that the woman could be admitted to await for her asylum hearing only if she could identify the specific individual who might rape her in Mexico, and not present a general fear.[34] The United States is making it easy for these migrants to be victimized in other ways as well. For example, it makes it easy for kidnappers to find and identify migrants because they send them back to the same place at the same time every day.[35]

The problem is widespread. Researcher Vicki Fox of the University of London, for example, reports that nine out of ten Central American migrants in Ixtepec "had been the victim of a serious crime in Southern Mexico, ranging from armed robbery and assault to gang rape and attempted murder. And, worse, they are often victims of violence and extortion from Mexican authorities."[36] Immigration attorney Taylor Levy told National Public Radio, "I have worked with asylum-seekers for 10 years . . . [and] I have never seen people as scared, who are just viscerally terrified while they're begging me, 'Please don't let me get sent back. Please don't let me get sent back.'"[37] Similarly, Linda Rivas, executive director of Las Americas Immigrant Advocacy Center, reports that she is terrified for what will happen to her clients who are returned to Juarez. "You're representing them, and you know they're going to be back in Juárez. . . . And you don't know if something's going to happen to them while they're waiting for the court or they're waiting for you to go out there and work on their asylum cases with them. Anything can happen. And it's happening."[38] As one asylum officer said, "You're literally sending people back to be raped and killed . . . that's what this is."[39]

While all migrants are being made vulnerable to this violence, things are especially dangerous for cisgendered heterosexual women and LBGTQ migrants, especially the risk of sexual assault. One Honduran woman who had been returned to Ciudad Juárez under the MPP, for example, was kidnapped and raped in mid-June. In a Mexican court hearing on June 17, she testified that Mexican federal police officers stormed into a house where migrants were staying and abducted her and two others, turning them over to a criminal group.[40] Sadly, her story is not unique. There is also Delfina M. (pseudonym), a twenty-year-old asylum seeker who fled Guatemala with her four-year-old son, who was grabbed and sexually assaulted by two men on the street in Cuidad Juárez after she was returned to Mexico as part of the MPP. They told her not to scream and threatened to kill her son. "I can still feel the dirtiness of what they did in my body,"[41] she told Human Rights Watch. And a *New York Times* investigation found "more than 100 documented reports of sexual assault of undocumented women along the border in the past two decades, a number that most likely only skims the surface."[42]

We find similarly alarming rates of violence against LBGTQ migrants in Mexico. The United Nations High Commissioner for Refugees said that "two thirds of the LBGTI refugees from Central America they spoke to in 2016 and 2017 had suffered sexual and gender-based violence in Mexico."[43] The *New York Times* article "'They Were Abusing Us the Whole Way': A Tough Path for Gay and Trans Migrants"[44] notes that many LBGTI Latinx migrants are fleeing violence and persecution in their home countries only to encounter it in force on their way to the United States and once they arrive, including by immigration officials themselves. They are raped, beaten, and humiliated by other migrants and migration officials alike.[45] All of these migrants are in this position because of the U.S. Remain in Mexico policy; if this policy were not in place, then they would not be vulnerable in these ways.

Again, though, this is not random or accidental. Mexico has said it will not protect these migrants because they want them to use government shelters. The United Nations will not step in because Mexico has yet to invite them.[46] And the United States knows that these migrants are vulnerable to violence in these ways. The State Department's own website reads,

> Violent crime, such as murder, armed robbery, carjacking, kidnapping, extortion, and sexual assault, is common. . . . Gang activity, including gun battles and blockades, is widespread. Armed criminal groups target public and private passenger buses as well as private automobiles traveling through Tamaulipas, often taking passengers hostage and demanding ransom payments.[47]

Beyond this, the State Department forbids U.S. government employees from traveling after dark on the grounds that they are safe in the very border cities they are sending migrants to because of widespread violent crime like kidnapping, robbery, and homicide.[48] Even U.S. federal asylum officers have said that "Mexico is simply not safe for Central American asylum seekers" and that "the risk of persecution in Mexico is even higher for the most vulnerable segments of asylum seekers," including ethnic minorities from Indigenous cultures, migrant women at large, and LGBTI migrants.[49] So the United States is knowingly placing these migrants in danger to advance its own objectives. In fact, it was so clear that this is an express goal of the policy (that is, using violence to deter Central Americans) that large numbers of asylum officers are resigning in protest.[50] One asylum officer said, "It's the first time that we have been asked to affirmatively do harm to people. You're not just saying 'I don't think you're eligible.' You're literally saying 'I believe what you're saying, I believe you're in danger. Go back to that danger.'"[51] Another said, "I feel in some ways this Administration has made me a human rights abuser."[52]

Finally, these policies also make these migrants vulnerable to epistemic violence because of how they quiet the testimony of the Central American migrants. Most asylum officers see their jobs as "trying to weed out the fakers, the ones trying to game the system."[53] Take the recent case of a Honduran woman who explicitly told authorities that she could not wait for her asylum claim court date in Mexico because, as a Honduran woman, Mexico was unsafe. The U.S. government refused to believe her and sent her back to Mexico, where she was kidnapped and raped by multiple assailants.[54] Similarly, David, another refugee from Honduras, said, crying, he "wanted to ask for asylum in the US, but the agents didn't listen to him. They just gave him documents to come back to a court date in December. He can't go back to Honduras."[55]

More generally, border and asylum officials begin the process on the assumption that these migrants have no epistemic credibility. But we also see it in how specific claims about fleeing violence or the dangers of Mexico are dismissed. Asylum officers conducting interviews with migrants say that even when they agree with the person that they should not be sent back, their supervisors overrule them.[56] And the only reason for this is because the U.S. government will only see them as untrustworthy liars who are trying to abuse the U.S. asylum system. In fact, the opening quote on an official White House briefing on this matter states, "The biggest loophole drawing illegal aliens to our borders is the use of fraudulent or meritless asylum claims to gain entry into our great country."[57] So the U.S. government has deemed the entire group of Central American migrants as untrustworthy out of hand, thus quieting their testimony and subjecting them to violence epistemically, physically, and emotionally, all because of where they come from.

In all of the ways just detailed, these policies come together, especially Plan Frontera Sur and the MPP, to oppress these migrants. And we must be clear that they are victims of *global* oppression in that the reasons these policies have been enacted and applied to them is precisely because of these migrants' national origins. Moreover, as we will now see, it is also to advance U.S. geopolitical interests in the region.

EXPORTING IMMIGRATION POLICY AS GLOBAL OPPRESSION AGAINST THE NATIONS OF MEXICO, GUATEMALA, HONDURAS, AND EL SALVADOR

The people of Central America are not the only targets of these policies though. I maintain that the nations of Mexico, Guatemala, Honduras, and El Salvador *themselves* face global oppression via the creation, enactment, and enforcement of these policies and plans. First, these policies place all of these nations into double-binds such that they either follow U.S. demands and their people suffer (for example, via infringement of human rights or lack of resources for other services in their home nations because funds are diverted to appease the United States) or they deny the United States and they and their people suffer via lack of aid, economic hardship, and international interference from the United States (like preventing them from access to loans or other international bodies). No matter what they do, they lose. And this is the exact purpose of the policies—to get the countries to bend to the will of the United States of America.

Second, these policies further global oppression against these nations by reflecting, reinforcing, and bolstering oppressive colonial relationships between the United States and Central America that date back to the Monroe Doctrine.[58] While I cannot rehearse this long history here, it is important to note that the United States has maintained dominant colonial relationships with all of these nations for almost two centuries—orchestrating a civil war in Colombia that resulted in Panama's independence and cleared the way for the United States to build the Panama Canal, imposing its Cold War agenda by organizing a CIA-led coup in Guatemala in 1954, using Honduras as a base for its military bases to wage the Contra War against Nicaragua, supporting military dictatorships in El Salvador, and by promoting the neoliberal trade agenda with NAFTA, CAFTA, and the Colombia Trade Promotion Agreement (CTPA/FTA). The policies under consideration here are part of this long-established pattern. The requirement that Mexico, Guatemala, El Salvador, and Honduras enforce and execute U.S immigration policy, then, is neither new nor the result of any of the specific actions these nations have taken but rather part of the larger U.S. project to maintain dominance in the region. Given this, these nations are being placed into double-binds *as nations*; they face these double-binds not because of their specific actions or policy decisions (as the Trump admin-istration claims) but rather because of their geopolitical location relative to the United States and its foreign and domestic policy objectives. This is the goal. And they accomplish this by perpetuating global oppression in spe-cific ways—namely by rendering Mexico and the nations of the Northern Triangle powerless and derivatizing them.

Powerlessness

Let's begin with powerlessness. Recall that powerlessness in the context of global oppression refers to a systemic lack of control and decision-making power for nations and their members. The policies under consideration in this chapter render Mexico, the nations of the Northern Triangle, and their people powerlessness. Let us look at Mexico's situation. Because of the enormous amount of trade between Mexico and the United States on which the Mexi-can economy depends, it cannot meaningfully resist U.S. tariff threats—at minimum, they must do something to appease the United States on immigra-tion because if 5 percent tariffs were imposed on Mexico's products entering the United States, their economy would be devastated. So the tariff threat in effect neutralized Mexico's decision-making abilities about what policy to adopt. For example, the United States announced this threat shortly after Mexico's election in which Manuel López Obrador was voted into power in part on a platform of implementing more humane policies toward migrants. And he was carrying this out—Mexico's will was clear here. But they were stripped of this power as soon as the tariffs were threatened because Mexico is not in a global position relative to the United States to carry out their own policy over the objections of their powerful neighbor to the North. The tariff threats thus rendered Mexico powerless.

Similarly, the MPP have rendered Mexico powerless to resist U.S. policy and carry out their own. Despite Mexican assertions that it would not ac-cept the MPP, the United States imposed the policy unilaterally. In fact, the United States even sent its own military to the border to prevent migrants from crossing and to force them to remain in Mexico. So even though Mexico resisted the policy, that resistance proved futile. That exemplifies powerlessness; the United States systematically and intentionally made it impossible for Mexico to execute its own will about what will happen to migrants in its territory via the creation and implementation of MPP. And the fact that Mexico resisted without effect shows that they were rendered powerless not because of their actions but rather because of its geopolitical location vis-à-vis the United States. Put differently, it is its position on the southern border in combination with its less powerful global position that made Mexico vulnerable in these actions.

We also see how these policies render Guatemala, El Salvador, and Honduras powerless. Human rights and international law along with deeply ingrained problems in their countries make it impossible for these nations to do what the United States is demanding. They cannot simply stop people from migrating or wave a magic wand and fix their nations so that people will stay. Even if you eliminate the corruption, these problems now have such a long history, it will take years to remedy them. So they need U.S. aid to help. But they cannot do it without signing meaningless, farcical agreements with which these nations cannot comply. So cutting off aid and pursuing safe third country agreements are making these nations powerless to make decisions on these matters for themselves by placing them into a double-bind such that they sign agreements they cannot fulfill or they lose needed aid for their nations.

Before concluding this section, I also want to note that these policies render all of these nations epistemically powerless. Mexico, for example, said it cannot accommodate these immigrants, but the United States simply gave them no epistemic credibility on this point and went forward. The same is true when Guatemala and Honduras denied any involvement in the migrant caravans. The United States simply does not trust these nations and consequently they cannot contribute knowledge about the circumstances, and these nations lack power to influence U.S. policy related to their own countries even though they are telling the truth. So the powerlessness goes beyond the political to the epistemic.

Derivatization

In addition to all of the ways that these policies promote, reflect, and further global oppression against these nations already discussed, they derivatize Mexico and the nations of Central America—thus reflecting, reinforcing, and perpetrating global oppression in yet another form. In short, what I want to say here is that, at their core, all of these policies ontologically erase Mexico and the nations of the Northern Triangle *as separate and distinct nations*. All of these policies reflect the fact that the United States fails to recognize Mexico, Guatemala, El Salvador, or Honduras as having their own existences, desires, fears, objectives, and cultures apart from the needs, desires, fears, and interests of the United States.

Central to all of these policies is the belief that these countries do not have interests that differ from those of the United States. And because their interests are inseparable from those of the United States, they *must* help fix U.S. problems. To see this, let us begin with the MPP. According to the Department of Homeland Security and Donald Trump himself, the MPP are being implemented because they see the number of Central American refugees trying to cross the southern border as a crisis; from their perspective, the United States is being "overwhelmed." So Mexico *has to help*. This attitude alone is derivatizing Mexico because it presumes Mexico's interest is to help the United States not feel overwhelmed regardless of the fact that it may not be in Mexico's interest to do so. But beyond this, the presumption only makes sense if either (1) Mexico also feels threatened (such that they have internal motivation to address the issue) or (2) Mexico is only conceptualized as an extension of the United States. I have already presented reason to deny the veracity of (1). With respect to (2), the facts seem more supportive, namely that before these policies, Mexico was looking at policy changes that allowed it to be more welcoming to migrants. And beyond this, there is a long history of the United States derivatizing Mexico in this way, including in the immigration context.

As historian Rachel St. John has shown, the United States and Mexico worked together before the border between them was drawn.[59] Granted, at first, this cooperation was minimal because from the end of the Mexican American War in the mid-1800s to the end of that century, the border with Mexico was not patrolled at all.[60] But this began changing during prohibition, when in an effort to stop U.S. citizens from crossing into Mexico to drink, the U.S. government pressured Mexico to stop the cross-border traffic.[61] Then during the Great Depression (when the United States did not want immigration from Mexico), *they asked Mexico to help prevent its citizens from leaving*, which Mexico did by creating checkpoints and confiscating the passports of Mexican nationals who sought to go north.[62] Mexican authorities were among the first to seek to work with U.S. immigration authorities to limit Mexican emigration to the United States, fighting coyotes, requiring Mexican passports to have U.S. visas, and charging extra fees to leave Mexico.[63] After further U.S. action in 1929, Mexico started to discourage Mexican emigration to the United States and *Mexican* migration officials created checkpoints and confiscated passports of Mexican nationals who sought to go north without proper authorization from the United States.[64] So even in the 1930s we see that "the regime of U.S. immigration control extended well south of the U.S.-Mexico border."[65] The fact that the Mexican government had little success in dissuading emigration did not change the fact that "the unsanctioned immigration of Mexican nationals into the United States was of concern to the Mexican government" because it drained Mexico of its supply of cheap labor.[66] As a result, post–World War II, "various Mexican interest groups pressured their government representatives to end unsanctioned Mexican migration across the U.S.-Mexico border."[67] These voices were joined by Bracero workers who saw undocumented immigration as a threat and other Mexicans who resented the loss of labor to the north. In response, the Mexican government pressured U.S. officials to intensify border patrols and enforcement.[68] And because mass deportations still did not resolve various issues, U.S. and Mexican authorities reached an agreement on January 11, 1945, to "control the return of undocumented Mexican migrants to Mexico through close U.S. and Mexican cooperation."[69] And as part of this effort, cross-border enforcement became prominent. For example,

> In the United States, those identified as illegal immigrants were subject to surveillance, detention, and deportation. In Mexico, they faced disruptions and anxieties of forced dislocation to unfamiliar places. In each location, however, the consequences of having committed the symbiotic trespasses of unauthorized exit from Mexico and illegal entry into the United States were bound together through the collaborative practices of U.S.-Mexican migration control.[70]

And this situation continues today. For example, the United States has pressured Mexico to require that anyone from Central America (except for Costa Ricans) to have visas to enter the country (something that is virtually not done anywhere in Latin America toward other Latin American citizens).[71] So U.S.-Mexican cooperation on immigration has a long history that did not start with these policies—the United States has long seen Mexico as being required to meet U.S. immigration objectives.

We should see that the current policies are part of this larger pattern. It makes no sense from the perspective of Mexico to assume responsibility for Central American migrants and refugees on behalf of the United States. The fact that they are expected to do so without so much as consultation or approval of the Mexican government—the fact that Mexico is just presumed responsible by default—only makes sense if the United States conceptualizes Mexico as a derivative of itself. If this were not the case, the United States would acknowledge that, as a separate nation, Mexico has no obligation to avoid a refugee problem for the United States! But MPP deny this, especially because Mexico voiced strong objections and the United States went ahead with it anyway. All the United States sees is its own political agenda and its feeling "overwhelmed" by the Central American refugee crisis and as a result fails to acknowledge the costs to Mexico or how their very policies create a crisis now overwhelming Mexico.

Second, the MPP derivatize Mexico in that they were implemented without consultation or approval of the Mexican government; it was simply presumed that Mexico would accept these migrants once the United States enacted the policy, despite objections to the contrary.[72] The head of Mexico's National Migration Institute, Tonatiuh Guillen, for example, stated that Mexico does not have the capacity to support the program.[73] His sentiments were echoed by the Mexican Secretariat of Foreign Affairs, who said that "the Mexican government doesn't agree with this unilateral measure implemented by the United States authorities"[74] and by Mexico's Undersecretary of Migration and Human Rights Alejandro Encinas, who, when questioned by the Mexican press about whether the López Obrador government would accept making Mexico the "safe third country" for the United States, bluntly replied, "No way."[75] Still, the United States went forward. I suggest this is only explicable if the United States perceives Mexico as a mere extension of its will and not as a nation with its own desires, needs, issues, and priorities; if the United States did see Mexico as a separate nation independent of the United States, it would have been consulted and worked with Mexican authorities to develop and implement the policy rather than simply impose it.

Let me be clear, though, Mexico is not a mere victim of the United States here, and the United States is not the only nation derivatizing another here; Mexico too seems to be derivatizing Central American migrants. Generally speaking, for example, Mexico is carrying out U.S. immigration policy in large swaths of the border, and Mr. López Obrador's administration has gone along with it on several fronts, including accepting women and children despite earlier promises to take only adult male asylum seekers.[76] The *New York Times* reports,

> The Mexican authorities are blocking groups of migrants at border towns, refusing to allow them onto international bridges to apply for asylum in the United States, intercepting unaccompanied minors before they can reach American soil, and helping to manage lists of asylum seekers on behalf of the American authorities to limit the number of people crossing the border.[77]

In carrying out these acts, I submit, Mexico is simultaneously derivatizing Central American nations in order to maintain their desired relationship with the United States.

A major reason the Mexican government is cooperating with MPP is the desire to avoid a public war with Donald Trump. "If we have to accept a handful of people back into Mexico, that's not really a problem for us, not even politically," said one official. "What we really want to avoid is a public fight with Trump."[78] From the perspective of Mexico, there is too much to lose in resisting the Trump administration's demands, such as elaborate regional trading arrangements and information sharing on border security, transnational crime, and terrorism. So as one official put it, López Obrador "has avoided a bruising and potentially costly public fight over the issue."[79] In the process, though, Mexico is conceptualizing Central American migrants as mere extensions of *its* needs, desires, and will, which is to maintain strong relations with the United States. These are no longer asylum seekers who have dreams of a safer life with more economic opportunity and safety for their children, they are paths to a strong relationship with the United States. And Mexico is treating them as such. For example, in Reynosa, Mexico, almost no one is allowed to cross the bridge to apply for asylum in neighboring McAllen, Texas. They are typically blocked or apprehended by Mexican officials, forcing migrants to try their luck in other towns.[80] And this is not limited to the MPP but also to actions with Plan Frontera Sur, as we saw earlier.

Now some might argue that I am being too hard on Mexico. After all, they are also trying to push a regional deal to help Central America and are lobbying the United States to commit $10 billion to the plan. They have also issued humanitarian visas and work permits to the Central American asylum seekers who are waiting for their hearing in the United States. And I do recognize this is light-years ahead of the U.S. response here. But in action, this does not cancel the reality—Mexico is treating Central America and its peoples as mere extensions of its own interests to achieve good relations with the United States, thus exposing another way MPP are unjust because they promote double derivatization—the United States derivatizes Mexico and Mexico derivatizes Central America and its citizens.

We also see derivatization via threats of tariffs, cutting off aid to Central American nations, and pursuing safe third country agreements. In response to cutting off aid to Central American nations, Trump stated, "We were paying them [Guatemala, Honduras, and El Salvador] tremendous amounts of money, and we're not paying them any more *because they haven't done a thing for us.*"[81] Similarly, State Department spokesperson Morgan Ortagus said that the United States "will not provide new funds until we are satisfied that those countries are taking concrete actions on reducing illegal migrants coming to the US border."[82] In all of these statements, the United States implies that these countries *must* do things for the United States, regardless of what they want or need. This can only make sense if the United States does not acknowledge these nations have interests apart from their own.

With respect to the tariffs, we also see derivatization of Mexico. When the tariffs were first threatened, for example, the White House said, "If the illegal migration crisis is alleviated through effective actions taken by Mexico, to be determined in our sole discretion and judgment, the tariffs will be removed."[83] Notice the language—*to be determined in our sole discretion and judgment.* This implies that Mexico must simply act as the United States wants or face the consequences; there is no suggestion that they are working together with another distinct nation. Mexico is treated as a mere extension of U.S. will.

Finally, the whole pursuit of safe third country agreements embodies derivatization. Putting aside the fact that asking nations deemed some of the most dangerous in the world to serve as "safe" countries for citizens fleeing violence from these very same nations is a cynical mockery of the idea of asylum, it is clear that the U.S. government is acting as if the nations of the Northern Triangle are mere extensions, ontologically, of the United States. The point of pursuing these agreements, as noted earlier, is that the United States wants to stop Central American immigration to the United States. This is a *U.S.* desire. But it is not clear how this would be in the national interest of Guatemala, Honduras, or El Salvador given that they cannot keep their own citizens safe and their economies benefit from remittances migrants send home. Accepting refuges from other nations, then, will only burden them further. Beyond this, there is deep and wide opposition to these agreements in these nations.[84] In fact, the Guatemalan Constitutional Court has ruled that the country cannot sign such an agreement. But rather than accept this nation's public opinion and legal system, Donald Trump responded to the decision by suggesting that the United States "would retaliate by blocking all Guatemalan immigrants and introducing a new tax on their remittances."[85] At the risk of sounding like a broken record, I must reiterate that in the face of such opposition, these responses can only be explained if the United States sees Guatemala and these other nations are mere extensions of their own will, needs, and desires.

Of course, one could deny what I am saying and suggest that these nations are acting in their own interests. After all, as we saw with the case of Mexico, they want good relations with the United States and are simply choosing to appease the United States for their own good. Beyond this, the United States is offering these nations aid in return for their cooperation, and they would not be doing that if they did not recognize the distinct needs, interests, and desires of those countries. So I am being disingenuous that the United States is treating them as mere derivatives with these agreements.

I maintain that this objection is without merit. First, the United States is not implementing these policies for the good of Mexico, Guatemala, Honduras, or El Salvador; it is doing it because it wants these nations to be seen as safe so they can deny more asylum claims—after all, people do not need asylum from safe countries. Second, and more important, the Trump administration has said that aid does not work and it is a waste of money. If that is the position, we cannot claim the United States is trying to help nations with aid; if it does not work, aid will not help. Instead the United States is using aid to coerce these nations to bend to its will in a way similar to using family separation to coerce parents not to migrate. So we should call this what it is: derivatization.

Beyond the derivatization just discussed, these policies also treat these nations as epistemic derivatives. Recall that the epistemically derivatized are epistemically harmed because they are not recognized as knowers in their own right; they are not recognized as being epistemic subjects who can generate knowledge that goes beyond the derivatizer's epistemic resources. The epistemically derivatized's subject can only be seen as epistemically credible when supporting the perpetuator's worldview; she cannot express or be seen as a knower about anything that goes beyond the perpetuator's understanding. This is precisely what is occurring in the cases of these policies.

One place this is clear is in cutting off aid to the nations of the Northern Triangle on the grounds that they are not doing enough to stem the flow of migrants from their countries. This is a refusal to give credibility to any evidence that contradicts their interpretation of the facts. For example, Article 13 of the United Nations Declaration of Human Rights guarantees the right to emigrate. So no matter what the United States does or wants, these nations cannot prohibit their people from moving. But they will not recognize that as valid (or as a valid constraint) because it contradicts the US (or at least Donald Trump's) worldview.

Beyond this, though, it turns out these countries have been trying to achieve the U.S. goals. After the unexpected 2014 surge of migrant children and families, the United States devised the Strategy for Engagement in Central America, a comprehensive multiyear approach to help Central American nations, especially those in the Northern Triangle.[86] This plan complimented and reinforced another, the Plan of the Alliance for Prosperity, in which the Northern Triangle governments promised to fund complementary investments, especially in infrastructure, education, and law enforcement. Both plans *explicitly aimed* to discourage emigration by expanding economic opportunities, increasing security, and improving government effectiveness.[87] According to Willis and Seiz, "In all, the Northern Triangle governments report having spent more than $4 billion from 2016 to 2018 to complement U.S. appropriations, funding numerous initiatives, from providing training and credit to small businesses to increasing support for returning emigrants."[88] So despite U.S. claims to the contrary, these nations have been trying to work with the United States. But the United States will not acknowledge any of this. There is a complete negation that these nations are trustworthy and to be believed. If they were recognized as knowers who had knowledge beyond that U.S. position, they would be believed (or at least consulted) before actions were taken that deny the facts.

This epistemic derivatization is even more apparent when we see that the distrust is selective, that these nations are being treated as certain kinds of epistemic subjects, namely trustworthy sources of knowledge when they express the U.S. worldview and untrustworthy when they do not. For example, when López Obrador says that Mexico can handle migrants or Guatemalan president Morales says his country can serve as a safe third country, they are believed.

They are only discredited when they contradict the U.S. position. In this way, the policies treat these nations and their citizens as epistemic derivatives—they are only recognized as epistemic subjects when they support the U.S. worldview. But if they express anything that contradicts or goes beyond the U.S. epistemic apparatus about immigration, they are denied epistemic authority.

And as a result of the derivatization, these nations are then victims of epistemic violence. The United States refuses to serve as a willing audience to listen to the claims of Mexico, Guatemala, Honduras, and El Salvador about what they can and cannot do and they quiet the testimony of governments when they report what they are indeed doing. This is evident in the threats to impose tariffs on Mexican goods. Despite Mexican assertions that they are acting to curb Central American migration (and the evidence supporting this claim), the United States denies them epistemic credibility and refuses to believe them. Despite executing Plan Frontera Sur, for example, Donald Trump stated, "Mexico is doing very little, if not NOTHING, at stopping people from flowing into Mexico through their Southern Border, and then into the U.S."[89] Similarly, Vice President Mike Pence repeated the claims that Mexico "must do more." And there is a similar pattern with Central American nations. Despite the fact that there is no evidence of government involvement in migrant caravans, for example, Trump said that the Honduran government was responsible for them,[90] stating, "We're giving hundreds of millions of dollars to these three countries. . . . And they arrange . . . these caravans. And they don't put their best people in those caravans, they put people in there that you don't want in the United States."[91] All of this illustrates how the U.S. government refuses to listen to these nations.

CONCLUSION

As this chapter has illustrated, the U.S. pattern of exporting its immigration policy reflects and perpetuates global oppression in numerous ways. It treats Mexico and the nations of Central America as mere derivatives of U.S. foreign policy and renders thousands of Central Americans vulnerable to systemic violence and powerless to resist the U.S. demands. These policies around immigration commit countless immigration injustices, further and reflect colonial power arrangements, and place thousands of migrants' lives at risk. This cannot stand. We must recognize the fact that Mexico and the nations of the Northern Triangle are not mere extensions of the United States but rather are nations with their own interests, goals, and projects. And the United States must not only treat them as such but also stop obligating them to further U.S. interests over their own.

NOTES

1. Adam Isacson, in Lorne Matalon, "Programa Frontera Sur: Tracking U.S Influence on Mexico's Southern Border Plan," May 28, 2017, http://lornematalon .com/2017/05/28/programa-frontera-sur-tracking-u-s-influence-on-mexicos-southern -border-plan/.

2. "Programa Frontera Sur: The Mexican Government's Faulty Immigration Policy," Council on Hemispheric Affairs, October 26, 2016, http://www.coha.org/ programa-frontera-sur-the-mexican-governments-faulty-immigration-policy/.

3. Jeff Abbott, "Keep Out! How the U.S. Is Militarizing Mexico's Southern Border," *Progressive Magazine*, October 2, 2017, https://progressive.org/magazine/ keep-out-how-the-us-militarizes-mexico-southern-border/.

4. Matalon, "Programa Frontera Sur," 7.

5. Molly O'Toole, "Goodbye Stranger: The Out Crowd," *This American Life*, National Public Radio, November 15, 2019, https://www.thisamericanlife.org/688/ the-out-crowd.

6. Ibid.

7. "Migrant Protection Protocols," Department of Homeland Security, January 24, 2019, https://www.dhs.gov/news/2019/01/24/migrant-protection-protocols.

8. O'Toole, "Goodbye Stranger."

9. "Migrant Protection Protocols."

10. Ibid.

11. Ibid.

12. Ira Glass, "Prologue: The Out Crowd," *This American Life*, National Public Radio, November 15, 2019, https://www.thisamericanlife.org/688/the-out-crowd.

13. Kristina Cooke, Mica Rosenberg, and Reade Levinson, "Exclusive: U.S. Migrant Policy Sends Thousands of Children, Including Babies, Back to Mexico," *Reuters*, October 11, 2019, https://www.reuters.com/article/us-usa-immigration-ba bies-exclusive/exclusive-u-s-migrant-policy-sends-thousands-of-children-including -babies-back-to-mexico-idUSKBN1WQ1H1; Glass, "Prologue."

14. Louise Radnofsky, William Mauldin, and David Luhnow, "Trump Threatens Tariffs on Mexican Imports in Response to Migrant Surge," *Wall Street Journal*, May 30, 2019, https://www.wsj.com/articles/trump-threatens-5-tariff-on-mexican -imports-beginning-june-10-11559260679.

15. Ayesha Rose and Bobby Allen, "Trump: U.S., Mexico Reach a Deal to Avoid New Tariffs," *National Public Radio*, June 7, 2019, https://www.npr.org/ 2019/06/07/730283772/trump-u-s-mexico-reaches-deal-to-avoid-new-tariffs.

16. "Trump Renews Mexico Tariff Threat Amid Row over Migration Deal," *Al Jazeera News*, June 10, 2019, https://www.aljazeera.com/news/2019/06/trump -renews-mexico-tariff-threat-row-migration-deal-190610212227154.html; "Trump Threatens to Reimpose Tariffs Against Mexico," *Telesur*, June 10, 2019, https:// www.telesurenglish.net/news/Trump-Threatens-to-Reimpose-Tariffs-Against-Mex ico-20190610-0003.html.

17. "Donald Trump Cuts off Aid to Central America," *The Economist*, April 4, 2019, https://www.economist.com/the-americas/2019/04/04/donald-trump-cuts-off

-aid-to-central-america; Julia Harte and Tim Reid, "Trump Cuts Aid to Central American Countries as Migrant Crisis Deepens," *Reuters*, March 30, 2019, https://www.reuters.com/article/us-usa-immigration-trump/trump-cuts-aid-to-central-american-countries-as-migrant-crisis-deepens-idUSKCN1RC013.

18. Julian Borger, "Trump Plans to Cut Central America Aid Blaming Countries for Migrant Caravans," *The Guardian*, April 3, 2019, https://www.theguardian.com/world/2019/apr/03/trump-to-sanction-central-american-nations-with-aid-cuts?CMP=share_btn_link.

19. Camilo Montoya-Galvez, "U.S. Cuts Millions in Aid to Central America, Fulfilling Trump Vow," *CBS News*, June 18, 2019, https://www.cbsnews.com/news/us-cuts-millions-in-aid-to-central-america-fulfilling-trumps-vow/.

20. Colleen Long and Astrid Galvin, "US, El Salvador Sign Asylum Deal, Details to be Worked Out," *Associated Press*, September 20, 2019, https://www.apnews.com/de6a00632755415fad2a952c7cd4bd72; Nick Miroff, "Trump Administration Reaches Deal to Send Asylum Seekers to El Salvador in An Effort to Deter Migrants from Entering the United States," *Washington Post*, September 20, 2019, https://www.washingtonpost.com/immigration/trump-administration-reaches-deal-to-send-asylum-seekers-to-el-salvador-in-an-effort-to-deter-migrants-from-entering-the-united-states/2019/09/20/17350a16-dbbd-11e9-ac63-3016711543fe_story.html; Zolan Kanno-Youngs and Elisabeth Malkin, "U.S. Agreement with El Salvador Seeks to Divert Asylum Seekers," *New York Times*, September 20, 2019, https://www.nytimes.com/2019/09/20/us/politics/us-asylum-el-salvador.html.

21. Hamed Aleaziz, "The Trump Administration Is Scrambling to Make Its 'Safe Third Country' Asylum Deal with Guatemala a Reality, A Memo Shows," *BuzzFeed*, July 30, 2019, https://www.buzzfeednews.com/article/hamedaleaziz/safe-third-country-asylum-deal-guatemala-obstacles-memo.

22. O'Toole, "Goodbye, Stranger."

23. Ibid.

24. Glass, "Prologue."

25. Emily Green, "Take the Long Way Home: The Out Crowd," *This American Life*, National Public Radio, November 15, 2019, https://www.thisamericanlife.org/688/the-out-crowd.

26. *Women on the Run: First-Hand Accounts of Refugees Fleeing El Salvador, Guatemala, Honduras, and Mexico*, United Nations Commissioner for Refugees, October 26, 2015, https://www.acnur.org/fileadmin/Documentos/Publicaciones/2015/10228.pdf.

27. Ibid.

28. John Burnett and Mara Liasson, "Trump Administration Mulls Tougher Immigration Policies Amid DHS Shake-Up," *National Public Radio*, April 9, 2019, https://www.npr.org/2019/04/09/711446892/trump-administration-mulls-tougher-immigration-policies-amid-dhs-shake-up.

29. Carlos Sandoval Garcia, *No Mas Muros: Exclusión y migración forzada en Centroamerica* (San José, Costa Rica: Editorial UCR, 2015).

30. Cedar Attanasio, "'It's Not Safe Here.' Migrants Detail Violence They Face as U.S. Makes Them Wait in Mexico," *Time*, June 27, 2019, https://time.com/5616370/migrants-detail-violence-mexico/.

31. Sandoval Garcia, *No Mas Muros*, 5.

32. Joel Rose and Laura Smitherman, "Fear, Confusion, and Separation as Trump Administration Sends Migrants Back to Mexico," *National Public Radio*, July 1, 2019, https://www.npr.org/2019/07/01/736908483/fear-confusion-and-separation-as-trump-administration-sends-migrants-back-tomex?utm_source=npr_newsletter&utm_medium=email&utm_content=20190701&utm_campaign=npr_email_a_friend&utm_term=storysh.

33. Glass, "Prologue."

34. O'Toole, "Goodbye, Stranger."

35. Green, "Take the Long Way Home."

36. Nick Schifrin, "On the Road in Mexico, Central American Migrants Face Uncertain Future," *PBS NewsHour*, April 13, 2017, https://www.pbs.org/newshour/show/road-mexico-central-american-migrants-face-uncertain-future.

37. Rose and Smitherman, "Fear, Confusion, and Separation."

38. Ibid.

39. Molly O'Toole, "Asylum Officers Rebel Against Trump Immigration Policies They Say Are Immoral and Illegal, *Los Angeles Times*, November 15, 2019, https://www.latimes.com/politics/story/2019-11-15/asylum-officers-revolt-against-trump-policies-they-say-are-immoral-illegal.

40. "We Can't Help You Here: US Returns Asylum Seekers to Mexico," Human Rights Watch, July 2, 2019, https://www.hrw.org/report/2019/07/02/we-cant-help-you-here/us-returns-asylum-seekers-mexico.

41. Ibid.

42. Manny Fernandez, "You Have to Pay with Your Body: The Hidden Nightmare of Sexual Violence on the Border," *New York Times*, March 3, 2019, https://www.nytimes.com/2019/03/03/us/border-rapes-migrant-women.html.

43. "Mexico/Central America: Authorities Turning the Backs on LGBTI Refugees," Amnesty International, November 27, 2017, https://www.amnesty.org/en/latest/news/2017/11/mexico-central-america-authorities-turning-their-backs-on-lgbti-refugees/.

44. Jose A. Del Real, "'They Were Abusing Us the Whole Way': A Tough Path for Gay and Trans Migrants," *New York Times*, July 11, 2018, https://www.nytimes.com/2018/07/11/us/lgbt-migrants-abuse.html.

45. "We Can't Help You Here."

46. Glass, "Prologue."

47. Attanasio, "'It's Not Safe Here.'"

48. "Mexico Travel Advisory," U.S. Department of State, April 2019, https://travel.state.gov/content/travel/en/traveladvisories/traveladvisories/mexico-travel-advisory.html.

49. "We Can't Help You Here."

50. O'Toole, "Goodbye, Stranger."

51. Ibid.

52. Ibid.

53. Ibid.

54. Rose and Smitherman, "Fear, Confusion, and Separation."

55. Green, "Take the Long Way Home."

56. O'Toole, "Goodbye, Stranger."

57. "Fact Sheet: President Donald J. Trump Is Working to Stop the Abuses of Our Asylum System and Address the Root Causes of the Border Crisis," The White House, April 29, 2019, https://www.whitehouse.gov/briefings-statements/president-donald-j-trump-working-stop-abuse-asylum-system-address-root-causes-border-crisis/.

58. Monroe Doctrine, 1823.

59. Rachel St. John, *Line in the Sand: A History of the Western U.S-Mexico Border* (Princeton, NJ, and Oxford: Princeton University Press, 2011).

60. Paul Ganster with David M. Lorey, *The U.S.-Mexican Border Today: Conflict and Cooperation in Historical Perspective*, third edition (Lanham, Boulder, New York, London: Rowman & Littlefield, 2016), 215; Kelly Lytle Hernández, *Migra! A History of the U.S. Border Patrol* (Berkeley, Los Angeles, and London: University of California Press, 2010).

61. St. John, *Line in the Sand*, chap. 6.

62. Hernández, *Migra!*, 94–95.

63. Ibid., 90.

64. Ibid., 94–95.

65. Ibid., 95.

66. Ibid., 109, 113.

67. Ibid., 114.

68. Ibid.; Nelson Copp, *"Wetbacks" and Braceros: Mexican Migrant Laborers and American Immigration Policy, 1930–1960* (San Francisco: R and E Research Associates, 1971).

69. Hernández, *Migra!*, 127.

70. Ibid., 129–30.

71. See Sandoval Garcia, *No Mas Muros.*

72. Joel Rose, "'Remain in Mexico' Policy Expands, but Slowly," *National Public Radio*, March 12, 2019, https://www.npr.org/2019/03/12/702597006/-remain-in-mexico-immigration-policy-expands-but-slowly; https://www.cnn.com/2019/03/12/politics/remain-in-mexico-expands/index.html.

73. Redacción Animal Político, "Extranjeros que soliciten asilo en EU se quedarán en México; INM dice que no hay capacidad para recibirlos," *Animal Político*, December 20, 2018, https://www.animalpolitico.com/2018/12/mexico-recibir-solicitantes-asilo-eu/.

74. "Mexico Rejects US Plan to Extend 'Stay in Mexico' Policy for Asylum Seekers," *Mexican News Daily*, March 13, 2019, https://mexiconewsdaily.com/news/mexico-rejects-us-plan/.

75. Redacción Animal Político, "Extranjeros."

76. Azam Ahmed and Kirk Semple, "Trump's Surprising New Ally in Mexico? The Government," *New York Times*, March 1, 2019, https://www.nytimes.com/2019/03/01/world/americas/mexico-migration-trump.html

77. Ibid.; Emily Green, "As Trump Knocks Mexico on Immigration, López Obrador Keeps Quiet," *Public Radio International*, April 2, 2019, https://www.pri.org/stories/2019-04-02/trump-knocks-mexico-immigration-l-pez-obrador-keeps-quiet.

78. Ahmed and Semple, "Trump's Surprising New Ally in Mexico?"

79. Ibid.

80. Ibid.

81. Demetri Sevastopulo, Aime Williams, and Jude Weber, "Donald Trump Cuts off Aid to Three Central American States," *Financial Times*, June 17, 2019, https://www.ft.com/content/f3cd73d2-9135-11e9-aea1-2b1d33ac3271; emphasis added.

82. Ibid.

83. Lauren Gambino and David Agren, "Trump Announces Tariffs on Mexico Until 'Immigration Remedied,'" *The Guardian*, May 31, 2019, https://www.theguardian.com/us-news/2019/may/30/trump-mexico-tariffs-migration.

84. Jonathon Blitzer, "How Trump's Safe-Third-Country Agreement with Guatemala Fell Apart," *The New Yorker*, July 15, 2019, https://www.newyorker.com/news/news-desk/how-trumps-safe-third-country-agreement-with-guatemala-fell-apart.

85. Nicole Narea, "Trump's Agreements in Central America Could Dismantle the Asylum System as we Know it," *Vox*, September 26, 2019, https://www.vox.com/2019/9/26/20870768/trump-agreement-honduras-guatemala-el-salvador-explained.

86. "U.S. Strategy for Engaging with Central America: Policy Issues for Congress," Congressional Research Service, June 12, 2019, https://fas.org/sgp/crs/row/R44812.pdf.

87. Eliza Willis and Janet Seiz, "Central American Governments Can't Stop Migration," *The Atlantic*, April 9, 2019, https://www.theatlantic.com/ideas/archive/2019/04/central-american-governments-cant-stop-migration/586726/.

88. Ibid.

89. American Shipper Staff, "Trump Threatens to End NAFTA if Mexico Doesn't Help on Immigration," *American Shipper*, April 2, 2018, https://www.americanshipper.com/news/trump-threatens-to-end-nafta-if-mexico-doesnt-help-on-immigration?autonumber=70981&infrom=right.

90. Borger, "Trump Plans to Cut Central America Aid Blaming Countries for Migrant Caravans."

91. Ibid.

Chapter Six

¡Nicas Fuera!

Colonialism, Cultural Imperialism, and Immigration Injustice in Costa Rica

In April 2018, anti-government protests erupted in Nicaragua in response to a plan to reform the country's social security system. Nicaragua's government reacted forcefully and violently, causing many to flee to Costa Rica. Since the violence broke out, 200 Nicaraguans have applied for asylum in Costa Rica each day;[1] Costa Rica had taken in over 68,000 Nicaraguans as of October 2019.[2]

A few months after, in August 2018, Costa Rica saw protests of a different sort against the newly arrived Nicaraguans. As Joshua Partlow explains, on August 18, "apparently motivated by false and inflammatory online messages,"[3] about five hundred Costa Rican protesters marched into Merced Park (a popular meeting place for Nicaraguans) waving Costa Rican flags, shouting "Nicaraguans get out!" (¡Nicas fuera!) and threatening migrants who were peacefully gathered in the park.[4] The Costa Rican men wore red shirts and marched in carrying knives, baseball bats, and glass bottles stuffed with gasoline-soaked rags.[5] Asked why she was protesting, Miria Gómez replied, "Nicaraguans only come to Costa Rica 'to commit crimes' and they wrongly 'receive free water and electricity. But Costa Ricans are also suffering and don't receive the same support.'"[6] More than forty people were arrested.

I was in shock. Costa Rica has long been known as a peaceful and welcoming nation that prides itself on the absence of these kinds of actions and attitudes. But as immigration expert and sociologist at the University of Costa Rica Carlos Sandoval Garcia said, "The xenophobic march was a turning point. Our whole image as a liberal nation changed."[7] How did this happen? What happened to "pura vida"?

Before going any further, I must pause to confess that this chapter is unusually painful for me to write. I love Costa Rica. It is where I discovered the splendor of Latin America and how much I feel connected to it. It is where I discovered my passion for its indescribably beautiful tropical beaches, thick forests, volcanos, and, of course, delicious gallo pinto. It is where I learned not only to speak Spanish but also to love Spanish. It is where my children have been welcomed by friends with the same openness and kindness with which they have welcomed me every year since the summer of 2002. In many ways, it was where I discovered myself. So it goes without saying that my views of Costa Rica are colored by deep affection and gratitude. But I also know that while my story may be typical for foreigners from the United States, Europe, and Canada, it vastly differs from the experience of many, and especially that of Nicaraguans like Mateo who I introduced at the outset of this book.

This chapter interrogates the different ways U.S. and European immigrants are treated in Costa Rica compared with Nicaraguans. As I will show, while Costa Rica should be (and rightly has been) lauded by the international community for many of its formal efforts to welcome Nicaraguan immigrants, Costa Rican society treats them unjustly and in ways that reflect and perpetuate global oppression. I will start with a brief overview of how the different immigrant groups are treated in the small Central American nation.

THE GRINGOS, THE EUROPEOS, AND THE "NICAS": CONTRASTING IMMIGRANT EXPERIENCES IN COSTA RICA

Treatment of Immigrants from the United States, Canada, and Europe in Costa Rica

Most immigration literature—within and outside of philosophy—focuses on immigration from the Global South to the Global North. While we are beginning to see an increased focus on South-South migration (such as Nicaraguans migrating to Costa Rica), there is almost nothing on North-South immigration (such as people from the United States, Canada, and Europe migrating to Costa Rica). Still, there are some things that we do know.

Welcoming Europeans immigrants and, to a lesser extent, people from the United States and Canada has a long history in Costa Rica. In the eighteenth century the Costa Rican government created various campaigns and incentives to try to attract immigration from these parts of the world as part of its quest to form a European national identity.[8] And they, like other nations of Latin America such as Argentina, justified these programs on the basis of Darwinism and eugenics.[9] While many of these efforts were unsuccessful, much of the rhetoric took hold and solidified the idea in Costa Rica that

Europeans and people from the United States and Canada are "desirable" immigrants and those from Asia, Africa, and Latin America are not.[10]

Costa Rica has become an increasingly popular destination for these groups, especially since 1990,[11] and according to the U.S. State Department, approximately 120,000 U.S. citizens now live there (many retirees) and over 1.4 million visit the country each year.[12] Most of these immigrants live in the capital city of San José (with a majority—30 percent—in Escazú), although U.S. and Canadian immigrants also live along the Central and Northern Pacific Coasts (like Flamingo, Jacó) and Europeans in the Southern Atlantic Coast (primarily Cahuita and Puerto Viejo).[13] Both groups constitute a significant presence in tourist communities, like Monteverde and Arenal.[14]

Consistent throughout their experiences is that these immigrants are largely welcomed, sometimes catered to, and at minimum are left alone to live without incident or negative interference from the Costa Rican people or government. In their recent study of the interactions between immigrants from the United States, Canada, and Europe and the local population in Nuevo Arenal, for instance, David Matarrita-Cascante and Gabriela Stocks found that there was an overall positive atmosphere that was welcoming of immigrants, likely influenced by the fact that there were "immediate and perceptible economic benefits that accompanied the international migrants."[15] The Costa Rican government increased services, like water and internet, and has approved the construction of housing developments especially for this population.[16] In Nuevo Arenal, there are at least "three gated communities, constructed where the topography allows for unimpeded lake views for the purpose of attracting foreign purchasers. These developments are relatively ostentatious, almost exclusively foreign-owned, and easily distinguished as self-contained residential areas."[17] So gringos and Europeos are not only treated well, but the government makes investments in those communities so that more come to Costa Rica. In fact, Carlos Sandoval notes, these populations are not even referred to as "immigrants"; they are "investors," "retirees," and "tourists," but never "immigrants," even when they reside in the country for decades.[18]

Now, this is not to say that all Costa Ricans take a rosy view of gringos or Europeans. There are plenty of negative stereotypes, for example, about the degree to which they drink and party, seek out sex with local women, or do not integrate into Costa Rican society. As philosopher Alexander Jiménez explains,

European and North American migrants who have come to Costa Rica have transformed the landscape of the country in many cities in the Central Valley and the beaches, even while their cultural and social integration into Costa Rican society has been minimal. In particular, the population of U.S. retirees that permanently reside in Costa Rica largely does not speak Spanish, socializes and lives amongst other people from the U.S. and Canada, consumes U.S. products,

26

Chapter Six

watched U.S. television and movies, and lives their same way of life. The only changes they make is that they do it while appreciating Costa Rica's beauty. For them, this is the land of sun, but they are not interested in anything other than Costa Rica as a great setting for a "successful retirement."[19]

Despite all of this, though, these stereotypes do not negatively impact the opportunities these migrants face or the treatment they receive. On the contrary, many areas, like Arenal, Jacó, Manuel Antonio, and Puerto Viejo, create businesses, hotels, and activities to cater to their desires rather than shun them. So even when there are obstacles, the communities are still embraced rather than rejected.

General Treatment of Nicaraguan Immigrants in Costa Rica

The experiences I just mentioned are markedly distinct from those of the country's largest immigrant population: Nicaraguans. It is currently estimated that Nicaraguans constitute about 600,000 of Costa Rica's roughly five million inhabitants.[20] And the Costa Rican government has tried to accommodate them in various ways. Nicaraguan immigrants, for example, have access to social services (like emergency health care and public education) and the Costa Rican government allows them to enter the country, often with only a brief detention of twenty-four hours or less (if at all), even if they do not have documents.[21] In response to the current influx, the government has built two shelters for recently arrived Nicaraguan refugees[22] and has requested help from the United Nations to process asylum requests more rapidly.[23] And in response to those anti-Nicaraguan protests I referenced at the chapter's outset, the government strongly condemned them with its First Vice President Epsy Campbell declaring, "We will protect our country in every way, but these acts are not welcome, nor will they be tolerated in any way. . . . We cannot permit even the smallest space to feed a xenophobic attitude."[24]

Despite all of these positive efforts, Nicaraguans' treatment is far inferior to that received by U.S. and European immigrants. For example, while the government and private developers build gated communities with lot of amenities for U.S. and European migrants, there is little housing for Nicaraguan immigrants, most of who live in San José in shantytown neighborhoods like La Carpio:

A neighborhood of cement and sheet-metal homes where sleeping quarters and a latrine often occupy a single space. Water is scarce, trash piles up in the streets and sewage flows in open channels. Even before the latest influx of Nicaraguan refugees, half of the estimated 18,000 people in the neighborhood lived in inadequate homes and 70 percent of households subsisted on less than $330 per month, according to a government study last year.[25]

Beyond the dangerous and squalid living conditions, Nicaraguan immigrants face discrimination, legal barriers, and the constant threat of violence.

Carlos Sandoval identifies these and other challenges facing the Nicaraguan community, including but not limited to poverty, malnutrition, low salaries, discrimination, hostility from the local Tico population, and "othering."[26] Widespread in Costa Rica are assertions that Nicaraguans are diseased,[27] animals with little to no culture or intelligence,[28] and violent.[29] Nicaraguan women are labeled as "dirty, stupid, prostitutes, who are diseased and the mother of (too) many children."[30] Luis Ángel López Ruiz and David Delgado Montaldo identify a principal source of this prejudice in the perception that Nicaraguans constitute competition for jobs.[31] This perception, they argue, leads to resentment because Costa Ricans think that although Nicaraguans are hard workers, they are not highly educated and thus are not as deserving as Costa Ricans (or other foreigners) to get jobs or access to social services.[32] As Nicaraguan immigrant Vincente told Sandoval, "According to the Ticos, we are like strange animals with no rights to anything Costa Rica has to offer; they discriminate against us, they humiliate us, they treat us terribly without recognizing the fact that this country's economy has risen in large measure because of Nicaraguan labor."[33]

Another source of prejudices and discriminatory attitudes is the idea that Nicaraguan immigrants are drains on public resources, despite ample evidence that they are not. In fact, Koen Voorend showed that Nicaraguans are actually *underutilizing* health care and other social services in Costa Rica.[34] Still, the stereotype persists that Nicaraguan women in particular come to Costa Rica to have babies and get access to the Costa Rican social services network.[35] As Kate Goldade reports, "One idea is that Nicaraguan women migrate when pregnant simply in order to access superior health services; another is that they become pregnant with the intention of garnering the newborn's legal entitlements to education and health care until age eighteen. Most extremely, there is the belief that Nicaraguan women migrate with the sole purpose to steal a husband, in order to have Costa Rican babies and thus ensure their own legal status."[36] In all cases, the stereotype is rampant that Nicaraguans are somehow taking advantage of Costa Rica's welfare system, and as a result it is crumbling.

Recent changes in Costa Rican law are also presenting challenges. While the 2010 General Law of Migration and Alien Affairs (no. 8,764) does place higher emphasis on protecting immigrants' human rights, Sandoval argues that it combines the human rights framework "with specific provisions that make the regularization of the migratory process even more cumbersome and grants powers—such as to extend detentions for more than 24 hours—to the executive branch that, according to the Constitution, properly belongs to the judicial branch."[37] For example, the new law requires Nicaraguan *workers* (as opposed to their employers) to obtain workers' comp insurance and establishes multiple fees to regularize immigration status.[38] There are also changes that target women specifically, such as the 2013 resolution from the Caja Costaricense de Seguro Social "stating that pregnant women with irregular migration status would not have routine access to health care"[39] but only to emergency care.

Finally, Nicaraguan immigrants face violence and the threat of violence in Costa Rica. The most infamous case of such violence occurred in 2005, when Navidad Canda, age twenty-four, was killed by two Rottweilers when he attempted to burglarize a mechanic's shop and car dealership. The attack—which was partially caught on tape by a local news team—lasted nearly two hours but was not stopped by police and other emergency officials who responded to the incident. Some said Canda deserved it because he was a Nicaraguan thief.

Thankfully, most violence against Nicaraguans does not rise to this level, though it is still deeply pervasive. As Caitlin Fouratt notes, "Nicaraguan immigrants often avoid speaking in public to avoid revealing their accent. They worry about being harassed on the bus."[40] It is common for Nicaraguans to face abuse in their jobs, on the streets, or even by authorities.

Women face these issues and more. Because they tend to work as maids and nannies in people's homes, for example, they are at increased risk for sexual assault. They are also at increased risk from violence by their own family members because they are too afraid to report the abuse.[41] Increasingly, they are victims of rape and other abuse by Costa Rican immigration authorities. One woman, for example, explained to Rocio Loría Bolaños,

> You don't even have to come by yourself for them to do whatever they want with you in those detention rooms, which are like pigpens. . . . When night falls and the bosses leave for the night, the party begins for those who are on night duty. The next day, nobody says anything. And who's going to talk? They threaten you that if you open your mouth . . . they'll send you back, and it is even worse if they send us back.[42]

Beyond this, Nicaraguan women are victims of reproductive injustice and attacks on their intimate lives, such as the denial of nonemergency prenatal and postnatal care. Worse, women tend not to get health insurance via employment and so it is often the case that they lack the state insurance needed to gain full access to the health care system or they receive inferior medical care and treatment.[43] One woman, Veronica, said, "I was so scared to go to the hospital to give birth because I thought, maybe, they would mistreat me. I have heard stories of other Nicaraguan women who were treated terribly in the maternity wards because they did not have insurance. . . . I heard that when they had contractions the nurses did note even pay attention to them or they would say stuff to them like 'Why are you complaining so much?'"[44] So Nicaraguan women face uniquely gendered violence in Costa Rica in addition to the threats of violence Nicaraguan men endure.

This is just a brief overview of the many challenges Nicaraguan immigrants face in Costa Rica. Far from being welcomed the way immigrants from the United States, Canada, and Europe are, Nicaraguan immigrants confront legal barriers to regularizing their status, discrimination, poor living conditions, reproductive injustice, and violence. The difference is palpable and undeniable.

WHY IS THIS HAPPENING? COLONIAL LOGIC, NATIONAL IDENTITY, AND GLOBAL OPPRESSION

What could explain the drastically different treatment just described? I submit that at least part of the answer lies in the colonial mindset and logic that pervades Costa Rica (and many parts of Latin America). According to this logic, Europe and the United States are superior to Latin America, Africa, or Asia. By extension, people from those regions are overvalued and Latin Americans, Africans, and Indigenous peoples are undervalued (or devalued completely). Therefore it is preferable to have immigration from the United States and Europe and they deserve better treatment than those from Latin America.

Enrique Dussel discusses the colonial geography of the center and the periphery. On this ontology, the center imposes itself on the periphery and is seen by all (including the periphery) as the source of knowledge, morals, culture, etc. Using the field of philosophy as one illustration, Dussel suggests that "the philosophy that has emerged from a periphery has always done so in response to a need to situate itself with regard to a center in total exteriority."[45] First, Latin American thought modeled the Spanish scholastics. When this model fell, it followed the path of European philosophy more broadly by sending its elites to study in Europe and then having them return to their homelands to train their own students in these colonial logics and ideas.[46] As Dussel explains,

Colonial elites were now systematically trained in the imperialist center. Oxford, Cambridge, and Paris were transformed into theaters of "reeducation," of brainwashing, until well into the twentieth century. The colonial oligarchies were brown, black, or yellow, and they applied the philosophy they had learned abroad. True puppets, they repeated in the periphery what their eminent professors of the great metropolitan universities had propounded. In Cairo, Dakkar, Saigon, and Peking as in Buenos Aires and Lima they taught their pupils the *ego cogito* in which they themselves remained constituted as an idea or thought, entities at the disposal of the "will to power," impotent, dominated wills, castrated teachers who castrated their pupils . . . the colonial philosophers of the periphery gaze at a vision foreign to them, one that is not their own. From the center they see themselves as nonbeing, nothingness; and they teach their pupils, who are something (although illiterate in the alphabets imposed on them), that really they are nothing, that they are like nothings walking through history. When they have finished their studies they, like their colonial teachers, disappear from the map—geopolitically and philosophically, they do not exist. This pathetic ideology given the name of philosophy is the one still taught in the majority of philosophy schools of the periphery by the majority of its professors.[47]

This example illustrates one instance of the broader phenomenon of how colonialization placed Europe, its idea, its philosophies, and its culture into the center of the universe and erased, devalued, destroyed the periphery. As part of this phenomenon, the elites in the periphery overvalue the center and devalue the periphery by continuing to mimic European (and later U.S.) ideals, sending its elites abroad to learn them (either literally or by establishing elite private schools to teach the language and ideals of the center), and then imposing those ideas and standards in their own countries. In the process, they denigrate their own culture, deny that it is theirs, and try to align themselves with Europe and the United States.

I think this is an especially apt description for what occurred in Costa Rica in the nineteenth and twentieth centuries and what continues to manifest in the way that Costa Rica treats different immigrant groups; Costa Rica is valuing the center and its people and devaluing the periphery and its people. As Ivan Molina explains in his book *Costariccense por dicha*, during the mid- and late 1800s, liberals took power in Costa Rica and instituted a series of "modernizing" reforms meant to create a Costa Rican national identity that was white and aligned with Europe and the distant South American countries (Argentina, Chile, and Uruguay) rather than with its neighbors on the isthmus, especially Nicaragua.[48] To accomplish this, they emphasized Costa Rica's connections to Europe by identifying with the white, Spaniard father and distancing themselves from the "nonwhite" (that is, Afro, Indigenous, and Nicaraguan) populations of the dry Pacific and Atlantic[49] by deriding, critiquing, and erasing these populations, their culture, and their morality from Costa Rica's national story. According to the Liberal Project, the Spanish are Costa Rica's true ancestors, and through them, Costa Ricans learned the virtues of individualism, democracy, simplicity, hard work, and civilized behavior. Put differently, because of their European ancestry and all of its virtues, Costa Rica is rightly understood as a white, European nation constituted by Western, rational, democratic men.

This, then, explains why Costa Rica is superior to its Central American, especially Nicaraguan, neighbors. Costa Ricans inherited their virtue, reason, and temperament from their Spanish father, whereas these other places did not. Because Costa Rica's connection is to the Spanish father and the Central Americans' to the Indigenous mother, Costa Rica is a nation of reason and peace, while their Central American neighbors are violent and disordered.[50]

This project to construct a white, European Costa Rican national identity also occurred in the intellectual sphere via what Alexander Jiménez denotes as "metaphysical ethnic nationalism." According to Jiménez, the recurring themes of the ethnometaphysical nationalists are rationality and destiny (as well as the whiteness and homogeneity that give rise to both). Unlike liberal nationalists, the ethnometaphysical nationalists claimed that the essence or being of the Costa Rican is white; for them, whiteness is so essential to being Costa Rican that one cannot be Costa Rican and not be white.[51] And they also suggest that it is *because* of this whiteness that Costa Rica has superior social and moral values and is the peaceful alternative to its violent Central American neighbors. In the process of aligning Costa Rican identity with the center, then, these ethnometaphysical nationalists define nonwhites, especially Nicaraguans, as inferior to Costa Ricans.[52]

Both the identity construction and "modernization projects" of the liberal and ethnometaphysical nationalists reflect and promote the modern colonial epistemic system. In constructing itself as a white society, Costa Rica simultaneously cast itself as a "modern" one—a society that is enlightened, progressive, and forward looking. In defining themselves in opposition to Nicaragua and other Central American neighbors, they simultaneously conceptualized Nicaraguans as "nonmodern,"[53] "primitive," and "barbaric." In doing so, these national identity-building projects define Costa Ricans and Nicaraguans oppositionally, such that the latter is a threat to the former; Costa Ricans and Nicaraguans are not just opposites, Nicaraguans are also a threat to Costa Rican society and aspirations.

In his book *Otros Amenazantes: Los nicaragüenses y la formació de identidades nacionales en Costa Rica*,[54] Carlos Sandoval describes the inherent connection between the formation and maintenance of Costa Rican identity and the parallel construction of Nicaraguans as "threatening others."[55] As is likely already evident, "Costa Rican" is fundamentally constructed in relation to "others"; it is not simply a desire to be European or American, it is also about *not being* Central American, and certainly not being Nicaraguan. More precisely, says Sandoval, the Other against which Costa Rican identity is constructed is the "nica."[56]

Being "nica" is a stigma in Costa Rica.[57] "Nicas" are said to be characterized by different ethnic markers that distinguish them from Costa Ricans:

"dark skin, poverty, and a violent character. On top of that, they do not speak 'standard Spanish.'"[58] Media and other pop culture sources portray "nicas" as violent invaders who are flooding the country, stealing jobs, draining public resources (like health care and education), and contaminating Costa Rica (literally with disease and metaphorically with poor values).[59] Because it has a specific referent, not all Nicaraguans are "nicas." For example, Nicaraguan intellectuals and business owners are not part of this classification.[60] Still, most do not differentiate because, from the Costa Rican imaginary, all Nicaraguans are immigrants and "los 'inmigrantes' son 'nicas.'"[61]

Given the Costa Rican project of constructing a white, European national identity and that Nicaraguans are constructed as brown, nonmodern Central Americans, it becomes clear that this ontology conceptualizes Nicaraguan immigrants as threats to the Costa Rican culture, identity, and nation itself. Sometimes they are threats to the homeland (as in the border disputes between Costa Rica and Nicaragua),[62] sometimes they are threats to the cultural imaginary (brown skin, "bad" Spanish, communist),[63] and sometimes they are seen as literal threats to economic and public health and safety (violent criminals stealing Costa Rican jobs).[64] But they are always threatening. As such, they cannot be integrated into Costa Rican society in the way immigrants from the United States, Canada, and Europe can because one can literally not be both Costa Rican and Nicaraguan (they are logically opposed), but one can be Costa Rican and white. We now see the fundamental reason that Nicaraguan immigrants are treated one way and immigrants from the United States and Europe another.

COLONIAL LOGIC, CULTURAL IMPERIALISM, AND INJUSTICE AGAINST NICARAGUANS FROM COSTA RICANS, GRINGOS, AND EUROPEANS

While I do not deny the key roles race, class, and media portrayals play in fundamentally shaping the constructions of Nicaraguan immigrants in Costa Rica, I think we would be remiss if we fail to see the connections between these constructions, global oppression, colonial logic, cultural imperialism, and the differential treatment of Nicaraguan, U.S.-born, and European immigrants.

Recall that cultural imperialism in the context of global oppression refers to various ways in which the cultural norms of a nation(s) are presented as normal, civilized, and superior in contrast to others, which are rendered deviant, primitive, barbaric, or odd. This occurs throughout Latin America in relation to the United States and Europe; the United States and Europe are depicted as civilized, educated, dynamic, and places of opportunity, whereas Latin America is seen as violent, poor, and stagnant. Or, less harsh but equally problematic, Europe and the United States are places of business, innovation, and electric energy, whereas Latin America is relaxed, naturally beautiful, and a place to escape the pressures of the modern world (thus implying it is nonmodern).

I think that cultural imperialism and the colonial logic described by Dussel in combination with a rehearsal of efforts to construct a specific white Costa Rican identity in opposition to Nicaraguans aptly explain at least part of why immigrants from the United States, Canada, and Europe are treated one way in Costa Rica and Nicaraguan immigrants a different way.

First, let us explore the connections to colonial logic and Nicaraguan immigration. Costa Rican identity is based on colonial notions about the superiority of Europe and the inferiority of Indigenous and Afro societies. These ideas led Costa Ricans to embark on a project to align themselves with Europe and distance themselves, their race, their ethnicity, and their values from Central America, especially Nicaragua. While much time has passed, these ideas still deeply permeate Costa Rican society, politics, and norms.

Costa Rica still defines itself in opposition to Nicaraguans. It still sees itself as the peaceful, rational democracy that stands in stark contrast to its violent, irrational neighbors. Yes, they will allow them to reside in their territory because that is what morally virtuous modern nations do—they save brown, violent neighbors from themselves—but Nicaraguans can never be Costa Ricans. They are not white, do not share the same values, and are ill equipped to advance Costa Rica's national projects. In fact, they are antithetical to them. As such, they can never truly become "Costa Ricans" —they are just too different.

By contrast, people from Europe, Canada, and the United States are fundamentally similar to Costa Ricans (at least as Costa Ricans see themselves)—white, educated, rational, and democratic. So they can both be easily assimilated into Costa Rican society and advance it. Therefore they should be courted.

This logic manifests itself, then, in cultural imperialism and the idea that Costa Rica is normal, white, civilized, educated, and modern and Nicaraguans are deviant, primitive, violent, poor, uneducated, and dark. And investigating the treatment of Nicaraguans through this lens reveals that they do not fit the mold of the modern subject and consequently they cannot be welcomed into Costa Rican society without threatening Costa Rica's self-image. In other words, the treatment of Nicaraguan immigrants can be explained as a manifestation of cultural imperialism and colonial logic in the Costa Rican imaginary that sees Costa Ricans and Nicaraguans not only as inherently opposite but also as incompatible.

I think this mindset and logic, intended or not, is clearly reflected in Costa Rica's immigration policies, practices, norms, laws, and systems, which favor those from Europe, the United States, and Canada. While they are putting out the red carpet for U.S. and European immigrants, Costa Rica only offers Nicaraguans formal relief—the ability to reside in Costa Rica—but no opportunity to improve their position or integrate into Costa Rican society. Instead they face exploitation, marginalization, and violence, sometimes at the hands of European and U.S. immigrants themselves, without response. Given this, the difference in treatment between the groups reflects and perpetuates cultural imperialism and thus constitutes immigration injustice.

I want to caution here that Costa Rica is not the only party involved in upholding colonial logic and cultural imperialism. The European, U.S., and Canadian immigrant communities are doing it as well. In one sense, these immigrants are furthering these culturally imperialist ideas indirectly by taking advantage of their status as "the right kind of immigrant." What I mean here is that these immigrants happily buy real estate, hire Nicaraguan maids and nannies, and live in wealthy areas without question of the consequences. They do not get involved with causes to fight for better treatment of other immigrant groups or reflect on the consequences of their pleasure on Costa Rican society, for example, on land or food prices (which have skyrocketed in conjunction with the rise of immigration from these countries), social mores, or the environment. Sometimes I hear these immigrants refer to Nicaraguans in the same derogatory way I have highlighted here. They presume that Costa Ricans are happy to have them, and they think they are right.

We can see all of this in the everyday acts and behaviors of European and U.S. immigrants. These groups, while they may believe the first version of cultural imperialism, seem to be acting according to the second version (that sees Europe and the United States as the centers of progress, innovation, business, and action and Central America as a relaxed, chill place with natural beauty where they can go to escape it all and find peace). They move to Costa Rica to live a certain kind of life, a life where they can relax on the beach and enjoy the mountains all while having access to cheap domestic (Nicaraguan) labor, gated communities, a high-quality, inexpensive health care system, and all of the comforts of home. But they refuse to integrate into Costa Rican society or adapt their habits to Costa Rican life. As we saw, most do not have Costa Rican friends and do not get involved outside their enclaves.

My point here is most clearly exemplified by the refusal of these migrants (as a whole) to learn Spanish. When I ask them why they do not want to learn Spanish, many answer "why should I?" or "I don't need to." And they want credit if they learn a few words. At the same time, however, many of these same immigrants often expect that Costa Ricans should speak English to them *even though they are in Costa Rica.* Sometimes they opt to take some Spanish classes but refuse to pay what the classes are worth or complain to the teacher that they charge too much, complain if the Spanish teacher is not bilingual, and almost always quit within six months.[65] In these and related actions, U.S. and European immigrants perpetrate cultural imperialism against Costa Ricans. They see English as the normal, civilized, and modern language and Spanish as the language of primitive, uncivilized people. As such, they do not need to speak Spanish, but Costa Ricans should learn English. This is just one example of how immigrant communities are perpetuating cultural imperialist logic and global oppression in Costa Rica.

Too many immigrants from Europe and the United States also often uphold this problematic logic by implicitly or explicitly taking advantage of their privileged status as "the right kind of immigrant" (that is, who is accepted and can live as they please without interference) to do terrible things to Costa Rican and Nicaraguan women. Sometimes they do this by paying exploitative wages to Nicaraguan women for domestic service work or to Costa Rican women for Spanish classes. Other times, it is via attitudes that they will find romantic partners who can be wooed by the allure of their being from the Global North. Others go further and engage in sex tourism so that Costa Rican and Nicaraguan women play to their ego, insecurities, and fantasies about masculinity, U.S. superiority, and their ability to conquer.[66] We see this reflected in interviews conducted by researcher Megan Rivers-Moore with men from the United States, who told her,

The Ticos make them work, the Ticos make them clean and do everything. They beat them; they make them work. So the gringo, as ugly, fat and smelly as he is still gets the good looking one because the Tico's worse than the smelly gringo. (Julio, 46)[67]

So many women have told me that I am so much nicer than the Costa Ricans they've been with. Costa Ricans are awful. We treat them one tenth nicer than the Costa Ricans and they're so happy with us. They really appreciate it because they're used to being treated badly. (Mark, 30)[68]

The Costa Ricans don't treat the women with all that much respect, which is really too bad. In some cases, at least that's what they tell me, and you can take it for what it is, that's why they prefer gringos or foreigner. (Roberto, 45, U.S. interview)[69]

I need an answer from you. I find that all this is . . . each group of guys is like a group of animals walking into the Prince Hotel. I want to know if each group of men you interview think they're special and that the rest of us are scum. Do they

say, "We're not like the rest of those guys because we're young and good looking. . . . We're not like the bad guy who goes to the elevator [to go up to a hotel
room] with a little one and she's just miserable"? Because they're all miserable.
Less miserable with guys that treat them right and are more fun. That's what I
think. (Curly, 58, U.S. tourist)[70]

As Rivers-Moore explains,

Almost none of the men interviewed seem to have thought critically about what
they have heard about Costa Ricans. They fail to consider what might motivate
sex workers to tell stories that present a very particular picture of Costa Rican
men. The tourists use these stories as evidence of their superiority and civilization in comparison with violent Costa Rican men, and they deploy these constructions in order to prove their own worth as good men.[71]

Now, as Rivers-Moore states, the idea of white men crossing borders to
have sex with or marry women of color is not new;[72] it is part and parcel of
colonial logic.[73] As Razack affirms, "The subject . . . is first and foremost a
colonial subject seeking to establish that he is indeed in control and lives in
a world where a solid line marks the boundary between himself and racial/
gendered Others."[74] But these and so many testimonies like them go farther to
reflect the way that U.S. and European men both take advantage of and promote colonial, racist, masculinist logic so they can benefit from their status as
"gringos." If Nicaraguan men behaved in this way, they would face violence,
incarceration, and deportation. But these men are left alone because of their
national identity so much so that sex tourism is promoted as part of a way to
attract them.[75] So the cultural imperialism is not only perpetuated by Costa
Ricans in how they treat immigrants but by the very "model immigrants"
Costa Rica has been trying to attract for over a century and a half. In this way,
the U.S., European, and Canadian immigrants are, at minimum, complicit in
Costa Rica's unjust treatment of Nicaraguans and the immigration injustice
that reflects and continually creates.

My affection for Costa Rica will always run deep. Still, it is undeniable that
the reasons I love it are deeply connected to my global and social location.
I began this chapter by reflecting on what I took as a disconnect—the Costa
Rican people and their government welcoming me and my co-patriots while
protesting, shunning, and abusing Nicaraguans. But after this reflection it is
clear to me that these two apparently divergent experiences are both expressions of the same globally oppressive colonial paradigm. I am treated well
because my presence bolsters the Costa Rican national story while the Nicaraguans do the opposite. As a colonial subject, I am welcomed, and as colonized, the Nicaraguans are shunned. And this is true even when Americans

and Europeans treat Costa Ricans themselves as colonized beings. As such, we should recognize this difference in treatment and attitude for what it is— global oppression in the form of cultural imperialism and coloniality—and thus as immigration injustice.

WHAT'S A GRINGA TO DO?

I have shown that the divergent treatment of Nicaraguan immigrants and those from the United States and Europe constitutes immigration injustice because of how it reifies, reflects, and furthers global oppression in the form of coloniality and cultural imperialism. As an academic, this leaves me with some satisfaction that I have a better understanding of something I found perplexing and difficult to identify and accept. And on that level, I am excited because I have little doubt that what I have just described helps explain what is going on not only in Costa Rica but also in many situations that appear to perplex in relation to South-South immigration more generally, like why Mexicans mistreat Guatemalans or Colombians mistreat Venezuelans, even as immigrants from these very nations suffer at the hands of U.S. and European immigration policies. But as someone who has spent so much time in Costa Rica and has enjoyed (and continues to enjoy) so many of its treasures, I admit to feeling disturbed and sickened. Inadvertent as it may be, I wonder how I am complicit in the injustices just detailed. What should I do in response?

Admittedly, I am not sure how to respond to my own musings here. I certainly do not think I have the space to do a proper analysis. But I would feel remiss if, before concluding, I did not suggest a few things. First, people from the United States and Europe who live in Costa Rica or who spend a lot of time there need to begin seeing themselves as connected to the Nicaraguan immigrant population and their struggles. At minimum, I think this implies that we cannot contribute to their exploitation and we ought to work with groups inside and outside of Costa Rica to fight for their just treatment.

Second, U.S. and European immigrant communities need to integrate themselves into Costa Rica society. We are a privileged group in Costa Rica and most of us have the means and the time to learn Spanish, volunteer in community groups, and learn the foods and customs of our hosts. To not do so is to maintain the very colonial logic and cultural imperialism that I am condemning—one that holds that we are superior, that we have the right to go wherever we want in the world and use it for our own purposes, and that we are simply using this glorious country to fulfill our fantasies about what the perfect vacation or retirement looks like. Failing to challenge this means that we are furthering global oppression while benefitting from its existence.

Third, it is critical that we resist colonial logics and ideologies. Our treatment and the treatment of Nicaraguan immigrants result from problematic, false, and dangerous ideas that Europe and the United States are culturally and morally superior to Latin America. These oppressive structures are also responsible for Costa Ricans thinking that they must send their children to private schools with European or U.S. curriculums; learn English, French, German, or Italian; and distance themselves from their Latin American histories and identities. This too is cultural imperialism—epistemic cultural imperialism—that devalues, erases, and coopts the knowledge of the Global South. So those of us who are academics must engage the decolonial projects within and outside of the academy as part of our struggle for immigration justice in the Americas.

What I have just outlined is just the beginning of a larger aspect of fighting for immigration justice in Costa Rica and many other nations of Latin America. And I am sure that it falls short. Still, we must realize that the struggles of all immigrants are connected and that sometimes immigrant groups contribute to the global oppression of others. That is what is going on here. It is not simply Costa Rica that is promoting global oppression toward Nicaraguans, it is also those from the United States and Europe are capitalizing on a colonial, globally oppressive system that affords us unearned privileges, and promoting it too. We must resist. At the very least, let us agree that we need to support (and join?) the fight so that Costa Ricans and all the immigrants who reside there can live *pura vida.*

NOTES

1. Carrie Kahn, "200 Nicaraguans Claim Asylum Daily in Costa Rica, Fleeing Violent Unrest," *National Public Radio*, August 26, 2018, https://www.npr.org/2018/08/26/641375695/200-nicaraguans-claim-asylum-daily-in-costa-rica-fleeing-violent-unrest; Spencer Feingold, "Costa Rica Overwhelmed with Nicaraguan Asylum Seekers," *CNN*, August 1, 2018, https://edition.cnn.com/2018/08/01/americas/costa-rica-overwhelmed-nicaraguan-asylum-seekers-unhcr/index.html.

2. Jenny Barchfield, "Nicaraguans Make Their Home in an Idle Costa Rican Factory," United Nations High Commission on Refugees, October 16, 2019, https://www.unhcr.org/news/stories/2019/10/5da655084/nicaraguans-home-idle-costa-rican-factory.html.

3. Joshua Partlow, "They Fled Violence in Nicaragua by the Thousands. What Awaits Them in Costa Rica?" *Washington Post*, September 2, 2018, https://www.washingtonpost.com/world/the_americas/they-fled-violence-in-nicaragua-by-the-thousands-what-awaits-them-in-costa-rica/2018/09/01/51d3f7ee-a62c-11e8-ad6f-080770dcddc2_story.html.

4. "Nicaragua Refugees: 'I Don't Understand Why People Hate Us," *BBC News*, April 18, 2019, https://www.bbc.com/news/world-latin-america-47934961.

5. Partlow, "They Fled Violence in Nicaragua by the Thousands."

6. "Nicaragua Refugees."

7. Ibid.

8. Patricia Alvarenga Venútolo, "La Inmigración Extranjera en la Historia Costariccence," in *El Mito Roto: Inmigración y Emigración en Costa Rica*, ed. Carlos Sandoval Garcia (San José, Costa Rica: Editorial UCR, 2015), 3–24.

9. Ibid.

10. Ibid., 10.

11. Flora V. Calderón-Steck and Roger E. Bonilla-Carrión, "Algunos aspectos sociodemográficos de los estadounidenses, canadienses y eurpeos residentes en Costa Rica según el Censo 2000," in *El Mito Roto*, ed. Carlos Sandoval Garcia, 78.

12. U.S. Department of State, "U.S. Relations with Costa Rica: Bilateral Relations Fact Sheet," October 24, 2019, https://www.state.gov/u-s-relations-with-costa-rica/.

13. Calderón-Steck and Bonilla-Carrión, "Algunos aspectos sociodemográficos," 64–65.

14. Marietta Morrissey, "Imaginaries of North American lifestyle migrants in Costa Rica," *Population Space Place* 24 (2018): 1–9, https://doi.org/10.1002/psp.2168.

15. David Matarrita-Cascante and Gabriela Stocks, "Amenity Migration to the Global South: Implications for Community Development," *GeoForum* 49 (2013): 96.

16. Calderón-Steck and Bonilla-Carrión, "Algunos aspectos sociodemográficos," 65.

17. Matarrita-Cascante and Stocks, "Amenity Migration to the Global South," 96.

18. Carlos Sandoval-Garcia, "El 'Otro' Nicaraguense en el imaginario colectivo costaricense: Algunos retos analítos y politicos," *Nómadas* 51 (October 2019): 157.

19. Alexander Jiménez Matarrita, *La vida en otra parte: Migraciones y cambios culturales en Costa Rica* (Editorial Arlekin, 2009), 57; translation mine.

20. "Costa Rica Population," World Population Review, accessed January 31, 2020, http://worldpopulationreview.com/countries/costa-rica-population/.

21. Kirk Semple, "Nicaraguan Migrants Fleeing Turmoil Test Costa Rica's Good Will," *New York Times*, September 22, 2018, https://www.nytimes.com/2018/09/22/world/americas/nicaragua-migrants-costa-rica.html.

22. AFP and Tico Times, "Costa Rica Sets up Shelters for Nicaraguan Migrants," *Tico Times*, July 20, 2018, https://ticotimes.net/2018/07/20/costa-rica-installs-shelters-for-nicaraguan-migrants.

23. Semple, "Nicaraguan Migrants Fleeing Turmoil Test Costa Rica's Good Will."

24. Partlow, "They Fled Violence in Nicaragua by the Thousands."

25. Mario Negrinia and Maria Verza, "Fate in Limbo, Many Nicaraguans Exiles Struggle in Costa Rica," *Associated Press*, April 1, 2019, https://apnews.com/de1f373d910e48258464e84c40a2814b.

26. Sandoval-Garcia, "El 'Otro' Nicaraguense el el imaginario colectivo costaricense," 153–55.

27. Jorge Ramirez Caro, "El Chiste de la Alteridad: La Pesadilla de ser otro," in *El Mito Roto*, ed. Carlos Sandoval Garcia, 318–19.

28. Ibid., 321, 322, 330.

29. Ibid., 322–25.

30. Kevin Masís Fernández and Laura Paniagua Arguedas, "Chistes Sobre Nicaragüenses en Costa Rica: barreras simbólicas, mecanismos de control social, constructores de identidades," in *El Mito Roto*, ed. Carlos Sandoval Garcia, 350; translation mine.

31. Luis Ángel López Ruiz and David Delgado Montaldo, "Actitudes y percepciones segmentadas: prejuicios hacia la población nicaragüense en Costa Rica," in *Migraciones en América Central: Políticas, territories y actores*, ed. Carlos Sandoval Garcia, (San José, Costa Rica: Editorial UCR, 2016), 245.

32. Ibid., 246.

33. Carlos Sandoval García, *Otros Amenazantes: Los nicaragüenses y la formació de identidades nacionales en Costa Rica* (San José, Costa Rica: Editorial UCR, 2008); translation mine.

34. Koen Voorend, "El sistema de salud como imán: La incidiencia de la población nicaragüense en los servicios de salud costarricenses," in *Migraciones en América Central*, ed. Carlos Sandoval Garcia, 202–3.

35. Kate Goldade, "Reproducción Transnacional: La salud reproductiva, las limitaciones, y las contradicciones para las migrantes laborales nicaragüenses en Costa Rica," in *El Mito Roto*, ed. Carlos Sandoval Garcia.

36. Ibid.

37. Carlos Sandoval Garcia, "Nicaraguan Immigration to Costa Rica: Tendencies, Policies, and Politics," *LASA Forum* XLVI, no. 4 (Fall 2015): 7–10.

38. Ibid.

39. Ibid.

40. Caitlin Fouratt, "The Rise of Anti-Immigrant Attitudes, Violence and Nationalism in Costa Rica," *The Conversation*, March 28, 2017, https://theconversation.com/the-rise-of-anti-immigrant-attitudes-violence-and-nationalism-in-costa-rica-73899.

41. Rocío Loría Bolaños, "Vulnerabilidad a la violencia en la inmigración," in *El Mito Roto*, ed. Carlos Sandoval Garcia, 224.

42. Ibid.

43. Goldade, "Reproducción Transnacional," 246.

44. Ibid., 245; translation mine.

45. Enrique Dussel, *Philosophy of Liberation* (New York: Orbis Books, 1985), 1.1.3.1.

46. Ibid., 1.2.2.1

47. Ibid., 1.2.4.2 and 1.2.2.4

48. Ivan Molina, *Costarricence por dicha: Identidad nacional y cambio cultural en Costa Rica durante los siglos XIX y XX* (San José, Costa Rica: Editorial UCR, 2002), 20; translation mine.

49. Ibid., 21.

50. Alexander Jiménez Matarrita, *El imposible país de los filósofos* (San José, Costa Rica: Editorial Universidad de Costa Rica, 2013).

51. Ibid., 218.

52. Ibid., 223.

53. Juan Ricardo Aparicio and Mario Blaser, "The 'Lettered City' and the Insurrection of Subjugated Knowledges in Latin America," *Anthropological Quarterly* 81, no. 1 (Winter 2008): 59–94.

54. Carlos Sandoval Garcia, *Threatening Others: Nicaraguans and the Formation of National Identities in Costa Rica*, (Columbus: Ohio University Press, 2004).

55. Ibid. See, for example, 35, 109, 112, 115, 168–69.

56. Ibid., 7.

57. Sandoval, *Otros Amenazantes*, 260–21.

58. Ibid., 261; translation mine.

59. Ibid., chap. 2.

60. Ibid., 262.

61. Ibid.

62. Ibid.

63. Ibid., 82, 169.

64. Ibid., 35, 71, 90, 96, 168.

65. Personal communications with various Spanish teachers in Costa Rica. One, who has a master's degree in Spanish, was told that she should charge $3 per hour.

66. Megan Rivers-Moore, "'They're Machistas, They Treat Them Badly': Comparative Transnational Masculinity in Sex Tourism," in *El Mito Roto*, ed. Carlos Sandoval Garcia; Robert Fletcher, *Romancing the Wild: Cultural Dimensions, of Ecotourism* (Durham, NC: Duke University Press, 2014).

67. Rivers-Moore, "'They're Machistas.'"

68. Ibid., 252.

69. Ibid., 253.

70. Ibid., 254.

71. Ibid., 252.

72. Ibid., 251.

73. María Lugones, "Heterosexualism and the Colonial/Modern Gender System," *Hypatia* 22, no. 1 (Winter 2007): 186–209.

74. Sherene H. Razack, "Introduction: When Place Becomes Race," in *Race, Space, and the Law: Unmapping a White Settler Society*, ed. Sherene H. Razack (Toronto: Between the Lines Press, 2002), 136.

75. Rivers-Moore, "'They're Machistas,'" 248.

Chapter Seven

"Nosotras no valemos nada acá en Colombia"

Seeing Femicide/Feminicide as Immigration Injustice

March 7, 2018: Two Venezuelan women were shot dead in the Colombian border province of North Santander in separate incidents. . . . Maribella Guerrero
Sanchez, 39, was with a group of family and friends in a pool hall in the San
Martin de Tibu neighborhood when a man reportedly entered, fired six shots,
and fled without a word. . . . Meanwhile, that same evening, Nancy Arlenys
Quiroz Aguilar, 22, was killed inside the Las Vegas brothel, where she was
employed. According to Quiroz's co-workers, an unknown man entered the
establishment and requested her services. The two made their way to one of the
rooms and gunshots were subsequently fired, which allegedly went unheard by
others on the premises due to the loud music.[1]

March 3, 2019: "La chama," or Yuli Mar Pérez, 45 years old, was killed by two
gunshots to the head in Las Maravillas. The Venezuelan woman was shot by two
assassins on a motorcycle.[2]

April 28, 2019: In downtown Villavicencio, two Venezuelan women, Achille
Yugeidy Hernández and Johana Ruiz Pérez were shot and killed. It appears the
women were sex workers.[3]

We have seen so many women go and never come back. Actually, a friend of
mine went to the house of a man she did not know for a job [sex work]. He beat
her and raped her and told her it was because she was Venezuelan and Venezuelans are worth nothing in Colombia.[4]

The violence just described is horrifying. And it is part of a pattern of
raping, torturing, and murdering Venezuelan migrant women in Colombia.
In fairness, the violence is not limited to Venezuelan women; on average,
"one Venezuelan died violently in Colombia each day in the first eight
months of 2019."[5] Still, in this chapter I want to focus on violence directed

at Venezuelan women. In particular, I will explore femicide of Venezuelan immigrants in Colombia and the responses to it in order to argue that femicide is a type of immigration injustice, a means to perpetrate immigration injustice, and a product of immigration injustice.

To defend these points, I will proceed as follows. I will begin by explaining what constitutes feminicide and provide a brief overview of feminicide against Venezuelan migrant women in Colombia. From there, I will explore the relationship between Colombian immigration policies, the international community's responses to the Venezuelan crisis, and the femicide of Venezuelan women to show that they are inadequate and create, reflect, and perpetuate global oppression. I conclude by showing how the femicide of Venezuelan immigrants in Colombia reveals how femicide is inherently connected to immigration injustice in the three ways referenced here.

WHAT IS FEMICIDE/FEMINICIDE?[6]

Although many believe that femicide simply refers to "men killing women,"[7] it is much more complex than that. As Julia E. Monárrez Fragoso explains, while it is true that all "violence culminating in the death of a girl or woman, and perpetrated by a man, constitutes feminicide insofar as the victim is a woman, it is necessary to point out that there are killings of women that cannot be considered feminicides."[8] Femicide, then, goes beyond men killing women.

Now feminists have long noted that violence against women is a complex, structural expression of patriarchy—take, for example, Susan Brownmiller's infamous analysis of rape as a crime of violence to enforce patriarchy,[9] or Andrea Dworkin's discussion of "gynocide" as "the systematic crippling, rape and/or killing of women . . . the relentless violence perpetrated by a gendered class of men upon a gendered class of women"[10]—but Diane E. H. Russell was one of the first to expressly use the term "femicide" to describe "the misogynist killing of women by men and a form of continuity of sexual assault, where you must take into account: the acts of violence, the motives and the imbalance of power between the sexes in political, social and economic environments."[11] Still, as Rosa-Linda Fregoso and Cynthia Bejarano explain, women's rights advocates, feminist scholars, researchers, and legal theorists really began widely using the terms "femicide" and "feminicide" to describe the horrors of waves of murders of women and girls in Cuidad Juárez, Mexico. Most notable among them was Julia E. Monárrez Fragoso.

Connecting the killings in Cuidad Juárez back to Jane Caputi's analysis in the *Age of Sex Crimes*, Monárrez explains that these and other twentieth-century forms of violence against women are distinct. She says,

Women-killing is usual in the patriarchy, yet, the 20th Century has been known for a new kind of crime against women, which includes torture, mutilation, rape and the murder of both women and girls. The frequency and upsurge of these acts has brought Caputi to call our times as the "era of sexual crimes." This age starts with "Jack the Ripper," the still unknown London killer who in 1888 murdered and mutilated five prostitutes (1989: 445). Through him and his crimes, a tradition of sexual murders and sexual killers is established, the purpose being "terrorizing women and inspiring and empowering men" (1990: 3–4; 1989: 445). Consequently, serial sexual murder is a ritualistic mythic act in the contemporary patriarchy where sex and violence combine, where an intimate relationship between manliness and pleasure are established because. . . . The murder of women and children—including torture and killings by husbands, lovers, and fathers, as well as those committed by strangers—are not an unexplainable crime or in the domain of "monsters" only.

According to Monárrez, then, we need to understand femicide as structural and systemic—femicide is not a random or individual act but rather an act that forms part of a larger patriarchal system designed to terrorize women and maintain male power. As such, it is not carried out by deranged actors, moral monsters, or violent criminals, it is carried out by normal men who are following patriarchal scripts to their logical conclusions. Within patriarchal logic—a logic that says that women are stupid, irrational, and emotional, that they must be subservient to men, that they must always be sexually available to men, that men have the rightful power to control women and "keep them in their place," and that women are not full human beings—committing femicide is simply men (husbands, fathers, brothers, nephews, sons) doing what they were taught to do: keeping women in their place and maintaining male power. It is the logical conclusion to "a progression of violent acts that range from emotional and psychological abuse, battery, verbal abuse, torture, rape, prostitution, sexual assault, child abuse, female infanticide, genital mutilation, domestic violence and all policies tolerated by the state that cause the death of women."[12] And as such, femicide is part of normal, patriarchal systems and not an aberration.

Building on these ideas, Marcela Lagarde y de los Ríos says that we should see femicide as an extreme form of the larger phenomenon of gender violence.[13] Like Monárrez, Lagarde maintains that femicide is systemic and "produced by the patriarchal, hierarchal, and social organization of gender, based on supremacy and inferiority, that creates gender inequality between women and men."[14] But as Fregoso and Bejarano note, it is not simply a gendered form of homicide but rather a gender-specific form of violence directed at women *as women*. Put differently, "unlike most cases of women's murders, men are not killed *because* they are men or as a result of their vulnerability as members of a subordinate gender; nor are men subjected to gender-specific forms of degradation and violation, such as rape and sexual torture, prior to their murder."[15]

Because feminicide is directed at women because they are women, while it obviously affects specific women, they are not targeted *as individuals*; feminicide is targeted at a member of a specific social group—WOMAN, TRANS-WOMAN, LESBIAN—in order to terrorize women as a whole. In fact, neither the victims nor the perpetrators are involved in feminicide as mere individuals; men commit feminicide as representatives of social groups (MEN) or organizations (drug cartels, gangs, organized crime) and women are victims as WOMEN. In this way, femicide is both a systemic and a "social phenomenon" that is connected to a patriarchal system that presupposes, to a greater or lesser degree, that women can be murdered simply for being women.[16]

With this in mind, Monserrat Sagot Rodríguez expands our understanding even farther by noting the connections between femicide and masculinity. Sagot affirms that "femicide represents the ultimate expression of masculinity as power, domination, and control over the lives of women. From this perspective, it is perpetrated by men on the basis of their sense of superiority over women, for sexual pleasure, and under the premise that they own women."[17] In other words, femicide is not only enforcing patriarchy, it is also affirming a certain conception of masculinity, one where masculinity is about projecting dominance, control, and power as well as the idea that women are objects to be owned. But focusing on patriarchy or masculinity in isolation yields too narrow of an understanding.

Sagot goes on to caution us that because of its complex motivations and manifestations, understanding femicide requires exploring its gendered dimensions and their connections to other oppressive systems. In other words, understanding femicide requires an intersectional analysis of its nature, causes, and expressions. Sagot suggests that such intersectional analyses would include explorations of the way neoliberalism and femicide are related.[18] Similarly, Monárrez suggests such investigations focus on the role of class and capitalism.[19] I contend this intersectional analysis must include the oppressive systems related to immigration and the treatment of immigrants.

Despite being well aware that femicide of immigrants is rampant, many analyses of femicide leave out, ignore, undertheorize, or underemphasize the connection between feminicide and immigration. To take just one example, Monárrez notes, "there is a descriptive generalization of memory taking place when it is said that some 400 young women, ranging in age from 16 to 24, *mainly immigrants*, often black, primarily students at commercial schools or computing centers or workers in free trade zones, have been mutilated, tortured, and raped, their bodies left abandoned in the desert surrounding the town."[20] But, she argues, we should not focus on the preponderance of femicide against migrant women because doing so "hinders making visible other representations of feminicide and elaborating a feminist policy that focuses on opposition strategies vis-à-vis the murder of women in all its forms."[21]

I disagree. I think that, in focusing on "other representations of femicide," we have lost sight of the connection between femicide and immigration. And I maintain that developing policies and strategies to stop "the murder of women in all of its forms" requires considering femicide in all of *its* forms, including femicides of immigrants and how they are deeply connected to immigration and immigration injustice. I will illustrate this by exploring femicides against Venezuelan women in Colombia.

FEMICIDE IN COLOMBIA

South America is in the midst of a Venezuelan migration millions strong. As of mid-2019, the United Nations and the International Organization of Migration report that over four million Venezuelans had left their country,[22] representing over 13 percent of Venezuela's total population.[23] By November 2019, the numbers increased to 4.6 million Venezuelans who had crossed the border in search of a new life elsewhere.[24] And if nothing drastically changes, the Organization of American States estimates that by the end of 2020 the number of Venezuelan immigrants will number between 7.5 and 8.2 million.[25] If this occurs, it will constitute the largest exodus in the world.[26]

While Venezuelans are going to various places—Peru, Ecuador, Costa Rica, and the United States—Colombia is by far the nation housing the largest number. As director of the Wilson Center's Latin American Program Cynthia J. Arnson highlights,

Colombia, which shares a long border with Venezuela, now hosts the largest number of refugees—1.3 million, up from about 300,000 just two years ago. Another 710,000 Venezuelans traveled through Colombian territory in 2018 in transit to other destinations farther south.[27]

In fact, as of November 2019, the numbers of Venezuelans in the South American nation surpassed 1.6 million.[28] And now Migración Colombia predicts that there will be over 2.2 million Venezuelans residing in Colombia by the end of 2020, if not more (though with the Covid-19 pandemic, the numbers appear stable for now).[29]

Colombia, however, is a nation with its own struggles. Despite the fact that its economy grew at a rate of 3 percent in early 2019,[30] Colombia struggles with severe inequality, low wages, and its unemployment rate hovered just under 11 percent in October 2019.[31] And this was before the Covid-19 pandemic hit. It is also trying to manage an internally displaced population of over 7.7 million, the largest in the world,[32] while simultaneously recovering from a fifty-plus-year civil war that only officially ended in 2016. And it is not always succeeding; the peace process is stalled, the displaced population remains high, and the country still grapples with security concerns around theft, drug violence, the resurgence of paramilitary forces, and homicide.[33] Over three hundred activists, Indigenous leaders, and community organizers have been murdered with hundreds more having received death threats since the peace accords were signed,[34] and femicide remains all too common.

Femicide was officially criminalized in Colombia in 2015 with the passage of the Law Against Femicide, commonly known as the "Ley de Rosa Elvira Cely."[35] At the time the law was passed, a woman was murdered in Colombia, on average, every two days.[36] Despite taking this important step, though, femicide remains a serious problem in the South American nation. According to the Observatorio Feminicidios Colombia, there were 666 femicides in Colombia in 2018 alone.[37] And as of May 2019, Observatorio Feminicidios Colombia reported 248.[38] Increasingly, femicide victims include Venezuelan immigrants.

Over 120 Venezuelan immigrant women have become victims of femicide outside of their home nation,[39] with the majority occurring in Colombia.[40] The victims ranged in age from a nine-year-old girl to women in their forties.[41] Venezuelan sociologist and activist Esther Pineda reports that "between April 2018 and April 2019, at least 22 femicides were committed against Venezuelan women in Colombian territory."[42] And the Red Feminista Antimilitarista reports that since early 2018 there have been at least two femicides of Venezuelan migrant women in Colombia per month, with no sign the trend is abating.[43] Most recently, Francisco de Vitoria identified eighty-three cases of femicide against Venezuelan migrants in Colombia.[44]

Here are the names of just some of the victims:

Maribella Guerrero Sanchez, 39
Nancy Arlenys Quiroz Aguilar, 22
Yuli Mar Pérez, 45
Achille Yugeidy Hernández
Johana Ruiz Pérez
María Laura Brito González, 17
Anngi Del Valle Ruiz Valbuena, 22
Greydis Orian Reyes Gonzalez, 18
Karen María Pinto Tirado, 21
Katerín Julieth González Moreno, 17
Érika Patricia Carpio Medrano, 17
Yuliana Gómez Quejada, 27

Yenny Liliana Pedraza
Maribella Guerrero Sánchez, 39
Nancy Arelia Quiroz Aguilar, 22
Mary Yelithza Castillo, 36
Keyra Yinete López Chico, 26
Nacielyz Violeta Hernández
Mana Sinai Gomez Perez, 22
Dubleisy Carolina Machado, 22
Estefany Paola, 27
Madelein Solemne Arteta Díaz, 19
Genesy Klertrojas Cuicas, 23
Yorgelis Andrea Colmenareas

Verónica Audrimar Raga Murillo, 22   Erika Patricia Carpio Medrano, 24
Iris Concepción Duarte, 53   Anyelys Coromoto Rivero, 25
Gabriela Andrea Romero Cabarcas, 18   Exdimar Iluth Flores Villegas, 25
Yulimar Carolina Hidalgo, 17   Elizabeth Coromoto Nava Wilches
Fraibelys Polanco, 16   Mayela René Pereira Hidalgo, 31
Lissette Josefina Chirinos Martínez, 44 Yissenia Jhoany Colina Vásquez, 25
Zuleika Gabriela Briceño   Lili

FEMINICIDE AS IMMIGRATION INJUSTICE

Clearly these are horrific acts that most would strongly condemn. But I condemn these murders not solely on the grounds that they are immoral and despicable expressions of gender violence but also because of their connections to global oppression and immigration injustice. In this section, I will highlight the Colombian and international community's response to the Venezuelan migration crisis in order to illuminate the connections between these responses, femicide, global oppression, and immigration injustice.

The Colombian Response

Colombia has taken many positive actions toward the Venezuelan immigrant population. It has allowed Venezuelans into their country, offered them special permissions to stay in the country with a work permit, and, in October 2019, announced that children born to Venezuelan parents on Colombian soil will receive Colombian citizenship.[45] "The measure will grant a path to Colombian passports to babies born to Venezuelan parents on Colombian territory from August 2015 until August 2021, making it easier for them to access education and health care, and preventing an explosion of statelessness in Colombia."[46] And in January 2020, Colombia announced a plan to work with local authorities to help Venezuelans get regularized, receive increased humanitarian assistance, and become socioeconomically integrated into Colombian society.[47] Colombia, then, is making some strong efforts to respond to the needs of Venezuelan immigrants.

Despite this, Venezuelan immigrants, especially those without formal documents, face profound and pervasive immigration injustices in Colombia. And as of late January 2020, over half of the immigrants do not have documents, with 719,189 Venezuelans in regularized status but 911,714 undocumented.[48] As the International Refugee Committee observes,

While some of these programs are facilitating access to minimum and basic services, there are challenges for those who do not have documentation. This includes no formal work, no access to non-emergency health care, no certification to proceed through education; as well as threats such as xenophobia; extortion; vulnerability to human trafficking, including sexual exploitation, and being less likely to report abuses to authorities.[49]

So while Colombia may be helping put those who have documents on the path to safety, a large portion of the population is left unprotected. Colombia's Department of Legal Medicine, for example, found that between January and June 2019, 233 Venezuelans were killed in Colombian territory, including 206 men and 27 women.[50] Much of this is said to be due to criminal gangs, xenophobia, and machismo that the government does not try to address or confront (and some would argue they promote). As public policy expert Jeisson Camacho explained, "Not creating employment, or access to certain conditions, causes a great many [Venezuelans] to become tied up criminal dynamics, but there are also elements of xenophobia in the country that accentuate this."[51]

For Venezuelan women, the challenges are especially great. They confront multiple forms of discrimination and violence, which include hypersexualizing girls and women, harassment, rape, sexual exploitation in exchange for food, water, medicine, personal hygiene products, and other basic goods. And there are sexual exploitation rings that recruit vulnerable Venezuelan women.[52] Venezuelan women constantly endure "men sexually harassing and verbally abusing them, attacking them as dirty foreigners and pressing them for sex while they work as waitresses or cleaners."[53] They are also constantly attacked for having too many children and seeking to come to Colombia just to have babies.[54] Despite this, the government does virtually nothing.

Now some might highlight that Colombia is a *machista* society that permits this kind of harassment of all women. But I reject the implication—the fact that Colombia perpetuates oppression of all women does not make it acceptable. Nor does it lessen the degree of the wrongs perpetrated against Venezuelan women. And this tolerance of machismo culture is inseparable from the fact that Venezuelans are subjected to violence.

Venezuelan women are also subjected to violence, including and especially sexual violence. Again, the International Refugee Committee found that

> all five female focus groups mentioned that sexual violence is occurring against Venezuelan women in Colombia, with some participants having experienced violence themselves. Two groups mentioned that the greatest risks were either at their workplace or when searching for work, saying "men trick women with job opportunities but in reality, they have intentions of some kind of exploitation," "other times women are drugged and taken advantage of."[55]

And Pineda points out what we already know—namely, that "Venezuelan women in Colombia are increasingly victims of femicide."[56]

Part of why Venezuelan women are falling prey to femicide is because the Colombian government's actions (or lack thereof) place them into especially dangerous situations through its immigration policies that make it difficult for migrants to obtain work permits or work in their chosen fields. For undocumented women, this almost always means being forced into sex work. As University of Oxford researcher Julia Zulver reports, thousands of desperate Venezuelan women turn to sex work to survive because there are no other options, despite the fact that most were educated and working as professionals in Venezuela. The International Refugee Committee found that "sex work was noted as a common coping strategy, with one focus group mentioning that even professionals, like doctors, have turned to sex work."[57] While volunteering at a free legal clinic, for example, a woman told me, "in Venezuela I was studying at the University, I never thought I would have to do this."[58] Another woman told Zulver, "I arrived with my young daughter and I simply couldn't find work, so one day I said to myself, 'I have to go into the street, because otherwise we won't eat.'"[59] And when we combine this with Colombia's lack of action to protect Venezuelan women and its acceptance of machismo culture, even Venezuelan women who are not sex workers confront harassment because people *presume* they are.[60] Venezuelan women, then, are consistently victims of violence and exploitation in various forms in Colombia, and yet almost nothing is being done to protect them. Pineda notes,

> From the moment that Venezuelan women begin the journey from their homes of origin to their destination, they face lack of protection and multiple forms of violence and gender inequality; among these it is possible to mention: prejudices, stereotypes, harassment, sexual violence, capture by trafficking networks for the purpose of sexual exploitation and feminicide.[61]

In not acting to stop these things (and some would argue even allowing them to occur), Colombia and its immigration policies around granting work permits support the conditions for femicide to flourish, despite officially criminalizing it.

The government's handling of the peace process also contributes to this phenomenon. The Duque administration refuses to fund many initiatives or programs to advance the peace process because it does not agree with many of its provisions. As a result, various armed groups, including Revolutionary Armed Forces of Colombia (FARC), Patriotic Forces of National Liberation (FPLN), and the National Liberation Army (ELN)[62] are continuing to operate throughout the country with impunity. They, not the Colombian government, are controlling large sections of the border with Venezuela. And this is significant because these groups take advantage of Venezuelan migrants, especially women. Zulver found that "*trochas*—the hundreds of [paths] where it's possible to cross the border illegally—are controlled by armed groups. These men charge bribes; if a female migrant doesn't have money . . . sex is demanded as payment."[63] Moreover, "perpetrators take advantage of the fact that [women] are almost invisible. . . . They know that they won't be held accountable and behave accordingly."[64] In other words, perpetrators know the women will not report the rapes and, even if they do, the government will likely do nothing in response. So the groups feel they have a free pass to do whatever they want to women. And in practice it appears they do.

In not actively working to further the peace process, take control over their borders, or create immigration policies that make it possible for Venezuelans to cross at official entry points rather than *trochas*, Colombia is complicit in the violence against Venezuelan women. Colombian actions and policies combine to place Venezuelan immigrant women into double-binds such that they have no good options—stay in Venezuela and starve, face violence, and endure a deeply inadequate health care system or go to Colombia and risk forced prostitution, sexual abuse, or femicide. Consequently, both Colombia's immigration policies (especially around obtaining work permits and protecting women's safety) and its lack of adequate actions to advance the peace accords are creating (or at least clearly contributing to the existence of) systemic barriers leading Venezuelan women to be vulnerable to femicide.

The International Response (or Lack Thereof)

The picture I just painted is overly simplistic. This is not to say that Colombia cannot or should not do more to combat femicide and sexual violence against all women its territory, including Venezuelans—it absolutely must—however, it must be recognized that even if Colombia wanted to do everything in its power to stop the feminicides, it could not do so because it lacks the resources. And pleas for help from the international community have fallen on deaf ears.

The rest of the world is neither taking in Venezuelans nor providing resources to help their process. Neighboring countries, like Peru, Chile, and Ecuador, have imposed strict new entrance requirements that most Venezuelans cannot meet, effectively closing their borders to thousands of them[65] and forcing more into Colombia. The United States is making it difficult for Venezuelans to go there, denying half of the 30,000 asylum petitions in 2018 and resisting bipartisan legislation to grant Venezuelans temporary protected status.[66] According to the Organization of American States, while "Colombia has granted legal residency to 1.6 million Venezuelans during the past five years . . . only about 221,000 Venezuelans have arrived in the United States during the same period . . . and most of them do not have legal residency papers."[67] And while the European Union consistently declares that member nations should accept Venezuelan migrants, because of the distance and the resources needed to get to Europe from Latin America, they only report receiving about 18,400 applications, which does not do much to alleviate the crisis.[68] Colombia is increasingly the only game in town.

In addition to failing to take in more Venezuelans, the world's wealthy nations are offering woefully inadequate financial assistance to help Colombia respond to the crisis. In fact, "only a fraction of the international assistance dedicated to other major crises has been devoted to helping Venezuelans."[69] In 2019, the United Nations High Commissioner for Refugees and International Organization for Migration have asked the international community for $738 million to assist migrant-receiving countries in Latin America and the Caribbean, "but as of July 2019, it had only received 23.9 percent of the funds needed."[70] Specific to Colombia, even though the World Bank estimates that it "had to spend roughly $900 million last year to meet only the basic needs of Venezuelan migrants, . . . a 2019 campaign by the World Bank to help raise funds to assist Colombia in settling Venezuelan migrants raised only $32 million."[71] Recently, the United States pledged $120 million to Colombia but, as we can see, this is a pittance of what Colombia needs or the United States could afford to give.[72]

Many have offered explanations for this poor showing—the world's resources are depleted, this is considered a political crisis of Venezuela's own making, the international community may be waiting on the sidelines to contribute to Venezuela's reconstruction after Maduro falls, "compassion fatigue" in Europe and the United States—but as Arnson notes, "compassion fatigue hasn't stopped the international community from providing more than $17 billion in assistance for Syrian refugees in less than a decade, approximately $3,000 per person, . . . [but] in the case of Venezuela, the Organization of American States estimates the number to be a scant $100 to $200 per individual."[73] In other words, the world is failing to step up and they are abandoning both Colombia and the Venezuelan migrants in the process.

The reason that all of these points are important is because they demonstrate how the response (or lack of it) to the Venezuelan issue, intended or not, creates, reflects, and perpetuates global oppression. First, it perpetuates global oppression against Colombia, which makes it unable to offer adequate assistance to Venezuelans. Let me state the obvious: Colombia is not the United States or Europe. Europe and the United States have abundant resources that they are choosing not to share, whereas Colombia has limited resources. Colombia does not have the

financial wherewithal to provide shelter, food, medical care, and employment to such large numbers of hungry and vulnerable people. Public health and education are already overextended and under-resourced . . . and recent migrants are sicker than in the past. Many arrive having walked thousands of kilometers through rugged terrain and needing urgent medical attention. Some carry infectious diseases, such as measles and tuberculosis. Public health officials have observed a rise in sexually transmitted diseases such as syphilis and HIV/AIDS.[74]

Consequently, as Felipe Muñoz, the Colombian official in charge of running the border zone, explains,

> Many schools in the border zone have taken in up to 300 students without adding new teachers. As migrants typically settle in the poorest areas of cities, schools with the fewest resources are bearing the heaviest load. And because Venezuelans have access to only limited emergency care at Colombian hospitals, waiting rooms and wards at clinics across the country have become overcrowded. With local housing stock unable to cope with the numbers of newcomers, many migrants can be found sleeping in town plazas.[75]

It is clear, then, that Colombia cannot handle the crisis alone. But as we saw, the international response has been abysmal, which has trapped Colombia in double-binds that force it to choose between its own people and its desperate neighbors. If Colombia directs resources to Venezuelan immigrants, then it cannot put resources into the peace process, strengthening its infrastructure, creating and funding social programs to alleviate vast inequalities within its population, and so forth. However, if it closes its borders to Venezuelans or reduces the resources dedicated to resettling them in order to direct them to its own population, then it defaults on moral obligations to help those in dire suffering and contributes to furthering global oppression against Venezuelans. The lack of response has left Colombia with no good options. They should not have been put into this position in the first place, and the fact that they are results from global oppression in the form of powerlessness and exploitation.

The lack of international assistance renders Colombia both politically and epistemically powerless. Recall that powerlessness in the context of global oppression refers to nations lacking control over various aspects of their affairs. And this is certainly happening in the case of Colombia. The international community's response to the Venezuelan crisis has put Colombia in a position where it lacks control over how to manage Venezuelan immigrants and lacks authority over what is happening in their territory. Most glaringly in this context, because other nations refuse to admit large numbers of Venezuelans, they increasingly have to go to Colombia, regardless of whether Colombia is equipped to accept them. Put differently, regardless of what Colombia wants, the actions of the international community leave desperate Venezuelans with nowhere else to go. So they continue to arrive in Colombia in very high numbers and Colombia is powerless to stop it. This is one way it lacks authority over its nation's affairs. And because the international community is refusing to provide resources, Colombia is not in a position to develop a strategy for integrating Venezuelans in ways that keep them safe or balance their needs with Colombian citizens. Everything has to be done as an emergency response. So they lack authority over how to manage the crisis.

The lack of international assistance also epistemically marginalizes Colombia in ways that render it epistemically powerless. Epistemic marginalization occurs when an entire nation is excluded from useful participation in the production and dissemination of knowledge by excluding nations and their members from international dialogue. And when a nation is excluded from the community of knowers, they are no longer able to contribute to that community's knowledge. In other words, their epistemic marginalization leads to their epistemic powerlessness. Again, the epistemically powerless lack epistemic credibility; they lack the ability to influence others, even if they are speaking the truth. As such, among other things, they cannot entrust others with what they know and they are excluded from cooperative interactions.

We see both Colombia's epistemic marginalization and powerlessness in the international community's response in at least two ways. First, the international community appears to be taking action about Venezuelans without consulting or considering Colombia's situation. In this way, they are excluding them from the conversation, which makes it impossible for Colombia to participate in intellectual dialogue on the crisis or contribute their knowledge to others. Second, the international community's failure to contribute even a minimally reasonable portion of the aid Colombia, the World Bank, or the UNHRC requested reflects the fact that Colombia lacks epistemic credibility on the global stage; Colombia lacks the ability to influence other nations, even when it speaks the truth. In at least these ways, Colombia is epistemically marginalized and powerless. All of this shows their lack of sway over the debate about Venezuelan migrants while also revealing global oppression manifest in the lack of global assistance.

The Global North is also exploiting Colombia by failing to respond. Because it refuses to help, Colombia's resources, energies, territory, and labor are all being transferred from Colombians to benefit the nations of the Global North; because they are withholding support, citizens in the Global North continue to benefit from their governments' spending programs, while Colombia's people are left with smaller portions of an already inadequate social net budget. And I submit that this is happening because of Colombia's global position relative to the Global North and Venezuela itself; because Colombia is a mid-income Global South nation that happens to border Venezuela, the world simply expects it to comply. At the same time, because it lacks resources, the nations of the Global North know that they will not face serious repercussions for their refusal to act. The lack of international response, then, reflects and perpetuates global oppression against these nations and contributes to deep immigration injustices to be perpetrated. And in this case, it is costing Venezuelan women their lives.

Before concluding this section, however, I want to highlight how the international response specifically perpetrates oppression, and thus immigration injustice, against Venezuelan women. The world is well aware that Venezuelan women are subjected to violence on Colombia's borders and inside its territory. The world knows that Colombia cannot be reasonably expected to take control of that border back from the FARC, ELN, FPLN, and other groups. The world knows Venezuelan women are being killed along the border. But it does almost nothing. The world knows that if Venezuelan women could get passports and birth certificates, then they would have options for work aside from prostitution, but they do not respond. And they know that those women cannot find adequate, safe shelter or food in Colombia, but they remain unmoved. I maintain that these actions (or lack thereof) demonstrate clearly that the world does not think the killings of Venezuelan migrant women are serious or concerning enough to warrant expending international resources.

Worse, though, is that I think it is clear that at least part of the reason these murders do not provoke international outcry is because of *who* the women are. If migrant women from the United States or Europe were being tortured, raped, and murdered in Colombia, there would be in an uproar and resources would be flowing into Colombia to protect them (along with a tide of negative publicity and economic damage). However, because these migrants are being murdered in the Global South by other citizens of the Global South, their lives are deemed less worthy. The lives of Latina and Latinx migrants are simply not seen as important enough to protect. Again, why is this? As we have seen in previous chapters, the colonial global order is operative that protects the privileged position of Europe, the United States, and their peoples and sees nations of the Global South and their people as disposable or as mere derivatives of the Global North and its interests. On this view, helping colonized beings[76] from the Global South only makes sense if it somehow benefits colonizers. Because there is no obvious benefit to the Global North to step up here, they simply do not seem to care about these women.

If I am even partially correct, then the fact that the world is not moved to respond to protect Venezuelan women reflects global oppression and, by definition, constitutes immigration injustice. The reason, in other words, for the lack of response is because of *who* the victims of the crime are. That means the world is, at least in part, determining who is worth protecting based on cultural imperialism. Put differently, the collective actions of the international community create, perpetuate, and reflect global oppression in various forms, including powerlessness, cultural imperialism, and epistemic marginalization, and thus constitute immigration injustice.

Femicide as Immigration Injustice

Let us take stock of where we are. I have shown that there is an increasing problem of femicide of Venezuelan immigrant women in Colombia, but neither Colombia nor the international community have done enough to stop it. On the one hand, while Colombia has done some positive things to help Venezuelan immigrants, efforts to protect the safety of Venezuelan women are inadequate. In fact, Colombia's immigration policies are themselves partially responsible for Venezuelan women's vulnerability to systemic violence and femicide. And intended or not, Colombian practices and policies, like not prosecuting crimes against Venezuelan women, sustain, if not directly promulgate, immigration injustice against this group.

On the other hand, however, Colombia is not entirely to blame here. To the contrary, the world has put Colombia into a terrible position because even though it is in no position to take many of the needed actions to protect Venezuelan women, international assistance has not materialized. And I suggest the reasons for this reflect and perpetuate global oppression against both Venezuelans and Colombia and, by extension, constitute immigration injustice in their own right.

While I have used the case of femicide to reveal various types of immigration injustices in this Colombia-Venezuelan context, I still have to show more explicitly how femicide and immigration injustice are connected. I will do so by using this case and what I have written thus far to note three connections in particular. First, feminicide is, itself, a form of immigration injustice. Second, feminicide is a means to perpetrate and enforce immigration injustices. Third, feminicide is a consequence of immigration injustice.

First, femicides against Venezuelan women in Colombia demonstrate that the act itself constitutes immigration injustice in the form of systemic violence. Recall that immigration injustice is present when a nation's immigration policies, practices, laws, norms, and systems create, reflect, or perpetuate global oppression. And global oppression may manifest itself in many forms, one of which is systemic violence. Systemic violence as a face of global oppression occurs when a group is systematically made vulnerable to violence or the threat of violence only because they are immigrants or have specific national identities. Our analysis shows that this is precisely what is going on when Venezuelan immigrant women are murdered.

Feminicide is expressly about maintaining and perpetuating oppression against Venezuelan immigrant women by rendering them vulnerable to violence due to their immigrant status and nationality. These women are not being killed only because they are women; they are being killed because they are immigrant women. As we saw, these women are targeted precisely because they are not protected and, as a result, they are seen as easy targets. In this sense, femicide is a form of immigration injustice because it creates, reflects, and perpetuates global oppression against immigrant women.

Still, feminicide is not simply about subjecting immigrant women to systemic violence, it is also about sending messages to others that they are not welcome; it is about communicating to would-be migrants that if they immigrate to Colombia and get "out of their place," then they will face the consequences. In this sense, though, we can see that femicide is not directed at all immigrant women (at least all immigrant women equally), it is only directed at women who are the "wrong kind of immigrant." And this leads to the second connection between feminicide and immigration injustice, namely that feminicide is a way to perpetuate immigration injustice and enforce oppressive systems against immigrants, in this case Venezuelan immigrants specifically. As we saw in the previous chapter, there is a long-held colonial attitude throughout Latin America that the "right kind of immigrant" is European or from the United States. That this permeates Colombian society as well is attested to by the fact that these groups are welcomed formally and informally throughout the society—there are countless private school options for educating children in their native languages (Colegio Nueva Granada, Anglo Colombiano, and the British School in English; the Liceo Francés and Colegio Helvetia for French; Colegio Andino for German; and Colegio Italiano Leonardo di Vinci for Italian), numerous restaurants and markets where these immigrants can find their favorite foods and other products from their native countries, and it is seen as an asset when applying for jobs to be from one of these places. Members of these groups rarely, if ever, face targeted attacks or harassment based on their nationality.[77] It is unheard of, for example, for someone to call me "gringa" in a dismissive and threatening way on the street or have people presume that I am sex worker, uneducated, or only in Colombia to take advantage of their welfare system. When people ask me why I came to Colombia, it is because they cannot believe I would want to leave the United States, not because they are implying negative things about me or my home nation.

This stands in stark contrast to the constant harassment endured by Venezuelans, especially Venezuelan women, who are constantly called *"puta"* or *"veneca,"* and are presumed to be uneducated sex workers who are only in Colombia to have babies and take advantage of the system. Whereas so many Colombians are grateful to have people from the United States and

Europe living in their country, they think Venezuelan women should be grateful to be living there; some think they should be grateful if they are not raped, tortured, or killed. This sentiment was actually expressed to a young twenty-three-year-old Venezuelan college student who was forced to migrate to help her family. She thought she was offered a job as a waitress in Bogotá, but when she arrived she realized that the job was to be a sex worker. When she pointed out that she accepted a waitress position and not a position in a brothel, the male boss threatened her and told her to be grateful that his was a good brothel because that was the only work she was going to be able to find in Colombia.[78] His threats made it clear that if she objected further, then she would be subjected to serious violence, forced prostitution, or worse.

There is a hierarchy among immigrants in the Colombian imaginary. And the threat of violence and feminicide is a means to enforce that hierarchy and to keep Venezuelan women in their place. Femicide in these instances, in other words, is about maintaining and enforcing global oppression against Venezuelan immigrants, which constitutes immigration injustice.

So femicide itself is a manifestation of immigration injustice and is a tool for executing immigration injustice; it is clearly used to exploit, marginalize, and render immigrant women powerless and vulnerable to systemic violence due to sexism and cultural imperialism, and thus it exemplifies global oppression. This leads to a third way femicide is connected to immigration injustice: it is a product of it.

Feminicide is a consequence of immigration injustice in that a major reason that Venezuelan women are vulnerable to it is the fact that they are treated unjustly to begin with. Put simply, when women are subjected to immigration injustice, their risk of femicide increases. As we have seen, this is the case in Colombia—feminicide is in part a result of Colombia's immigration policies, lack of action to protect Venezuelan women, and the lack of international assistance. For example, as we saw earlier, femicide is at least a partial consequence of Colombia not prosecuting crimes against Venezuelan women (such that it is seen as something that people can get away with) or Venezuelan women being forced into sex work because Colombia will not issue them work permits. As such, feminicide is in part a result of immigration injustice.

To summarize: femicide and immigration are deeply connected. First, femicide is a form of immigration injustice as systemic violence that expressly targets specific immigrant women because they have fewer rights and protections. Second, femicide is a tool to maintain and enforce immigration hierarchies. These women are targets for femicide because they are *Venezuelan* women specifically, and it is employed to send a message about which immigrants are welcome and which are not. Third, a major reason that Venezuelan immigrants are vulnerable to violence and feminicide in the first place is because Colombia and the international community fail to protect them. And part of why they fail to protect them is because they are *Venezuelan* immigrants rather than immigrants from other places. So they are vulnerable to feminicide precisely because they are not treated justly in the first place. In this way, femicide is also a consequence of immigration injustice. In all of these ways, femicide creates, perpetuates, and reflects global oppression and thus immigration injustice.

CONCLUSION

At the outset of the chapter, we read Diana's testimony that many Venezuelans see their violent treatment as a sign that they "are worth nothing in Colombia." That is exactly the message that feminicide is intended to send—immigrant women and their lives are worth less than those of others. And because they are worth nothing, they can demand nothing. If they do have the audacity to demand something—even if it is simply the right to safety and respect—then they must be taught a lesson. And this lesson is increasingly taught via femicide. Sadly, the lack of systemic efforts by the Colombian state or the international community to protect these women seems to reinforce that message.

I have tried to show throughout this chapter that we need to see feminicide and immigration injustice as inherently connected in at least three ways: (1) feminicide as a form of immigration injustice, (2) femicide as a tool to enforce and perpetuate immigration injustice, and (3) feminicide as a consequence of immigration injustice. Given these connections, feminicide cannot be completely understood or challenged without considering its connections to immigration and immigration policies, practices, laws, and norms. And conversely, practices and policies related to immigration cannot be considered just if they do not help to protect migrant women's lives and bodily integrity. Once we see that, feminists and immigration activists can do a better job joining forces to show Diana, and countless other Venezuelan women, that their lives are, indeed, worth a lot.

NOTES

1. Lucas Koerner, "Two Venezuelan Women Killed in Northern Colombia," *Venezuelanalysis*, March 7, 2018, https://venezuelanalysis.com/news/13706.
2. "Boletín Vivas Nos Queremos: Femicidios de Migrantes Venezolanas en Colombia Enero a Abril 2019," Observatorio Feminicidios Colombia, accessed December 20, 2019, http://observatoriofeminicidioscolombia.org/attachments/article/391/Bolet%C3%ADn%20Vivas%20Nos%20Queremos%20-%20Feminicidio%20de%20

mujeres%20migrantes%20venezolanas%20en%20territorio%20colombiano%20
-%20Enero%20.pdf; "'La Chama' Fue Asesinada de Dos Balazos en Las Maravillas," *La Lengua Caribe*, March 3, 2019, https://www.lalenguacaribe.co/2019/judicial/
la-chama-fue-asesinada-de-dos-balazos-en-las-maravillas/.

3. Ibid.; "En el centro de Villavicencio atacaron a bala a trabajadoras sexuales
venozalanas," *HSBNoticias.com*, April 28, 2019, https://hsbnoticias.com/noticias/
judicial/en-el-centro-de-villavicencio-atacaron-bala-trabajadoras-522093.

4. "Diana," personal communication, November 27, 2019.

5. Reuters, "Violent Deaths of Venezuelans in Colombia Said on the Rise, Averaging One a Day Since the Year's Start," August 26, 2019, https://www.japantimes
.co.jp/news/2019/08/26/world/crime-legal-world/violent-deaths-venezuelans-colom
bia-said-rise-averaging-one-day-since-years-start/#.Xf1FgNZKi1s.

6. I will use the terms "femicide" and "feminicide" interchangeably. As Rosa-
Linda Fregoso and Cynthia Bejarano explain in the introduction to their edited col-
lection *Terrorizing Women: Feminicide in the Américas* (Durham and London: Duke
University Press, 2010), there is no consensus among Latin American scholars about
which term to prefer. Some, like Marcela Lagarde y de los Ríos, prefer "feminicide"
to emphasize the role of the state in failing to protect women from these crimes,
while others, like Monserrat Sagot, argue that we need a broader term to capture the
crimes and violence, regardless of whether the state is involved or not. Still others,
like Fregoso and Bejarano, prefer "feminicide" to emphasize that the Spanish translation of "femicide," *feminicidio*, and the Latin American scholars who employ it have
advanced our knowledge of the concept. Because I see the points of both sides of the
issue, I will not choose one term over the other.

7. "Understanding and Addressing Violence Against Women: Femicide," *World
Health Organization*, 2012.

8. Julia E. Monárrez Fragoso, "Feminicidio Sexual Serial en Cuidad Juárez: 1993–
2001," *Debate Feminista* 25, no. 13 (April 2002): 279–305, trans. omenontheborder
.org/2011/06/julia-monarrez-serial-sexual-femicide/.

9. Susan Brownmiller, *Against Our Will: Men, Women, and Rape* (New York:
Fawcett Books, 1975).

10. Jane Caputi, *The Age of Sex Crime* (Bowling Green, OH: Bowling Green University Popular Press, 1987), 3.

11. Diana Russell, *Making Violence Sexy: Feminist Views on Pornography* (London: Open University, 1993).

12. Monárrez Fragoso, "Serial Sexual Feminicide."

13. Marcela Legarde y de los Ríos, "Preface," in *Terrorizing Women*, ed. Rosa-
Linda Fregoso and Cynthia Bejarano, xxii.

14. Ibid., xxi.

15. Fregoso and Bejarano, "Introduction," 7.

16. Monárrez Fragoso, "Serial Sexual Femicide."

17. Monserrat Sagot Rodríguez, "¿Un mundo sin femicidios? Las propuestas del
feminismo para erradicar la violencia contra las mujeres," in *Feminismos, Pensamiento Crítico y Propuestas Alternativas en América Latina*, edited by Monserrat Sagot
Rodríguez (Buenos Aires: CLACSO, 2017), 62; translation mine.

18. Ibid.

19. Monárrez Fragoso, "Serial Sexual Femicide."

20. Ibid.; emphasis mine.

21. Ibid.

22. "Refugees and Migrants from Venezuela Top 4 Million," *UNHCR*, June 7, 2019, https://www.unhcr.org/en-us/news/press/2019/6/5cfa2a4a4/refugees-migrants -venezuela-top-4-million-unhcr-iom.html; Merrit Kennedy, "Venezuelan Refugees and Migrants Top 4 Million, U.N Says," *National Public Radio*, June 7, 2019, https:// www.npr.org/2019/06/07/730687807/u-n-says-more-than-4-million-people-have -left-venezuela.

23. *Report to Address the Regional Crisis Caused by Venezuela's Migrant and Refugee Flows*, Organization of American States Report, June 2019, http://www .oas.org/documents/eng/press/OAS-Report-to-Address-the-regional-crisis-caused -by-Venezuelas-migrant.pdf.

24. Christina Armario, "UN Envy: As Venezuela Exodus Drags on Many Won't Go Back," *Associated Press*, November 14, 2019, https://apnews.com/867e10f67177 4bc59a2dd8885c91f241.

25. *Report to Address the Regional Crisis Caused by Venezuela's Migrant and Refugee Flows*.

26. Armario, "UN Envy."

27. Cynthia J. Arnson, "The Venezuelan Refugee Crisis Is Not Just a Regional Problem: Latin American Neighbors Are Pulling More than Their Weight," *Foreign Affairs*, July 26, 2019, https://www.foreignaffairs.com/articles/venezuela/2019-07-26/ venezuelan-refugee-crisis-not-just-regional-problem.

28. Armario, "UN Envy."

29. Ricardo Ajiaco, "Migrantes Venozolanos llegarían a 2 milliones en 2020," *El Tiempo*, January 22, 2020, https://www.eltiempo.com/politica/partidos-politicos/lo -restos-de-colombia-frente-a-una-migracion-venezolana-que-no-cesa-453616?.

30. "Country Report: Colombia," *World Bank*, October 2019, https://www.world bank.org/en/country/colombia/overview.

31. Adriaan Alsema, "Colombia's Unemployment Surges to 10.8%, Highest Since 2010," *Colombia Reports*, October 3, 2019, https://colombiareports.com/colombias -unemployment-spikes-to-10-8-highest-since-2010/.

32. "Colombia," UNHCR, https://www.unhcr.org/en-us/colombia.html.

33. "Crime and Security in Bogotá," *Colombia Reports*, July 19, 2019, https:// colombiareports.com/bogota-crime-security-statistics/.

34. Fabio Andres Diaz and Magda Jiménez, "Colombia's Murder Rate Is at an All-Time Low But Its Activists Keep Getting Killed," *The Conversation*, April 6, 2018, http://theconversation.com/colombias-murder-rate-is-at-an-all-time-low-but -its-activists-keep-getting-killed-91602.

35. Anastasia Moloney, "Colombia Confronts Femicide, the 'Most Extreme Form of Violence against Women,'" *Reuters*, August 20, 2015, https://www.reuters.com/ article/us-colombia-women-murder/colombia-confronts-femicide-the-most-extreme -form-of-violence-against-women-idUSKCN0QP0CM20150820.

36. Ibid.

37. "666 feminicidios en Colombia en el año 2018 [INfográfico]," *Red Feminista Antimilitarista*, February 2, 2019, http://redfeministaantimilitarista.org/novedades/item/666-feminicidios-en-colombia-en-2018-infografico.

38. "These Are the Numbers of Feminicides in Latin America," *Latin American Post*, August 24, 2019, https://latinamericanpost.com/29792-these-are-the-numbers-of-feminicides-in-latin-america.

39. Diego Battistessa, "Una masacre silenciosa: La venezolanas muertas en el extranjero," *El Pais*, September 3, 2019, https://elpais.com/elpais/2019/09/02/planeta_futuro/1567434636_760205.html?fbclid=IwAR3MF2gjEDLJSGX8FOIIz5 l7N_eh3yZPz3_BALq_2Uah3g3hp-GWZEj-hUE.

40. Ibid.

41. Claudia Yurley Quintero Rolón, "Suenos Rotos," http://ovidiohoyos.com/node/29187; translation mine.

42. Esther Pineda, "Explotadas y asesinadas: la vulnerabilidad de las mujeres venezolanas," *El Espectador*, December 20, 2019, https://www.elespectador.com/colombia2020/opinion/explotadas-y-asesinadas-la-vulnerabilidad-de-las-migrantes-venezolanas-columna-892839; translation mine.

43. "Boletín Vivas Nos Queremos."

44. Beverly Goldberg, "La mayoria de muertes de venezolanas en el país, entre 2018 y 2019, fueron feminicidios," *El Espectador*, January 29, 2020, https://www.elespectador.com/noticias/nacional/la-mayoria-de-muertes-de-venezolanas-en-el-pais-entre-2018-y-2019-fueron-feminicidios-articulo-902062.

45. Jenny Bartsfield, "Colombia Gives Venezuela Newborns a Start in Life, *United Nations Refugee Agency*, October 14, 2019, https://www.unhcr.org/en-us/news/stories/2019/10/5da42be64/colombia-gives-venezuela-newborns-start-life.html; Anatoly Kurmanaev and Jenny Carolina González, "Colombia Offers Citizenship to 24,000 Children of Venezuelan Refugees," *New York Times*, August 5, 2019, https://www.nytimes.com/2019/08/05/world/americas/colombia-citizenship-venezuelans.html.

46. Kurmanaev and González, "Colombia Offers Citizenship to 24,000 Children of Venezuelan Refugees."

47. Ajiaco, "Migrantes Venozolanos llegarían a 2 milliones en 2020."

48. Ibid.

49. "Needs Assessment Report: Venezuelan Migrants in Colombia," International Refuge Committee, November 6, 2018, https://www.rescue.org/sites/default/files/document/3302/ircassessment-venezuelansincolombianov2018.pdf.

50. Lucas Koerner and Ricardo Vaz, "One Venezuelan Migrant Killed Every Day in Colombia," *Venezuelanalysis*, August 28, 2019, https://venezuelanalysis.com/news/14641; Reuters, "Violent Deaths of Venezuelans in Colombia Said on the Rise."

51. Koerner and Vaz, "One Venezuelan Migrant Killed Every Day in Colombia."

52. Pineda, "Explotadas y asesinadas."

53. Julia Zulver, "At Venezuela's Border with Colombia, Women Suffer Extraordinary Levels of Violence," *Washington Post*, February 26, 2019, https://www.washingtonpost.com/politics/2019/02/26/venezuelas-border-with-colombia-women-suffer-extraordinary-levels-violence/.

54. Claudia Palacios, "Paren de parir," *El Tiempo*, June 12, 2019, https://www
.eltiempo.com/opinion/columnistas/claudia-palacios/paren-de-parir-columna-de
-claudia-isabel-palacios-giraldo-374742.

55. "Needs Assessment Report."

56. Pineda, "Explotadas y asesinadas."

57. "Needs Assessment Report."

58. Personal communication.

59. Zulver, "At Venezuela's Border with Colombia."

60. Ibid.

61. Esther Pineda, "Migrar y Morir: El Feminicidio de venezolanas en Colombia," *Tribuna Feminista*, November 18, 2019, https://tribunafeminista.elplural
.com/2019/11/migrar-y-morir-el-feminicidio-de-venezolanas-en-colombia/.

62. Human Rights Watch, *"The Guerrillas Are the Police": Social Control and
Abuses by Armed Groups in Colombia's Arauca Province and Venezuela's Apure
State*, January 22, 2020, https://www.hrw.org/report/2020/01/22/guerrillas-are-police/
social-control-and-abuses-armed-groups-colombias-arauca.

63. Zulver, "At Venezuela's Border with Colombia."

64. Ibid.

65. Anastasia Moloney, "Is South America Closing Its 'Open Door' On Venezuelans?" *Reuters*, August 8, 2019, https://www.reuters.com/article/us-venezuela-
migration-analysis/is-south-america-closing-its-open-door-on-venezuelans-idUSKC-
N1UY27D; Joshua Collins, "Venezuelans Stranded as Ecuador Imposes New Visa
Rules," *Al Jazeera News*, August 26, 2019, https://www.aljazeera.com/news/2019/08/
venezuelans-stranded-ecuador-imposes-visa-rules-190826134509203.html; Dylan
Baddour, "Ecuador Shuts Its Border to Venezuelan Refugees Amid Historical Exodus," *Washington Post*, August 20, 2018 https://www.washingtonpost.com/world/
the_americas/ecuador-shuts-its-border-to-venezuelan-refugees-amid-historic-exodus/
2018/08/20/28223fec-a48c-11e8-ad6f-080770dcddc2_story.html.

66. Molly O'Toole, "Venezuela, Now a Top Source of U.S. Asylum Claims, Poses
a Challenge for Trump," *Los Angeles Times*, June 5, 2019, https://www.latimes.com/
politics/la-na-pol-trump-venezuela-asylum-immigration-20190605-story.html.

67. Andres Oppenheimer, "Millions Are Fleeing Venezuela. Why Won't President
Trump Give Refugees TPS?" *Miami Herald*, October 11, 2019, https://www.miamiher
ald.com/news/local/news-columns-blogs/andres-oppenheimer/article235948032.html.

68. Francesco Guarascio, "Asylum Applications in EU Rise as More Venezuelans Seek Refuge," *Reuters*, June 24, 2019, https://www.reuters.com/article/us
-europe-refugees/asylum-applications-in-eu-rise-as-more-venezuelans-seek-refuge
-idUSKCN1TP0LQ; Mirra Banchon, "EU Lawmakers Issue Call to Take in Venezuelan Migrants," *DW.com*, June 7, 2018, https://www.dw.com/en/eu-lawmakers-issue
-call-to-take-in-venezuelan-migrants/a-44556414.

69. Arnson, "The Venezuelan Refugee Crisis Is Not Just a Regional Problem."

70. Oriana Van Praag, "Understanding the Venezuelan Refugee Crisis," *Latin
American Program Woodrow Wilson Center*, September 13, 2019, https://www.wil
soncenter.org/article/understanding-the-venezuelan-refugee-crisis.

71. Kurmanaev and González, "Colombia Offers Citizenship to 24,000 Children of Venezuelan Refugees."

72. Julia Simmons Cobb, "U.S. Gives Additional $120 Million to Help Venezuelan Migrants," *Reuters*, September 4, 2019, https://www.reuters.com/article/us-colombia-usa/u-s-to-give-additional-120-million-to-help-venezuelan-migrants-idUSKCN1VP30F.

73. Arnson, "The Venezuelan Refugee Crisis Is Not Just a Regional Problem."

74. Ibid.

75. Dylan Baddour, "Colombia Welcomes Millions of Venezuelans Fleeing Chaos," *The Atlantic*, January 30, 2019, https://www.theatlantic.com/international/archive/2019/01/colombia-welcomes-millions-venezuelans-maduro-guaido/581647/.

76. María Lugones, "Heterosexualism and the Colonial/Modern Gender System," *Hypatia* 22, no. 1 (Winter 2007): 186–209.

77. This is not to say that they may not hear comments or see graffiti, especially against the United States. It is common to hear comments like "Go home Yankee" or "Gringo go home" or to see depictions of someone defecating on the United States. But we must be clear that these are not about immigration but rather about imperialism; the message is for the United States to stop interfering in Latin American affairs, especially in Colombia after over a century of military and political intervention. I want to thank Catalina González and Lisímaco Parra for bringing these points to my attention.

78. Personal communication.

Concluding Thoughts

June 25, 2019, I landed at Bogotá, Colombia's El Dorado International Airport with my family, ironically enough, to become immigrants ourselves. I admit, I always thought that if I moved to Latin America, it would be to Costa Rica (where I had friends, adopted family, and experience). But when the opportunity presented itself, I was intrigued and quickly developed a deep affection, respect, and admiration for the South American nation's stunning green mountains, Caribbean beaches, colonial towns, and wonderfully warm, reflective, and friendly people. So we set off for Bogotá, and, like all immigrants, we were filled with hope, dreams, uncertainty, and trepidation.

Our entry process was uneventful—we went through customs, all of our passports were easily stamped with ninety-day tourist visas, and a team of three large cars met us after midnight to help us with our twenty-eight suitcases and take us to the short-term apartment we rented. Both my husband and I had jobs waiting for us, and, as a result, we had both security that many immigrants lack and a support system in place that helped us secure our work visas and find apartments, advised us about where to shop, and ensured we had plans for lunches, coffees, and watching soccer games. I do not want to idealize too much—it was deeply stressful getting our *cédulas* and waiting for those visas, my family is working hard to learn Spanish and navigate making friends in another culture (not always successfully), and we miss our house, family, and friends in the United States. But let's be real, these are an expected part of the process and they will pass. No doubt my story is a privileged one.

As might be imagined, I could not help but observe the difference between my family's immigration experiences and those of others. This is not only because I have heard and read countless immigrants' stories over the three years that I have been working on this book but also because immigration is a visible, dominant issue in Colombia. Every single day I see recent (and not so recent) arrivals from Venezuela, often with their young children, on the streets, in the park, or on the bus, asking for money, food, or clothes. The pleas quickly become routine and predictable: "Madre, por favor, ayúdame";[1] "Puede colaborarme con un poco de comida?" "Por favor, no quiero dinero, pero si tienes ropa extra en tu casa (o comida o algo para tomar o pañales) para los chicos."[2] On TransMilenio (the public bus system), I have almost memorized the long monologue recited by Venezuelans on my way to work— they are sorry to disturb us, they don't mean to be a bother, they want to work but can't find any, they are "not like other Venezuelans," *they* are honest, educated, and just need a little help if we could find it in our hearts. May G-d bless us. I remember one young man actually showed us his high school diploma to prove he was telling the truth. Another man performed magic tricks with his young daughter, clearly trying to keep a smile on both their faces in the middle of what was a terrible time.

When I can, I stop to talk to the different immigrants I pass. I met one woman a few blocks from where we rented our apartment. She had only been in the country for three weeks and told me coming to Colombia was her only hope for providing for her daughter. One day we were talking as she nursed her infant daughter in front of an upscale shopping area, and I asked her where she slept. She told me she tries to collect at least 20,000 pesos a night[3] by begging so that she can rent a room in the southern part of Bogotá (where many recent Venezuelan migrants live). Often she gets it but, if she doesn't, she "has to find other ways to pay."

Another woman I met in line when I was picking up my *cédula.* She told me that she was a nurse in Venezuela but did not have a passport so she had not been able to work in Colombia. After two years, she was getting a work permit. "How long have you been waiting?" she asked. I was almost ashamed to answer "two weeks," so I just responded "much less time than that."

The encounter that stands out to me the most, though, is when I met Beto,[4] his wife, and his two-year-old son when I went to the grocery store three days after our arrival. They looked so sad and lost, both with bloodshot eyes, as they asked if I could spare 1,000 pesos[5] to help them. I asked Beto how long they had been in Bogotá, and he responded, "three days." Then he told me with tears in his eyes: "I didn't think it would be this hard—we have no money, no cell phone, no food, no diapers, and we can't talk to our family. I am so sad." The contrast was so stark. How was it that Beto and his family spent their first three days in Bogotá so drastically different from the way my family and I had spent ours?

I will be blunt—none of this is fair. It is not fair that families who have lived in the United States for years now have to fear deportation. It is not fair that border agents rip children from their parents' arms only because they did not have proper authorization to enter the United States. It is not fair that the

United States can impose its will on Mexico, Guatemala, Honduras, and El Salvador just because the United States feels "overwhelmed" by the influx of immigrants from those nations or prefers more immigrants from "countries like Norway." It is not fair that immigrants from Europe and the United States (like my family) are treated so demonstrably better than Latinx immigrants. It is not fair that Central American and Venezuelan women are forced into prostitution, raped, or murdered just for trying to make a better life for themselves. In this book, I have tried to explain precisely *why* these and so many other things, are so unfair—because they create, reflect, and perpetuate oppression domestically and globally.

Now that I have offered such an explanation, we must act. Immigration justice, after all, is not about creating a perfect policy, it is about recognizing immigration injustice and getting to work to make it better. It is about trying to improve immigrants' lives. It is about creating more humane immigration policies and more services to help immigrants settle. It is about reducing and eliminating the violence immigrants face at the hand of ICE, the border patrol, and on the streets. It is about getting more immigrants access to good legal counsel to argue their asylum claims, creating citizen networks in our neighborhoods to help families who fear deportation, and sending resources to help migrants get across the desert without dying. Immigration justice is about fighting for paying undocumented immigrants decent wages and for safe work conditions and standing up when we hear racist or anti-immigrant jokes or comments. It is about voting for politicians who respect immigrants' rights, teaching English classes, and volunteering at legal and medical clinics. Is it about recognizing the humanity in the immigrants asking us for help on the street and inviting kids from other countries in our own children's school classes over for playdates. It is about using our talents and interests (be they philosophizing, painting, writing, driving, caregiving, studying, working, playing music and sports) to do our part to help create societies that welcome the stranger. I have tried to do that here and I hope the words I have written not only show us where the problems lie but also inspire actions that help Mateo, Beto, and their families and put us on the path to achieving just immigration in the Americas.

NOTES

1. "Ma'am, please help me."
2. "Please, I don't want money, but if you have some extra clothes, you could bring me for my children (or food or water or diapers)."
3. About $5.50 in U.S. dollars.
4. Name changed to protect anonymity.
5. About 30 cents.

Bibliography

Abbott, Jeff. "Keep Out! How the U.S. Is Militarizing Mexico's Southern Border." *Progressive Magazine*, October 2, 2017. https://progressive.org/magazine/keep -out-how-the-us-militarizes-mexico-southern-border/.

Abizadeh, Arash. "The Special-Obligations Challenge to More Open Borders." In *Migration in Political Theory: The Ethics of Movement and Membership*, edited by Sarah Fine and Lea Ypi. New York and Oxford: Oxford University Press, 2016.

AFP and Tico Times. "Costa Rica Sets up Shelters for Nicaraguan Migrants." *Tico Times*, July 20, 2018. https://ticotimes.net/2018/07/20/costa-rica-installs-shelters -for-nicaraguan-migrants.

Ahmed, Azam. "Women Are Fleeing Death at Home. The U.S. Wants to Keep Them Out." *New York Times*, August 18, 2019. https://www.nytimes.com/2019/08/18/ world/americas/guatemala-violence-women-asylum.html.

Ahmed, Azam, and Kirk Semple. "Trump's Surprising New Ally in Mexico? The Government." *New York Times*, March 1, 2019. https://www.nytimes.com/2019/03/01/ world/americas/mexico-migration-trump.html.

Ainsley, Julia Edwards. "Exclusive: Trump Administration Considering Separating Women, Children at Mexican Border." *Reuters*, March 3, 2017. https://www.re uters.com/article/us-usa-immigration-children-idUSKBN16A2ES.

Ajiaco, Ricardo. "Migrantes Venozolanos llegarían a 2 milliones en 2020." *El Tiempo*, January 22, 2020. https://www.eltiempo.com/politica/partidos-politicos/ lo-restos-de-colombia-frente-a-una-migracion-venezolana-que-no-cesa-453616?.

Akee, Randall. "Outdated Immigration Laws Increase Violence Toward Women." *Brookings Institute*, May 20, 2019. https://www.brookings.edu/opinions/outdated -immigration-laws-increase-violence-toward-women/.

Aleaziz, Hamed. "The Trump Administration Is Scrambling to Make Its 'Safe Third Country' Asylum Deal with Guatemala a Reality, A Memo Shows." *BuzzFeed*, July 30, 2019. https://www.buzzfeednews.com/article/hamedaleaziz/safe-third-country -asylum-deal-guatemala-obstacles-memo.

Alguilera, Jasmine. "Everything to Know About the Status of Family Separation." *Time*, September 21, 2019. https://time.com/5678313/trump-administration-fam ily-separation-lawsuits/.

Al Jazeera News. "Trump Renews Mexico Tariff Threat Amid Row Over Migration Deal." June 10, 2019. https://www.aljazeera.com/news/2019/06/trump-renews -mexico-tariff-threat-row-migration-deal-190610212227154.html.

Alsema, Adriaan. "Colombia's Unemployment Surges to 10.8%, Highest Since 2010." *Colombia Reports*, October 3, 2019. https://colombiareports.com/colom bias-unemployment-spikes-to-10-8-highest-since-2010/.

Alvarenga Venútolo, Patricia. "La Inmigración Extranjera en la Historia Costaric-cence." In *El Mito Roto: Inmigración y Emigración en Costa Rica*, edited by Carlos Sandoval Garcia, 3–24. San José, Costa Rica: Editorial UCR, 2015.

American Civil Liberties Union. "ACLU Obtains Documents Showing Widespread Abuse of Child Immigrants in U.S. Custody." May 22, 2018. https://www.aclu .org/news/aclu-obtains-documents-showing-widespread-abuse-child-immigrants -us-custody.

American Immigration Lawyers Association. "Deaths at Adult Detention Centers." Accessed January 9, 2020. https://www.aila.org/infonet/deaths-at-adult-detention -centers.

American Shipper Staff. "Trump Threatens to End NAFTA If Mexico Doesn't Help on Immigration." *American Shipper*, April 2, 2018. https://www.americanshipper .com/news/trump-threatens-to-end-nafta-if-mexico-doesnt-help-on-immigration ?autonumber=70981&infrom=right.

Amnesty International. "Fleeing for Our Lives." https://www.amnestyusa.org/fleeing -for-our-lives-central-american-migrant-crisis/.

———. "Mexico/Central America: Authorities Turning the Backs on LGBTI Refu-gees." November 27, 2017. https://www.amnesty.org/en/latest/news/2017/11/ mexico-central-america-authorities-turning-their-backs-on-lgbti-refugees/.

———. "USA: Policy of Separating Children from Parents Is Nothing Short of Tor-ture." June 18, 2018. https://www.amnesty.org/en/latest/news/2018/06/usa-family -separation-torture/.

Aparicio, Juan Ricardo, and Mario Blaser. "The 'Lettered City' and the Insurrection of Subjugated Knowledges in Latin America." *Anthropological Quarterly* 81, no. 1 (Winter 2008): 59–94.

Aratani, Lauren, and Agencies. "'Inexplicable Cruelty': US Government Sued over Family Separations at Border." *The Guardian*, February 12, 2019. https://www.the guardian.com/us-news/2019/feb/11/immigrant-families-sue-us-government-over -family-separation.

Arellano, Gustavo. "1994 California Proposition 187: Timeline of Anti-Immigrant Law." *Los Angeles Times*, October 29, 2019. https://www.latimes.com/california/ story/2019-10-06/proposition-187-timeline.

Armario, Christina. "UN Envy: As Venezuela Exodus Drags on Many Won't Go Back." *Associated Press*, November 14, 2019. https://apnews.com/867e10f67177 4bc59a2dd8885c91f241.

Arnson, Cynthia J. "The Venezuelan Refugee Crisis Is Not Just a Regional Problem: Latin American Neighbors Are Pulling More than Their Weight." *Foreign Affairs*, July 26, 2019. https://www.foreignaffairs.com/articles/venezuela/2019-07-26/ven ezuelan-refugee-crisis-not-just-regional-problem.

Attanasio, Cedar. "'It's Not Safe Here.' Migrants Detail Violence They Face as U.S. Makes Them Wait in Mexico," *Time*, June 27, 2019. https://time.com/5616370/ migrants-detail-violence-mexico/.

Baddour, Dylan. "Colombia Welcomes Millions of Venezuelans Fleeing Chaos." *The Atlantic*, January 30, 2019. https://www.theatlantic.com/international/ar chive/2019/01/colombia-welcomes-millions-venezuelans-maduro-guaido/581647/.

———. "Ecuador Shuts Its Border to Venezuelan Refugees Amid Historical Exo-dus." *Washington Post*, August 20, 2018. https://www.washingtonpost.com/world/ the_americas/ecuador-shuts-its-border-to-venezuelan-refugees-amid-historic-exod us/2018/08/20/28223fec-a48c-11e8-ad6f-080770dcddc2_story.html.

Bader, Veit. "The Ethics of Immigration." *Constellations* 12, no. 3 (2005): 331–61. https://doi.org/10.1111/j.1351-0487.2005.00420.x.

Bailey, Alison. "On Anger, Silence, and Epistemic Injustice." *Royal Institute of Philosophy Supplements* 84 (November 2018): 93–115. https://doi.org/10.1017/ S1358246118000565.

———. "Tracking Privilege-Preserving Epistemic Pushback in Feminist and Criti-cal Race Philosophy Classes." *Hypatia* 32, no. 4 (Fall 2017): 876–92. https:doi/ pdf/10.1111/hypa.12354.

———. "The Unlevel Knowing Field: An Engagement with Dotson's Third-Order Epistemic Oppression." *Social Epistemology Review and Reply Collective* 3, no. 10 (2014): 62–68.

Bala, Nila, and Arthur Rizer. "Trump's Family Separation Policy Never Ended. Here's Why." *NBC News*, July 1, 2019. https://www.nbcnews.com/think/opinion/ trump-s-family-separation-policy-never-really-ended-why-ncna1025376.

Balibar, Etienne. "Outlines of a Topography of Cruelty: Citizenship and Civility in the Era of Global Violence." *Constellations* 8, no. 1 (2001): 15–29.

———. *Politics and the Other Scene*. New York: Verso Books, 2012.

Banchon, Mirra. "EU Lawmakers Issue Call to Take in Venezuelan Migrants." *DW.com*, June 7, 2018. https://www.dw.com/en/eu-lawmakers-issue-call-to-take -in-venezuelan-migrants/a-44556414.

Barajas, Joshua. "How Trump's Family Separation Policy Has Become What It Is Today." *PBS Newshour*, June 14, 2018. https://www.pbs.org/newshour/nation/ how-trumps-family-separation-policy-has-become-what-it-is-today.

Barchfield, Jenny. "Nicaraguans Make Their Home in an Idle Costa Rican Factory." United Nations High Commission on Refugees, October 16, 2019. https://www .unhcr.org/news/stories/2019/10/5da655084/nicaraguans-home-idle-costa-rican -factory.html.

Baron, Dennis. "Official American: English Only." *PBS*, August 6, 2014. https:// www.pbs.org/speak/seatosea/officialamerican/englishonly/.

Barrett, Devlin. "DHS Secretary Kelly Says Congressional Critics Should 'Shut Up' or Change Laws." *Washington Post*, April 18, 2017. https://www.wash

ingtonpost.com/world/national-security/dhs-secretary-kelly-says-congressional
-critics-should-shut-up-or-change-laws/2017/04/18/8a2a92b6-2454-11e7-b503
-9d616bd5a305_story.html?utm_term=.c4f79cec3d4c.

Bartsfield, Jenny. "Colombia Gives Venezuela Newborns a Start in Life." *United Nations Refugee Agency*, October 14, 2019. https://www.unhcr.org/en-us/news/stories/2019/10/5da42be64/colombia-gives-venezuela-newborns-start-life.html.

Battistessa, Diego. "Una masacre silenciosa: La venezolanas muertas en el extranjero." *El Pais*, September 3, 2019. https://elpais.com/elpais/2019/09/02/planeta_futuro/1567434636_760205.html?fbclid=IwAR3MF2gjEDLJSGX8FOIIz5l7N_eh3yZPz3_BALq_2Uah3g3hp-GWZEj-hUE.

BBC News. "Nicaragua Refugees: 'I Don't Understand Why People Hate Us.'" April 18, 2019. https://www.bbc.com/news/world-latin-america-47934961.

Benhabib, Seyla. *The Rights of Others: Aliens, Residents, and Citizens*. Cambridge and New York: Cambridge University Press, 2004.

Berenstain, Nora. "Epistemic Exploitation." *Ergo: An Open Access Journal of Philosophy* 3 (2016): 569–90.

Bernstein, Hamutal, Dulce Gonzalez, Michael Karpman, and Stephen Zuckerman. "Adults in Immigrant Families Report Avoiding Routine Activities Because of Immigration Concerns." *Urban Institute*, July 24, 2019. https://www.urban.org/research/publication/adults-immigrant-families-report-avoiding-routine-activities-because-immigration-concerns.

Berry, Brian, and Robert Goodin, eds. *Free Movement: Ethical Issues in Transnational Migration of People and Money*. State College, PA: Pennsylvania State University Press, 1992.

Blitzer, Jonathon. "How Trump's Safe-Third-Country Agreement with Guatemala Fell Apart." *The New Yorker*, July 15, 2019. https://www.newyorker.com/news/news-desk/how-trumps-safe-third-country-agreement-with-guatemala-fell-apart.

Blunt, Mitch. *Systemic Indifference: Dangerous and Substandard Care in US Immigration Detention*. Human Rights Watch, 2017.

Bolaños, Rocío Loría. "Vulnerabilidad a la violencia en la inmigración." In *El Mito Roto: Inmigración y Emigración en Costa Rica*, edited by Carlos Sandoval Garcia, 221–31. San José, Costa Rica: Editorial UCR, 2015.

Borger, Julian. "Trump Plans to Cut Central America Aid Blaming Countries for Migrant Caravans." *The Guardian*, April 3, 2019. https://www.theguardian.com/world/2019/apr/03/trump-to-sanction-central-american-nations-with-aid-cuts?CMP=share_btn_link.

Bort, Ryan. "Trump Wants to Bring Back 'Large-Scale' Family Separations." *Rolling Stone*, April 8, 2019. https://www.rollingstone.com/politics/politics-news/mexico-border-family-separation-homeland-security-trump-819195/.

Brownmiller, Susan. *Against Our Will: Men, Women, and Rape*. New York: Fawcett Books, 1975.

Bump, Philip. "Here Are the Administration Officials Who Have Said that the Family Separation Policy Is Meant as a Deterrent." *Washington Post*, June 19, 2018. https://www.washingtonpost.com/news/politics/wp/2018/06/19/here-are-the-administration-officials-who-have-said-that-family-separation-is-meant-as-a-deterrent/.

Burnett, John, and Richard Gonzalez. "Thousands of Migrant Children Reported Sexual Abuse While in Custody." *National Public Radio*, February 26, 2019.

Burnett, John, and Mara Liasson. "Trump Administration Mulls Tougher Immigration Policies Amid DHS Shake-UP." *National Public Radio*, April 9, 2019. https://www.npr.org/2019/04/09/711446892/trump-administration-mulls-tougher-immigration-policies-amid-dhs-shake-up.

Bush, Laura. "Laura Bush: Separating Children from Their Parents at the Border 'Breaks My Heart.'" *Washington Post*, June 17, 2018. https://www.washingtonpost.com/opinions/laura-bush-separating-children-from-their-parents-at-the-border-breaks-my-heart/2018/06/17/f2df517a-7287-11e8-9780-b1dd6a09b549_story.html?noredirect=on&utm_term=.df7882ab2112.

Cahill, Ann J. *Overcoming Objectification: A Carnal Ethic*. New York: Routledge, 2012.

Calderón-Steck, Flora V., and Roger E. Bonilla-Carrión. "Algunos aspectos sociodemográficos de los estadounidenses, canadienses y eurpeos residentes en Costa Rica según el Censo 2000." In *El Mito Roto: Inmigración y Emigración en Costa Rica*, edited by Carlos Sandoval Garcia, 51–88. San José, Costa Rica: Editorial UCR, 2015.

Caputi, Jane. *The Age of Sex Crime*. Bowling Green, OH: Bowling Green University Popular Press, 1987.

Carens, Joseph. "Aliens and Citizens: The Case for Open Borders." *The Review of Politics* 49, no. 2 (Spring 1987): 251–73.

———. *Ethics of Immigration*. New York and Oxford: Oxford University Press, 2014.

Castro-Gómez, Santiago. "(Post)Coloniality for Dummies: Latin American Perspectives on Modernity, Coloniality, and the Geopolitics of Knowledge." In *Coloniality at Large: Latin America and the Postcolonial Debate*, edited by Mabel Moraña, Enrique Dussell, and Carlos A. Jáuregui. Durham and London: Duke University Press, 2008.

Center for the Study of Social Policy. "Zero Tolerance Immigration Policy Is a Cruel and Immoral Human Rights Violation." June 19, 2018. https://www.cssp.org/media-center/press-releases/zero-tolerance-immigration-policy-is-a-cruel-and-immoral-human-rights-violation.

Cohen, Elizabeth. "Pediatricians Share Migrant Children's Disturbing Drawings of the Time in US Custody." *CNN*, July 4, 2019. https://edition.cnn.com/2019/07/03/health/migrant-drawings-cbp-children/index.html.

Cole, Phillip, and Christopher Heath Wellman. *Debating the Ethics of Immigration: Is There a Right to Exclude*. Oxford and New York: Oxford University Press, 2011.

Collins, Joshua. "Venezuelans Stranded as Ecuador Imposes New Visa Rules." *Al Jazeera News*, August 26, 2019. https://www.aljazeera.com/news/2019/08/venezuelans-stranded-ecuador-imposes-visa-rules-190826134509203.html.

Collins, Randall. "Three Faces of Cruelty: Towards a Comparative Sociology of Violence." *Theory and Society* 1, no. 4 (Winter 1974): 415–40.

Colombia Reports. "Crime and Security in Bogotá." July 19, 2019. https://colombiareports.com/bogota-crime-security-statistics/.

Congressional Research Service. "U.S. Strategy for Engaging with Central America: Policy Issues for Congress." June 12, 2019. https://fas.org/sgp/crs/row/R44812.pdf.

Conley, Julia. "Immigrant Groups Mobilize to Combat Trump Administration's Plan to End DACA." *Common Dreams News*, September 4, 2017. https://www.com mondreams.org/news/2017/09/04/immigrant-groups-mobilize-combat-trumps -cruel-and-heartless-plan-end-daca.

Cooke, Kristina, Mica Rosenberg, and Reade Levinson. "Exclusive: U.S. Migrant Policy Sends Thousands of Children, Including Babies, Back to Mexico." *Reuters*, October 11, 2019. https://www.reuters.com/article/us-usa-immigration-babies -exclusive/exclusive-u-s-migrant-policy-sends-thousands-of-children-including -babies-back-to-mexico-idUSKBN1WQ1H1.

Copp, Nelson. *"Wetbacks" and Braceros: Mexican Migrant Laborers and American Immigration Policy, 1930–1960*. San Francisco: R and E Research Associates, 1971.

Council on Hemispheric Affairs. "Programa Frontera Sur: The Mexican Government's Faulty Immigration Policy." October 26, 2016. http://www.coha.org/ programa-frontera-sur-the-mexican-governments-faulty-immigration-policy/.

Dart, Tom. "Fearing Deportation, Undocumented Immigrants Wary of Reporting Crimes." *The Guardian*, March 23, 2017. https://www.theguardian .com/usnews/2017/mar/23/undocumented-immigrants-wary-report-crimes deportation?CMP=share_btn_link.

Davis, Jeffrey. "US 'Zero-Tolerance' Immigration Policy Still Violating Fundamental Human Rights Laws." *The Conversation*, June 27, 2018. https://theconversation .com/us-zero-tolerance-immigration-policy-still-violating-fundamental-human -rights-laws-98615.

Del Real, Jose A. "'They Were Abusing Us the Whole Way': A Tough Path for Gay and Trans Migrants." *New York Times*, July 11, 2018. https://www.nytimes .com/2018/07/11/us/lgbt-migrants-abuse.html.

Department of Homeland Security. *FY19 Budget Brief*. https://www.dhs.gov/sites/ default/files/publications/DHS%20BIB%202019.pdf.

———. "Migrant Protection Protocols." January 24, 2019. https://www.dhs.gov/ news/2019/01/24/migrant-protection-protocols.

Diaz, Daniella. "Kelly: DHS Is Considering Separating Undocumented Children from Their Parents at the Border." *CNN*, March 7, 2017. https://www.cnn .com/2017/03/06/politics/john-kelly-separating-children-from-parents-immigra tion-border/index.html.

Diaz, Fabio Andres, and Magda Jiménez. "Colombia's Murder Rate Is at an All-Time Low But Its Activists Keep Getting Killed." *The Conversation*, April 6, 2018. http://theconversation.com/colombias-murder-rate-is-at-an-all-time-low-but-its -activists-keep-getting-killed-91602.

Dickerson, Caitlyn. "Hundreds of Immigrant Children Have Been Taken from Parents at U.S. Border." *New York Times*, April 20, 2018. https://www.nytimes .com/2018/04/20/us/immigrant-children-separation-ice.html.

Dickerson, Caitlyn, and Zolan Kanno-Youngs. "Thousands Are Targeted as ICE Prepares to Raid Undocumented Migrant Families." *New York Times*, July 7, 2019. https://www.nytimes.com/2019/07/11/us/politics/ice-families-deport .html?smid=nytcore-ios-share.

Dinan, Stephen. "Secretary Kelly Tells DHS Critics to 'Shut Up,' Let Agents do Their Jobs." *Washington Times*, April 18, 2017. https://www.washingtontimes.com/news/2017/apr/18/dhs-chief-critics-shut-up-let-agents-do-their-jobs/.

Dotson, Kristie. "A Cautionary Tale: On Limiting Epistemic Oppression." *Frontiers: A Journal of Women Studies* 33, no. 1 (2012): 24–47.

———. "Conceptualizing Epistemic Oppression." *Social Epistemology* 28, no. 2 (2014): 115–38.

———. "How Is This Paper Philosophy?" *Comparative Philosophy* 3, no. 1 (2012): 3–29.

———. "Tracking Epistemic Violence, Tracking Practices of Silencing." *Hypatia* 26, no. 2 (Spring 2011): 236–57.

Dussel, Enrique. *Philosophy of Liberation*. New York: Orbis Books, 1985.

Economist, The. "Donald Trump Cuts off Aid to Central America." April 4, 2019. https://www.economist.com/the-americas/2019/04/04/donald-trump-cuts-off-aid-to-central-america.

Escobar, Natalie. "Family Separation Isn't New." *The Atlantic*, August 14, 2018. https://www.theatlantic.com/family/archive/2018/08/us-immigration-policy-has-traumatized-children-for-nearly-100-years/567479/.

"Fact Sheet: The Cost of Immigration Enforcement and Border Security." *American Immigration Council*, October 14, 2019. https://www.americanimmigrationcouncil.org/research/the-cost-of-immigration-enforcement-and-border-security.

Feingold, Spencer. "Costa Rica Overwhelmed with Nicaraguan Asylum Seekers." *CNN*, August 1, 2018. https://edition.cnn.com/2018/08/01/americas/costa-rica-overwhelmed-nicaraguan-asylum-seekers-unhcr/index.html.

Fernandez, Manny. "You Have to Pay with Your Body: The Hidden Nightmare of Sexual Violence on the Border." *New York Times*, March 3, 2019. https://www.nytimes.com/2019/03/03/us/border-rapes-migrant-women.html.

Fine, Sarah. "The Ethics of Immigration: Self-Determination and the Right to Exclude." *Philosophy Compass* 8, no. 3 (2013): 254–68.

Fine, Sarah, and Lea Ypi, eds. *Migration in Political Theory: The Ethics of Movement and Membership*. New York and Oxford: Oxford University Press, 2016.

Fletcher, Robert. *Romancing the Wild: Cultural Dimensions, of Ecotourism*. Durham, NC: Duke University Press, 2014.

Fouratt, Caitlin. "The Rise of Anti-Immigrant Attitudes, Violence and Nationalism in Costa Rica." *The Conversation*, March 28, 2017. https://theconversation.com/the-rise-of-anti-immigrant-attitudes-violence-and-nationalism-in-costa-rica-73899.

Frazee, Gretchen. "Why Trump Wants to Detain Immigrant Children Longer." *PBS Newshour*, August 21, 2019. https://www.pbs.org/newshour/nation/why-trump-wants-to-detain-immigrant-children-longer.

Fregoso, Rosa-Linda, and Cynthia Bejarano. "Introduction." In *Terrorizing Women: Femicide in the Américas*, edited by Rosa-Linda Fregoso and Cynthia Bejarano, 1–42. Durham and London: Duke University Press, 2010.

Frej, Willa. "Laura Ingraham Compares Child Immigrant Detention Centers to Summer Camps." *HuffPost*, June 19, 2018. https://www.huffingtonpost.com/entry/laura-ingraham-immigrant-summer-camp_us_5b28b769e4b0f0b9e9a4840c.

Fricker, Miranda. *Epistemic Injustice: Power and Ethics of Knowing*. New York and London: Oxford University Press, 2009.

Frye, Marilyn. *The Politics of Reality*. California: The Crossing Press, 1983.

Frye Jacobson, Matthew. *Whiteness of a Different Color: European Immigrants and the Alchemy of Race*. Cambridge, MA: Harvard University Press, 1999.

Gambino, Lauren, and David Agren. "Trump Announces Tariffs on Mexico Until 'Immigration Remedied.'" *The Guardian*, May 31, 2019. https://www.theguardian.com/us-news/2019/may/30/trump-mexico-tariffs-migration.

Ganster, Paul, with David M. Lorey. *The U.S.-Mexican Border Today: Conflict and Cooperation in Historical Perspective*. Third edition. Lanham, Boulder, New York, London: Rowman & Littlefield, 2016.

Garcia, Dulce. "We Can't Go Back to the Shadows: Six Dreamers Tell Their Stories." *Mother Jones*, September 26, 2018. https://www.motherjones.com/politics/2018/09/we-cant-go-back-to-the-shadows-six-dreamers-tell-their-stories/.

Gatto, Madeleine. "Pregnant Women Are Being Abused and Neglected in Immigration Detention Centers." *Ms.*, July 13, 2018. http://msmagazine.com/blog/2018/07/13/pregnant-women-abused-neglected-immigration-detention-centers/.

Gervis, Rick, and Alan Gomez. "Trump Administration Has Separated Hundreds of Children from Their Migrant Families Since 2018." *USA Today*, May 2, 2019. https://www.usatoday.com/story/news/nation/2019/05/02/border-family-separations-trump-administration-border-patrol/3563990002/.

Glass, Ira. "Prologue: The Out Crowd." *This American Life*, National Public Radio, November 15, 2019. https://www.thisamericanlife.org/688/the-out-crowd.

Goldade, Kate. "Reproducción Transnacional: La salud reproductiva, las limitaciones, y las contradicciones para las migrantes laborales nicaragüenses en Costa Rica." In *El Mito Roto: Inmigración y Emigración en Costa Rica*, edited by Carlos Sandoval Garcia, 233–59. San José, Costa Rica, Editorial UCR, 2015.

Goldberg, Beverly. "La mayoria de muertes de venezolanas en el país, entre 2018 y 2019, fueron feminicidios." *El Espectador*, January 29, 2020. https://www.elespectador.com/noticias/nacional/la-mayoria-de-muertes-de-venezolanas-en-el-pais-entre-2018-y-2019-fueron-feminicidios-articulo-902062.

Gonzalez, Richard. "ACLU Report: Detained Immigrant Children Subjected to Widespread Abuse By Officials." *National Public Radio*, May 23, 2018. https://www.npr.org/sections/thetwo-way/2018/05/23/613907893/aclu-report-detained-immigrant-children-subjected-to-widespread-abuse-by-officia.

Goodstein, Laurie. "I Know I'll Be Criticized: The Latino Evangelical Who Advises Trump on Immigration." *New York Times*, March 27, 2018. https://www.nytimes.com/2018/03/27/us/evangelical-dreamers-rodriguez.html.

Grabell, Michael. "Exploitation at the Chicken Plant." *New Yorker*, May 8, 2017. https://www.newyorker.com/magazine/2017/05/08/exploitation-and-abuse-at-the-chicken-plant.

Graham, David. "Are Children Being Kept in 'Cages' at the Border?" *The Atlantic*, June 18, 2018. https://www.theatlantic.com/politics/archive/2018/06/ceci-nest-pas-une-cage/563072.

Green, Emily. "As Trump Knocks Mexico on Immigration, López Obrador Keeps Quiet." *Public Radio International,* April 2, 2019. https://www.pri.org/sto ries/2019-04-02/trump-knocks-mexico-immigration-l-pez-obrador-keeps-quiet.

———. "Take the Long Way Home: The Out Crowd." *This American Life,* National Public Radio, November 15, 2019. https://www.thisamericanlife.org/688/the-out -crowd.

Guarascio, Francesco. "Asylum Applications in EU Rise as More Venezuelans Seek Refuge." *Reuters,* June 24, 2019. https://www.reuters.com/article/us-eu rope-refugees/asylum-applications-in-eu-rise-as-more-venezuelans-seek-refuge -idUSKCN1TP0LQ.

Gumbel, Andrew. "'They were laughing at us': Immigrants Tell of Cruelty, Illness and Filth in US Detention." *The Guardian,* September 12, 2018. https://www.theguard ian.com/us-news/2018/sep/12/us-immigration-detention-facilities.

Haag, Matthew. "Thousands of Immigrant Children Said They Were Sexually Abused in U.S. Detention Centers, Report Says." *New York Times,* February 27, 2019. https://www.nytimes.com/2019/02/27/us/immigrant-children-sexual-abuse.html.

Habib, Yamily. "Violence and Abuse: The Daily Life of Immigrants in Detention Centers." *Al Día,* July 20, 2018. http://aldianews.com/articles/politics/immigration/ violence-and-abuse-daily-life-immigrants-detention-centers/53396.

Harte, Julia, and Tim Reid. "Trump Cuts Aid to Central American Countries as Migrant Crisis Deepens." *Reuters,* March 30, 2019. https://www.reuters.com/ar ticle/us-usa-immigration-trump/trump-cuts-aid-to-central-american-countries-as -migrant-crisis-deepens-idUSKCN1RC013.

Haslanger, Sally. "Changing the Ideology and Culture of Philosophy: Not by Rea-son (Alone)." *Hypatia* 23, no. 2 (2008): 210–23. https://doi.org/10.1111/j.1527 -2001.2008.tb01195.x.

Hauslohner, Abigail. "ICE Agents Raid Mississippi Work Sites, Arrest 680 People in Largest-Scale Single State Immigration Enforcement Action in U.S. History." *Washington Post,* August 7, 2019. https://www.washingtonpost.com/immigration/ ice-agents-raid-miss-work-sites-arrest-680-people-in-largest-single-state-immi gration-enforcement-action-in-us-history/2019/08/07/801d5cfe-b94e-11e9-b3b4 -2bb69e8c4e39_story.html.

Helmore, Edward. "More Major US Immigration Raids Likely Despite Outcry." *The Guardian,* August 10, 2019. https://www.theguardian.com/us-news/2019/aug/10/ ice-raids-us-immigration-workplaces.

Hernández, Kelly Lytle. *Migra! A History of the U.S. Border Patrol.* Berkeley, Los Angeles, and London: University of California Press, 2010.

Hinojosa Hernández, Leandra. "Feminist Approaches to Border Studies and Gender Violence: Family Separation as Reproductive Injustice." *Women's Studies in Com-munication* 42, no. 2 (2019): 120–24.

Holder, Sarah. "The Real Intention Behind the Recent ICE Raids Is Intimidation." *Pacific Standard,* July 30, 2019. https://psmag.com/social-justice/the-real-intention -behind-the-recent-ice-raids-is-intimidation.

HSBNoticias.com. "En el centro de Villavicencio atacaron a bala a trabajadoras sexuales venozalanas." April 28, 2019. https://hsbnoticias.com/noticias/judicial/en-el-centro-de-villavicencio-atacaron-bala-trabajadoras-522093.

Human Rights Watch. *"The Guerrillas Are the Police": Social Control and Abuses by Armed Groups in Colombia's Arauca Province and Venezuela's Apure State.* January 22, 2020. https://www.hrw.org/report/2020/01/22/guerrillas-are-police/social-control-and-abuses-armed-groups-colombias-arauca.

———. "We Can't Help You Here: US Returns Asylum Seekers to Mexico." July 2, 2019. https://www.hrw.org/report/2019/07/02/we-cant-help-you-here/us-returns-asylum-seekers-mexico.

"ICE Raids: 300 People Released Amid Outrage over Mississippi Arrests." *BBC News*, August 9, 2019. https://www.bbc.com/news/world-us-canada-49283157.

Immigration Reform and Control Act, 1986.

Incite! "Immigration and Border Policies." Accessed January 26, 2020. http://www.incite-national.org/page/immigration-policing-border-violence.

Inspector General of the Department of Homeland Security. "Concerns About ICE Detainee Treatment and Care at Detention Facilities." December 11, 2017. https://www.oig.dhs.gov/sites/default/files/assets/2017-12/OIG-18-32-Dec17.pdf.

International Refuge Committee. "Needs Assessment Report: Venezuelan Migrants in Colombia." November 6, 2018. https://www.rescue.org/sites/default/files/document/3302/ircassessment-venezuelansincolombianov2018.pdf.

Jiménez Matarrita, Alexander. *El imposible país de los filósofos.* San José, Costa Rica: Editorial Universidad de Costa Rica, 2013.

———. *La vida en otra parte: Migraciones y cambios culturales en Costa Rica.* Editorial Arlekin, 2009.

Jordan, Miriam. "ICE Arrests Hundreds in Mississippi Raids Targeting Immigrant Workers." *New York Times*, August 7, 2019. https://www.nytimes.com/2019/08/07/us/ice-raids-mississippi.html.

———. "Judge Blocks Trump Administration Plan to Detain Migrant Children." *New York Times*, September 27, 2019. https://www.nytimes.com/2019/09/27/us/migrant-children-flores-court.html.

———. "More than 2000 Migrants Were Targeted in Raids. 35 Were Arrested." *New York Times*, July 23, 2019. https://www.nytimes.com/2019/07/23/us/ice-raids-apprehensions.html.

Jordan, Miriam, and Caitlyn Dickerson. "U.S. Continues to Separate Migrant Families Despite Rollback of Policy." *New York Times*, March 9, 2019. https://www.nytimes.com/2019/03/09/us/migrant-family-separations-border.html.

Jurecic, Quinta. "A Choice Between Cruelty and Mercy." *The Atlantic*, June 18, 2018. https://www.theatlantic.com/politics/archive/2018/06/border-policies-antigone/563126/.

Kahn, Carrie. "200 Nicaraguans Claim Asylum Daily in Costa Rica, Fleeing Violent Unrest." *National Public Radio*, August 26, 2018. https://www.npr.org/2018/08/26/641375695/200-nicaraguans-claim-asylum-daily-in-costa-rica-fleeing-violent-unrest.

Kang, Deborah. "15 Years After Its Creation, Critics Want to Abolish ICE." Interview by Meghna Chakrabarti. *Here and Now*, NPR, June 25, 2018. http://www.wbur.org/hereandnow/2018/06/25/immigration-abolish-ice.

Kanno-Youngs, Zolan, and Elisabeth Malkin. "U.S. Agreement with El Salvador Seeks to Divert Asylum Seekers." *New York Times*, September 20, 2019. https://www.nytimes.com/2019/09/20/us/politics/us-asylum-el-salvador.html.

Kelly, John. "Full Interview with DHS Secretary John Kelly." Interview by Wolf Blitzer. *The Situation Room*, *CNN*, March 6, 2017. Video, 9:39. https://edition.cnn.com/videos/politics/2017/03/06/john-kelly-dhs-trump-travel-ban-wiretap-tsr-intv-full.cnn.

———. "White House Chief of Staff John Kelly's Interview with NP." Interview by John Burnett. *National Public Radio*, May 11, 2018. https://www.npr.org/2018/05/11/610116389/transcript-white-house-chief-of-staff-john-kellys-interview-with-npr.

Kennedy, Merrit. "Venezuelan Refugees and Migrants Top 4 Million, U.N Says." *National Public Radio*, June 7, 2019. https://www.npr.org/2019/06/07/730687807/u-n-says-more-than-4-million-people-have-left-venezuela.

Khan, Mahwish. "CHARTS: Border/Enforcement Spending and Deportation Levels Continue to Skyrocket Under Obama." *America's Voice*, May 25, 2019. https://americasvoice.org/research/charts_enforcement_spending_and_deportation_levels_continue_to_skyrock/.

Koerner, Lucas. "Two Venezuelan Women Killed in Northern Colombia." *Venezuelanalysis*, March 7, 2018. https://venezuelanalysis.com/news/13706.

Koerner, Lucas, and Ricardo Vaz. "One Venezuelan Migrant Killed Every Day in Colombia." *Venezuelanalysis*, August 28, 2019. https://venezuelanalysis.com/news/14641.

Kriel, Lomi, and Dug Begley. "Trump Administration Still Separating Hundreds of Migrant Children at the Border through Often Questionable Claims of Danger." *Houston Chronicle*, June 22, 2019. https://www.houstonchronicle.com/news/houston-texas/houston/article/Trump-administration-still-separating-hundreds-of-14029494.php.

Kteily, Nour, and Emile Bruneau. "Backlash: The Politics and Real-World Consequences of Minority Group Dehumanization." *Personality and Social Psychology Bulletin* 43, no. (2017): 87–104.

Kukathas, Chandran. "Are Refugees Special?" In *Migration in Political Theory: The Ethics of Movement and Membership*, edited by Sarah Fine and Lea Ypi. New York and Oxford: Oxford University Press, 2016.

Kurmanaev, Anatoly, and Jenny Carolina González. "Colombia Offers Citizenship to 24,000 Children of Venezuelan Refugees." *New York Times*, August 5, 2019. https://www.nytimes.com/2019/08/05/world/americas/colombia-citizenship-venezuelans.html.

La Lengua Caribe. "'La Chama' Fue Asesinada de Dos Balazos en Las Maravillas." March 3, 2019. https://www.lalenguacaribe.co/2019/judicial/la-chama-fue-asesinada-de-dos-balazos-en-las-maravillas/.

Latin American Post. "These Are the Numbers of Feminicides in Latin America." August 24, 2019. https://latinamericanpost.com/29792-these-are-the-numbers-of -feminicides-in-latin-america.

Legarde y de los Ríos, Marcela. "Preface." In *Terrorizing Women: Femicide in the Américas*, edited by Rosa-Linda Fregoso and Cynthia Bejarano, xi–xxv. Durham and London: Duke University Press, 2010.

Limbaugh, Rush. "Without Zero Tolerance America Will Cease to Be." *The Rush Limbaugh Show*, June 21, 2018. https://www.rushlimbaugh.com/daily/2018/06/21/ without-zero-tolerance-our-culture-will-be-erased/.

Lind, Dara. "The First Immigration Raids of the Trump Era, Explained." *Vox*, February 14, 2017. https://www.vox.com/policy-and-politics/2017/2/14/14596640/immi gration-ice-raids.

Linthicum, Kate. "Salvadoran Immigrant Held at Adelanto ICE Facility Dies." *Los Angeles Times*, April 7, 2015. https://www.latimes.com/local/lanow/la-me-ln -detainee-death-20150407-story.html.

Liu, Amy H., and Ananda Edward Sokhey. "When and Why Do U.S. States Makes English Their Official Language?" *Washington Post*, June 18, 2014. https:// www.washingtonpost.com/news/monkey-cage/wp/2014/06/18/when-and-why -do-u-s-states-make-english-their-officialanguage/?noredirect=on&utm_term= .d3937fb44928.

Long, Colleen, and Astrid Galvin. "US, El Salvador Sign Asylum Deal, Details to Be Worked Out." *Associated Press*, September 20, 2019. https://www.apnews.com/ de6a00632755415fad2a952c7cd4bd72.

Lopez, German. "The Research on Race Explains Trump's Family Separation Policies." *Vox*, June 19, 2018. https://www.vox.com/identities/2018/6/19/17478970/ trump-family-separation-immigration-policy-racism.

López Ruiz, Luis Ángel, and David Delgado Montaldo. "Actitudes y percepciones segmentadas: prejucios hacia la población nicaragüense en Costa Rica." In *Migraciones en América Central: Políticas, territorios y actores*, edited by Carlos Sandoval Garcia, 237–59. San José, Costa Rica: Editorial UCR, 2016.

Lou, Michelle. "Tucker Carlson: Keeping Immigrant Families Together Threatens 'Your Country.'" *Huffington Post*, June 19, 2018. https://www.huffingtonpost.com/ entry/tucker-carlson-immigration-separation_us_5b28f904e4b05d6c16c7536e

Lugones, María. "Heterosexualism and the Colonial/Modern Gender System." *Hypatia* 22, no. 1 (Winter 2007): 186–209.

———. "Toward a Decolonial Feminism." *Hypatia* 25, no. 4 (Fall 2010): 742–59.

Macías-Rojas, Patrisia. *From Deportation to Prison: The Politics of Immigration Enforcement in Post-Civil Rights America*. New York: New York University Press, 2016.

"Man Threatens to Call ICE on Servers Speaking Spanish." *NBC News*, May 17, 2018.

"Man Yells at People in Restaurant for Speaking Spanish || ViralHog." YouTube Video, 0:55. "ViralHog," May 17, 2018. https://www.youtube.com/watch?v= -wGOV2jGk6E.

"Man Yells at Stranger for Speaking Spanish|CNN." YouTube Video, 1:35. *CNN*, May 23, 2017. https://www.youtube.com/watch?v=_a-NSz_CzIM.

Masís Fernández, Kevin, and Laura Paniagua Arguedas. "Chistes Sobre Nicaragüenses en Costa Rica: barreras simbólicas, mecanismos de control social, constructores de identidades." In *El Mito Roto: Inmigración y Emigración en Costa Rica*, edited by Carlos Sandoval Garcia, 339–55. San José, Costa Rica: Editorial UCR, 2015.

Matalon, Lorne. "Programa Frontera Sur: Tracking U.S Influence on Mexico's Southern Border Plan." May 28, 2017. http://lornematalon.com/2017/05/28/programa-frontera-sur-tracking-u-s-influence-on-mexicos-southern-border-plan/.

Matarrita-Cascante, David, and Gabriela Stocks. "Amenity Migration to the Global South: Implications for Community Development." *GeoForum* 49 (2013): 91–102.

Matthews, Chris. "Matthews: Trump's Family Separation Policy Is Cruel." *NBC News*, June 18, 2018. https://www.nbcnews.com/dateline/video/matthews-trump-s-family-separation-policy-is-cruel-1258664515965.

McDonnell, Patrick J. "Mexico Blasts U.S. Family Separation Policy as 'Violation of Human Rights." *Los Angeles Times*, June 19, 2018. http://www.latimes.com/world/mexico-americas/la-fg-mexico-family-separation-20180619-story.html.

McKinnon, Rachel. "Allies Behaving Badly: Gaslighting as Epistemic Injustice." In *Routledge Handbook on Epistemic Injustice*, edited by Gaile Pohlhaus Jr., Ian James Kidd, and Jose Medina. New York: Routledge, 2017.

Medina, José. *Epistemologies of Resistance: Gender and Racial Oppression, Epistemic Injustice, and Resistant Imaginations.* London and New York: Oxford University Press, 2011.

Mendoza, José Jorge. "Illegal: White Supremacy and Immigration Status." In *The Ethics and Politics of Immigration: Core Issues and Emerging Trends*, edited by Alex Sager, 201–20. New York and London: Rowman & Littlefield, 2016.

———. *Moral and Political Philosophy of Immigration: Liberty, Security, and Equality.* Lanham, Boulder, New York, and London: Lexington Books, 2017.

Merchant, Nomann. "Immigrant Kids Seen Held in Fenced Cages at Border Facility." *Associated Press*, June 18, 2018. https://www.apnews.com/6e04c6ee01dd46669ed dba9d3333f6d5/Immigrant-kids-seen-held-in-fenced-cages-at-border-facility.

Merkley, Jeff. *America Is Better than This: Trump's War Against Migrant Families.* New York and Boston: Twelve, 2019.

Mexico News Daily. "Mexico Rejects US Plan to Extend 'Stay in Mexico' Policy for Asylum Seekers." March 13, 2019. https://mexiconewsdaily.com/news/mexico-rejects-us-plan/.

Miller, David. "Is There a Human Right to Migrate?" In *Migration in Political Theory: The Ethics of Movement and Membership*, edited by Sarah Fine and Lea Ypi. New York and Oxford: Oxford University Press, 2016.

———. *Strangers in Our Midst: The Political Philosophy of Immigration.* Cambridge, MA, and London: Harvard University Press, 2016.

Mills, Charles. *The Racial Contract.* New York: Cornell University Press, 1999.

Mindock, Clark. "UN Says Trump Separation of Migrant Children with Parents 'May Amount to Torture,' in Damning Condemnation." *Independent*, June 22, 2018.

https://www.independent.co.uk/news/world/americas/us-politics/un-trump-children
-family-torture-separation-border-mexico-border-ice-detention-a8411676.html.

———. "US Workplace Immigration Raids Surge 400% in 2018." *Independent*, December 12, 2018. https://www.independent.co.uk/news/world/americas/us-politics/
ice-immigration-workplace-migrants-undocumented-immigrants-raids-trump
-obama-2018-a8678746.html.

Miroff, Nick. "Trump Administration Reaches Deal to Send Asylum Seekers to El
Salvador in an Effort to Deter Migrants from Entering the United States." *Washington Post*, September 20, 2019. https://www.washingtonpost.com/immigration/
trump-administration-reaches-deal-to-send-asylum-seekers-to-el-salvador-in-an
-effort-to-deter-migrants-from-entering-the-united-states/2019/09/20/17350a16-db
bd-11e9-ac63-3016711543fe_story.html.

Molina, Ivan. *Costarricence por dicha: Identidad nacional y cambio cultural en Costa
Rica durante los siglos XIX y XX*. San José, Costa Rica: Editorial UCR, 2002.

Moloney, Anastasia. "Colombia Confronts Femicide, the 'Most Extreme Form of
Violence against Women.'" *Reuters*, August 20, 2015. https://www.reuters.com/ar
ticle/us-colombia-women-murder/colombia-confronts-femicide-the-most-extreme
-form-of-violence-against-women-idUSKCN0QP0CM20150820.

———. "Is South America Closing Its 'Open Door' on Venezuelans?" *Reuters*, August 8, 2019. https://www.reuters.com/article/us-venezuela-migration-analysis/
is-south-america-closing-its-open-door-on-venezuelans-idUSKCN1UY27D.

Monárrez Fragoso, Julia. "Feminicidio Sexual Serial en Cuidad Juárez: 1993–2001."
Debate Feminista 25, no. 13 (2002): 279–305.

Monroe Doctrine, 1823.

Montoya-Galvez, Camilo. "U.S. Cuts Millions in Aid to Central America, Fulfilling
Trump Vow." *CBS News*, June 18, 2019. https://www.cbsnews.com/news/us-cuts
-millions-in-aid-to-central-america-fulfilling-trumps-vow/.

Morrissey, Marietta. "Imaginaries of North American Lifestyle Migrants in Costa
Rica." *Population Space Place* 24 (2018): 1–9. https://doi.org/10.1002/psp.2168.

Narea, Nicole. "Trump's Agreements in Central America Could Dismantle the
Asylum System as We Know It." *Vox*, September 26, 2019. https://www.vox
.com/2019/9/26/20870768/trump-agreement-honduras-guatemala-el-salvador
-explained.

Naturalization Act of 1790. https://www.mountvernon.org/education/primary
-sources-2/article/naturalization-acts-of-1790-and-1795/.

Navas, Gregory. 1983. El Norte. English. Public Broadcasting Service.

Negrinia, Mario, and Maria Verza. "Fate in Limbo, Many Nicaraguans Exiles
Struggle in Costa Rica." *Associated Press*, April 1, 2019. https://apnews.com/
de1f373d910e48258464e84c40a2814b.

Ngai, Mae. *Impossible Subjects: Illegal Immigrants and the Making of Modern
America.* Princeton, NJ: Princeton University Press, 2004.

Oberman, Kieran. "Immigration, Global Poverty, and the Right to Stay." *Political
Studies* 59 (2011): 253–68.

Observatorio Feminicidios Colombia. "Boletín Vivas Nos Queremos: Femicidios
de Migrantes Venezolanas en Colombia Enero a Abril 2019." Accessed Decem-

ber 20, 2019. http://observatoriofeminicidioscolombia.org/attachments/article/391/
Bolet%C3%ADn%20Vivas%20Nos%20Queremos%20-%20Feminicidio%20
de%20mujeres%20migrantes%20venezolanas%20en%20territorio%20colombi
ano%20-%20Enero%20.pdf.

Ochoa Espejo, Paulina. "Taking Place Seriously: Territorial Presence and the Rights
of Immigrants." *The Journal of Political Philosophy* 24, no. 1 (2016): 67–87.

O'Connor, Ema, and Nidhi Prakash. "Pregnant Women Say They Miscarried in
Immigration Detention and Didn't Get the Care They Needed." *BuzzFeed*, July
9, 2018. https://www.buzzfeednews.com/article/emaoconnor/pregnant-migrant
-women-miscarriage-cpb-ice-detention-trump.

Office of the Inspector General, Department of Homeland Security. "Management
Alert—DHS Needs to Address Dangerous Overcrowding and Prolonged Detention
of Children and Adults in the Rio Grande Valley." July 2, 2019.

Olorunnipa, Toluse, Tamara Thueringer, and Jennifer Epstein. "President Trump
Says Family Separations May Deter Illegal Immigration." *Time*, October 14, 2018.
https://time.com/5424225/trump-family-separation-illegal-immigration/.

Oppenheimer, Andres. "Millions Are Fleeing Venezuela. Why Won't President Trump
Give Refugees TPS?" *Miami Herald*, October 11, 2019. https://www.miamiherald
.com/news/local/news-columns-blogs/andres-oppenheimer/article235948032.html.

Organization of American States. *Report to Address the Regional Crisis Caused
by Venezuela's Migrant and Refugee Flows.* June 2019. http://www.oas.org/
documents/eng/press/OAS-Report-to-Address-the-regional-crisis-caused-by
-Venezuelas-migrant.pdf.

O'Toole, Molly. "Asylum Officers Rebel Against Trump Immigration Policies They
Say Are Immoral and Illegal." *Los Angeles Times*, November 15, 2019. https://
www.latimes.com/politics/story/2019-11-15/asylum-officers-revolt-against-trump
-policies-they-say-are-immoral-illegal.

———. "Goodbye Stranger: The Out Crowd." *This American Life*, National Public
Radio, November 15, 2019. https://www.thisamericanlife.org/688/the-out-crowd.

———. "Venezuela, Now a Top Source of U.S. Asylum Claims, Poses a Challenge
for Trump." *Los Angeles Times*, June 5, 2019. https://www.latimes.com/politics/
la-na-pol-trump-venezuela-asylum-immigration-20190605-story.html.

O'Toole, Molly, and Molly Hennesy-Fiske. "Trump Administration Plans to End Limits on Child Detention." *Los Angeles Times*, August 21, 2019. https://www.latimes
.com/politics/story/2019-08-21/trump-child-detention-limits-flores-agreement.

Owen, David. "In Loco Civitatis: On the Normative Basis of the Institution of Refugeehood and Responsibilities for Refugees." In *Migration in Political Theory: The
Ethics of Movement and Membership*, edited by Sarah Fine and Lea Ypi. New York
and Oxford: Oxford University Press, 2016.

Partlow, Joshua. "They Fled Violence in Nicaragua by the Thousands. What
Awaits Them in Costa Rica?" *Washington Post*, September 2, 2018. https://www
.washingtonpost.com/world/the_americas/they-fled-violence-in-nicaragua-by-the
-thousands-what-awaits-them-in-costa-rica/2018/09/01/51d3f7ee-a62c-11e8-ad6f
-080770dcddc2_story.html.

Palacios, Claudia. "Paren de parir." *El Tiempo*, June 12, 2019. https://www.eltiempo
.com/opinion/columnistas/claudia-palacios/paren-de-parir-columna-de-claudia
-isabel-palacios-giraldo-374742.

Perry, David M. "ICE Keeps Raiding Hospitals and Mistreating Disabled Children."
Pacific Standard, January 15, 2018. https://psmag.com/social-justice/ice-keeps
-raiding-hospitals-and-harming-disabled-children.

Phillips, Kristine. "ICE Arrests Nearly 150 Meat Plant Workers in Latest Immigration Raid in Ohio." *Washington Post*, June 20, 2018. https://www.washingtonpost
.com/news/post-nation/wp/2018/06/20/ice-arrests-nearly-150-meat-plant-workers
-in-latest-immigration-raid-in-ohio/.

Pineda, Esther. "Explotadas y asesinadas: la vulnerabilidad de las mujeres venezolanas." *El Espectador*, December 20, 2019. https://www.elespectador.com/
colombia2020/opinion/explotadas-y-asesinadas-la-vulnerabilidad-de-las-migrantes
-venezolanas-columna-892839.

———. "Migrar y Morir: El Feminicidio de venezolanas en Colombia." *Tribuna
Feminista*, November 18, 2019. https://tribunafeminista.elplural.com/2019/11/
migrar-y-morir-el-feminicidio-de-venezolanas-en-colombia/.

Pohlhaus Jr., Gaile. "Discerning the Primary Epistemic Harm in Cases of Testimonial
Injustice." *Social Epistemology: A Journal of Knowledge, Culture and Policy* 28,
no. 2 (2014): 99–114.

Pramuk, Jacob. "Trump Administration Ending DACA Program, Which Protected
800,000 Children of Immigrants." *CNBC*, September 5, 2017. https://www.cnbc
.com/2017/09/05/trump-administration-is-ending-daca-immigration-program-ag
-sessions-says.html.

Price, Kimala. "What Is Reproductive Justice? How Women of Color Activists Are
Redefining the Pro-Choice Paradigm." *Meridians: Feminism, Race, Transnationalism* 10, no. 2 (2010): 42–65.

Quijano, Aníbal. "Colonialidad y Modernidad/Racionalidad," in *Los Conquistadores:
1492 y la población indígena de las Américas*, ed. Robin Blackburn and Heraclio
Bonilla (Tercer Mundo Editores, 1992).

Radnofsky, Louise, William Mauldin, and David Luhnow. "Trump Threatens Tariffs
on Mexican Imports in Response to Migrant Surge." *Wall Street Journal*, May 30,
2019. https://www.wsj.com/articles/trump-threatens-5-tariff-on-mexican-imports
-beginning-june-10-11559260679.

Ralph, Pat. "Rivera Rips Trump's Zero-Tolerance Policy in Sean Hannity Interview that Went Off the Rails." *Business Insider*, June 20, 2018. https://www.busi
nessinsider.com/geraldo-rivera-rips-trump-zero-tolerance-policy-on-fox-news
-hannity-2018-6.

Ramirez Caro, Jorge. "El Chiste de la Alteridad: La Pesadilla de ser otro." In *El Mito
Roto: Inmigración y Emigración en Costa Rica*, edited by Carlos Sandoval Garcia,
313–37. San José, Costa Rica: Editorial UCR, 2015.

Rappleye, Hannah, and Lisa Riordan Seville. "24 Immigrants Have Died in ICE
Custody During the Trump Administration." *NBC News*, June 9, 2019. https://www
.nbcnews.com/politics/immigration/24-immigrants-have-died-ice-custody-during
-trump-administration-n1015291.

Razack, Sherene H., ed. *Race, Space, and the Law: Unmapping a White Settler Society*. Toronto: Between the Lines Press, 2002.

Red Feminista Antimilitarista. "666 feminicidios en Colombia en el año 2018 [INfográfico]." February 2, 2019. http://redfeministaantimilitarista.org/novedades/item/666-feminicidios-en-colombia-en-2018-infografico.

Redacción Animal Político. "Extranjeros que soliciten asilo en EU se quedarán en México; INM dice que no hay capacidad para recibirlos." *Animal Político*, December 20, 2018. https://www.animalpolitico.com/2018/12/mexico-recibir-solicitantes-asilo-eu/.

Reed-Sandoval, Amy. "The New Open Borders Debate." In *The Ethics and Politics of Immigration: Core Issues and Emerging Trends*, edited by Alex Sager, 13–28. New York and London: Rowman & Littlefield, 2016.

———. *Socially Undocumented: Identity and Immigration Justice*. New York: Oxford University Press, 2020.

Reuters. "Violent Deaths of Venezuelans in Colombia Said on the Rise, Averaging One a Day Since the Year's Start." August 26, 2019. https://www.japantimes.co.jp/news/2019/08/26/world/crime-legal-world/violent-deaths-venezuelans-colombia-said-rise-averaging-one-day-since-years-start/#.Xf1FgNZKi1s.

Rivers-Moore, Megan. "'They're Machistas, They Treat Them Badly': Comparative Transnational Masculinity in Sex Tourism." In *Shattering Myths on Immigration and Emigration in Costa Rica*, edited by Carlos Sandoval Garcia. Translated by Kari Meyers. New York: Lexington Books, 2010.

Rizzo, Salvador. "Jeff Merkley's Claims about Immigrant Children in 'Cages,' Access to a Texas Shelter." *Washington Post*, June 6, 2018. https://www.washingtonpost.com/news/fact-checker/wp/2018/06/06/does-the-u-s-keep-immigrant-children-incages/?utm_term=.04050bf69e66.

Rodriguez, Gregory. "Illegal? Better If You're Irish." *Los Angeles Times*, April 8, 2007. www.latimes.com/la-op-rodriguez8apr08-column.html.

Roediger, David. *Working Towards Whiteness: How America's Immigrants Became White*. New York: Basic Books, 2005.

Roller, Emma. "Trump Implies Asylum Seekers Are Liars, So It's Not Hard to See Where This Goes Next." *Splinter*, June 21, 2018. https://splinternews.com/trump-implies-asylum-seekers-are-liars-so-its-not-hard-1827016969.

Romo, Vanessa, Martina Stewart, and Brian Naylor. "Trump Ends DACA, Calls on Congress to Act." *National Public Radio*, September 5, 2017. https://www.nytimes.com/2017/09/05/us/politics/trump-daca-dreamers-immigration.html.

Rose, Ayesha, and Bobby Allen. "Trump: U.S., Mexico Reach a Deal to Avoid New Tariffs." *National Public Radio*, June 7, 2019. https://www.npr.org/2019/06/07/730283772/trump-u-s-mexico-reaches-deal-to-avoid-new-tariffs.

Rose, Joel. "'Remain in Mexico' Policy Expands, but Slowly." *National Public Radio*, March 12, 2019. https://www.npr.org/2019/03/12/702597006/-remain-in-mexico-immigration-policy-expands-but-slowly.

Rose, Joel, and Laura Smitherman. "Fear, Confusion, and Separation as Trump Administration Sends Migrants Back to Mexico." *National Public Radio*,

July 1, 2019. https://www.npr.org/2019/07/01/736908483/fear-confusion
-and-separation-as-trump-administration-sends-migrants-back-tomex?utm_
source=npr_newsletter&utm_medium=email&utm_content=20190701&utm_
campaign=npr_email_a_friend&utm_term=storysh.

Rosenberg, Mica. "Exclusive: Nearly 1,800 Families Separated at U.S.-Mexico Border in 17 Months through February." *Reuters*, June 8, 2018. https://www.reuters
.com/article/us-usa-immigration-children-exclusive/exclusive-nearly-1800-families
-separated-at-us-mexico-border-in-17-months-through-february-idUSKCN1J42UE.

Ross, Loretta, and Rickie Solinger. *Reproductive Justice: An Introduction*. Los Angeles: University of California Press, 2017.

Rubin, Jennifer. "Ending DACA Would Be Trump's Most Evil Act." *Washington Post*, September 4, 2017. https://www.washingtonpost.com/blogs/right-turn/
wp/2017/09/04/trump-ending-daca-would-be-cruelty-wrapped-in-a-web-of-lies/.

Russell, Diana. *Making Violence Sexy: Feminist Views on Pornography*. London:
Open University, 1993.

Sagot Rodríguez, Monserrat. "¿Un mundo sin femicidios? Las propuestas del femi-
nismo para erradicar la violencia contra las mujeres." In *Feminismos, Pensamiento
Crítico y Propuestas Alternativas en América Latina*, edited by Monserrat Sagot
Rodríguez. Buenos Aires: CLACSO, 2017.

Sánchez, Carlos Alberto. "On Brutality: Or, Toward a Philosophy of Excessive Violence" *A Sense of Brutality: Philosophy and Narco Culture*. Amherst, CA: Amherst
College Press, 2020 (forthcoming).

———. "'Illegal' Immigrants: Law, Fantasy, and Guts." *Philosophy in the Contemporary World* 21, no. 2 (Spring 2014).

Sandoval García, Carlos. "El 'Otro' Nicaraguense el el imaginario colectivo costaricense: Algunos retos analítos y politicos." *Nómadas* 51 (October 2019): 153–59.

———. "Nicaraguan Immigration to Costa Rica: Tendencies, Policies, and Politics."
LASA Forum XLVI, no. 4 (Fall 2015): 7–10.

———. *No Mas Muros: Exclusión y migración forzada en Centroamerica*. San José,
Costa Rica: Editorial UCR, 2015.

———. *Otros Amenazantes: Los nicaragüenses y la formación de identidades nacionales en Costa Rica*. San José, Costa Rica: Editorial UCR, 2008.

———. *Threatening Others: Nicaraguans and the Formation of National Identities
in Costa Rica*. Columbus: Ohio University Press, 2004.

Savage, Martin, Tristan Smith, and Emanuella Grinberg. "What Trump Supporters
Think of Family Separations at the Border." *CNN*, June 20, 2018. https://www.cnn
.com/2018/06/19/us/trump-voters-family-separation/index.html.

Scheler, Max. *The Nature of Sympathy*. Revised edition. New York: Transaction
Publishers, 2008.

Schifrin, Nick. "On the Road in Mexico, Central American Migrants Face Uncertain
Future." *PBS NewsHour*, April 13, 2017. https://www.pbs.org/newshour/show/
road-mexico-central-american-migrants-face-uncertain-future.

Schmidt, Samantha. "'Utter Chaos': ICE Arrests 114 Workers in Immigration Raid
at Ohio Gardening Company." *Washington Post*, June 9, 2018. https://www.wash
ingtonpost.com/news/morning-mix/wp/2018/06/06/utter-chaos-ice-arrests-114
-workers-in-immigration-raid-at-ohio-gardening-company/.

Semple, Kirk. "Nicaraguan Migrants Fleeing Turmoil Test Costa Rica's Good Will." *New York Times*, September 22, 2018. https://www.nytimes.com/2018/09/22/world/americas/nicaragua-migrants-costa-rica.html.

Sergent, James, Elinor Aspegren, Elizabeth Lawrence, and Olivia Sanchez. "Chilling First-Hand Reports of Migrant Detention Centers Highlight Smell of 'Urine, Feces,' Overcrowded Conditions." *USA Today*, July 17, 2019. https://www.usatoday.com/in-depth/news/politics/elections/2019/07/16/migrant-detention-centers-described-2019-us-government-accounts/1694638001/.

Serwer, Adam. "The Cruelty Is the Point: President Trump and His Supporters Find Community by Rejoicing in the Suffering of Those They Hate and Fear." *The Atlantic*, October 3, 2018.

Sessions, Jeff. "Speech to the National Sheriffs' Association." *Department of Justice*, June 18, 2018. https://www.justice.gov/opa/speech/attorney-general-sessions-delivers-remarks-national-sheriffs-association-annual.

———. "Statement to End DACA." *PBS Newshour*, September 5, 2017. https://www.pbs.org/newshour/politics/read-sessions-full-remarks-daca.

Sevastopulo, Demetri, Aime Williams, and Jude Weber. "Donald Trump Cuts off Aid to Three Central American States." *Financial Times*, June 17, 2019. https://www.ft.com/content/f3cd73d2-9135-11e9-aea1-2b1d33ac3271.

Shear, Micheal, and Julie Hirschfeld Davis. "Trump Moves to End DACA and Calls on Congress to Act." *New York Times*, September 5, 2017. https://www.nytimes.com/2017/09/05/us/politics/trump-daca-dreamers-immigration.html.

Shoichet, Catherine E. "ICE Raided a Meatpacking Plant. More than 500 Kids Missed School the Next Day." *CNN*, April 12, 2018. https://edition.cnn.com/2018/04/12/us/tennessee-immigration-raid-schools-impact/index.html.

Silva, Grant J. "Embodying a 'New' Color Line: Racism, Anti-Immigrant Sentiment and Racial Identities in the 'Postracial' Era." *Knowledge Cultures* 3, no. 1 (2015): 65–90.

Simmons Cobb, Julia. "U.S. Gives Additional $120 Million to Help Venezuelan Migrants." *Reuters*, September 4, 2019. https://www.reuters.com/article/us-colombia-usa/u-s-to-give-additional-120-million-to-help-venezuelan-migrants-idUSKCN1VP30F.

Sinclair, Harriet. "Pregnant Women Detained by ICE Miscarried and Did Not Get Medical Care, Report Claims." *Newsweek*, July 10, 2018. https://www.newsweek.com/pregnant-women-detained-ice-miscarried-babies-and-didnt-get-medical-care-1015676.

SisterSong: Women of Color Reproductive Justice Collective. Accessed January 18, 2013. http://sistersong.net/reproductive_justice.html.

Somin, Ilya. "The Case for Keeping DACA." *New York Times*, September 4, 2017. https://www.washingtonpost.com/news/volokh-conspiracy/wp/2017/09/04/the-case-for-daca/.

Song, Sarah. "The Significance of Territorial Presence and the Rights of Immigrants." In *Migration in Political Theory: The Ethics of Movement and Membership*, edited by Sarah Fine and Lea Ypi. New York and Oxford: Oxford University Press, 2016.

Speri, Alice. "Detained, then Violated." *The Intercept*, April 11, 2018. https://theinter cept.com/2018/04/11/immigration-detention-sexual-abuse-ice-dhs/.

Stilz, Anna. "Is There an Unqualified Right to Leave?" In *Migration in Political Theory: The Ethics of Movement and Membership*, edited by Sarah Fine and Lea Ypi. New York and Oxford: Oxford University Press, 2016.

St. John, Rachel. *Line in the Sand: A History of the Western U.S-Mexico Border*. Princeton, NJ, and Oxford: Princeton University Press, 2011.

Sullivan, Kate, and Devin Cole. "Democrats, including Nancy Pelosi and Joe Biden, Slam ICE Raids." *CNN*, July 14, 2019. https://edition.cnn.com/2019/07/14/politics/ ice-raids-democrats-reactions-2020-presidential-nominees/index.html.

Tapi-Fuselier, Nicolas, and Jemimah L. Young. "Texas Community Colleges Respond to the Threatened End of DACA: A Document Analysis." *Community College Journal of Research and Practice* 43, no. 10–11 (2019): 807–11. doi-org.ezproxy .uniandes.edu.co:8443/10.1080/10668926.1600605.

Telesur. "Trump Threatens to Reimpose Tariffs Against Mexico." June 10, 2019. https://www.telesurenglish.net/news/Trump-Threatens-to-Reimpose-Tariffs -Against-Mexico—20190610-0003.html.

Tillett, Emily. "Jeff Sessions Mocks Liberals on 'Lunatic Fringe' over Family Sepa-ration." *CBS News*, June 27, 2018. https://www.cbsnews.com/news/jeff-sessions -mocks-liberals-on-lunatic-fringe-over-family-separation/.

Towney, Cynthia. "Trust and the Curse of Cassandra: An Exploration of the Value of Trust." *Philosophy in the Contemporary World* 10, no. 2 (Fall–Winter 2003).

United Nations Commissioner for Refugees. "Colombia." https://www.unhcr.org/ en-us/colombia.html.

———. "Refugees and Migrants from Venezuela Top 4 Million." June 7, 2019. https://www.unhcr.org/en-us/news/press/2019/6/5cfa2a4a4/refugees-migrants -venezuela-top-4-million-unhcr-iom.html.

———. *Women on the Run: First-Hand Accounts of Refugees Fleeing El Salvador, Guatemala, Honduras, and Mexico*. October 26, 2015. https://www.acnur.org/ fileadmin/Documentos/Publicaciones/2015/10228.pdf.

United States v. Bhagat Singh Thind, 261 U.S. 204 (1923).

U.S. Citizenship and Immigration Services. "Approximate DACA Recipients as of June 30, 2019." Accessed January 28, 2020. https://www.uscis.gov/sites/default/ files/USCIS/Resources/Reports%20and%20Studies/Immigration%20Forms%20 Data/Static_files/DACA_Population_Receipts_since_Injunction_Jun_30_2019.pdf.

———. "Consideration of Deferred Action for Childhood Arrivals (DACA)." Ac-cessed January 28, 2020. https://www.uscis.gov/archive/consideration-deferred -action-childhood-arrivals-daca.

———. "2014 Executive Actions on Immigration." Accessed January 28, 2020. https://www.uscis.gov/archive/2014-executive-actions-immigration.

U.S. Department of State. "Mexico Travel Advisory." April 2019. https://travel.state .gov/content/travel/en/traveladvisories/traveladvisories/mexico-travel-advisory.html.

———. "U.S. Relations with Costa Rica: Bilateral Relations Fact Sheet." October 24, 2019. https://www.state.gov/u-s-relations-with-costa-rica/.

U.S. House of Representatives Staff. "Child Separations from the Trump Administration." *Committee on Oversight and Reform U.S. House of Representatives*, July 2019. oversight.house.gov.

Valladarez, Michelle. "We Can't Go Back to the Shadows: Six Dreamers Tell Their Stories." *Mother Jones*, September 26, 2018. https://www.motherjones.com/poli tics/2018/09/we-cant-go-back-to-the-shadows-six-dreamers-tell-their-stories/.

Van Praag, Oriana. "Understanding the Venezuelan Refugee Crisis." *Latin American Program Woodrow Wilson Center*, September 13, 2019. https://www.wilsoncenter .org/article/understanding-the-venezuelan-refugee-crisis.

Voorend, Koen. "El sistema de salud como imán: La incidiencia de la población nicaragüense en los servicios de salud costarricenses." In *Migraciones en América Central: Políticas, territorios y actores*, edited by Carlos Sandoval Garcia, 195–215. San José, Costa Rica: Editorial UCR, 2016.

Walzer, Michael. *Spheres of Justice*. New York: Basic Books, 1982.

Warikoo, Niraj. "Dad Deported to Mexico after 30 Years in U.S." *Detroit Free Press*, January 16, 2018. https://www.freep.com/story/news/local/michigan/ wayne/2018/01/15/jorge-garcia-daca-deported-mexico-immigration/1033296001/.

———. "ICE Defends Deportation of Garcia to Mexico." *Detroit Free Press*, January 17, 2018. https://www.freep.com/story/news/2018/01/17/immigration-customs -enforcement-ice-jorge-garcia-mexican-immigrant-deported/1039806001/.

"What Do Donald Trump's Immigration Raids Accomplish?" *The Economist*, August 22, 2019. https://www.economist.com/united-states/2019/08/22/what-do-donald -trumps-immigration-raids-accomplish.

Wheeler, Lydia, and Raphael Bernal. "Sessions Orders 'Zero Tolerance' Policy at Southwest Border." *The Hill*, April 2, 2018. http://thehill.com/regulation/ administration/381991-sessions-orders-zero-tolerance-policy-at-southwest-border.

White House, The. "Fact Sheet: President Donald J. Trump Is Working to Stop the Abuses of Our Asylum System and Address the Root Causes of the Border Crisis." April 29, 2019. https://www.whitehouse.gov/briefings-statements/president-donald -j-trump-working-stop-abuse-asylum-system-address-root-causes-border-crisis/.

Wilcox, Shelley. "Immigrant Admissions and Global Relations of Harms." *Journal of Social Philosophy* 38, no. 2 (2007): 274–91.

———. "The Open Borders Debate on Immigration." *Philosophy Compass* 4, no. 5 (2009): 813–21. https://doi.org/10.1111/j.1747-9991.2009.00230.x.

Willis, Eliza, and Janet Seiz. "Central American Governments Can't Stop Migration." *The Atlantic*, April 9, 2019. https://www.theatlantic.com/ideas/archive/2019/04/ central-american-governments-cant-stop-migration/586726/.

Wolf, Allison B. "Dying in Detention as an Example of Oppression." *APA Newsletter on Hispanic/Latino Issues in Philosophy* 19, no. 1 (Fall 2019): 2–8.

———. "Dying in Detention: Where Are the Bioethicists?" In *Applying Nonideal Theory to Bioethics: Living and Dying in a Nonideal World*, edited by Elizabeth Victor and Laura Guidry-Grimes. Springer, 2020.

———. "'Quit trying to make us feel teary-eyed for the children!' Constructions of Emotion, Anger, and Immigration Injustice." Colloquio: Emociones en las Ciencias Sociales. La Universidad de los Andes, Bogotá, Colombia, August 28, 2018.

World Bank. "Country Report: Colombia." October 2019. https://www.worldbank .org/en/country/colombia/overview.

World Health Organization. "Understanding and Addressing Violence Against Women: Femicide." 2012.

World Population Review. "Costa Rica Population." Accessed January 31, 2020. http://worldpopulationreview.com/countries/costa-rica-population/.

Young, Iris Marion. *Justice and the Politics of Difference*. Princeton, NJ: Princeton University Press, 1990.

Ypi, Lea. "Justice in Migration: A Closed Borders Utopia?" *The Journal of Political Philosophy* 16, no. 4 (2008): 391–418.

Yurley Quintero Rolón, Claudia. "Suenos Rotos." http://ovidiohoyos.com/node/29187.

Zaidi, Danish, and Mark Kuczewski. "Ending DACA Has Pragmatic and Ethical Implications for U.S. Health Care." *Hastings Center Report* 47, no. 6 (2017): 14–15. https://doi.org/10.1002/hast.780.

Zulver, Julia. "At Venezuela's Border with Colombia, Women Suffer Extraordinary Levels of Violence." *Washington Post*, February 26, 2019. https://www.washing tonpost.com/politics/2019/02/26/venezuelas-border-with-colombia-women-suffer -extraordinary-levels-violence/.

Index

About the Author

Allison B. Wolf, PhD, is an associate professor of philosophy and faculty member of the Center for Immigration Studies (Centro de Estudios de Migración) at Universidad de los Andes in Bogotá, Colombia, where she teaches political philosophy, philosophy of immigration, and feminist philosophy. Her research focuses on philosophy of immigration and immigration justice in the United States and Latin America, feminist philosophy, and feminist bioethics (specifically, philosophical issues in childbirth and maternity care).

Her work has been published in various journals and collections, including *Hypatia, Comparative Studies in Asian and Latin American Philosophies, Hispanic/Latino Issues in Philosophy Newsletter of the American Philosophical Association, International Journal of Feminist Approaches to Bioethics, International Journal of Applied Philosophy, Journal of Medical Humanities* (with Sonya Charles), *Philosophical Inquiry into Pregnancy, Childbirth, and Mothering: Maternal Subjects* (with Jennifer Benson), *Queer Philosophy: Presentations of the Society of Lesbian and Gay Philosophy, 1998–2008,* and *Journal of Global Ethics.* She is currently working on projects about obstetric violence and immigration and philosophical issues in immigration related to Colombia. She is also coediting an anthology titled *Incarnating Feelings, Constructing Communities: Experiencing Emotions in the Americas through Education, Violence, and Public Policy* with Ana María Forero Angel and Catalina González Quintero, to be published by Palgrave Macmillan in late 2020.

www.ingramcontent.com/pod-product-compliance
Lightning Source LLC
Chambersburg PA
CBHW031132270326
41929CB00011B/1590